THE CONCEPT
OF IDENTITY

THE CONCEPT
OF IDENTITY

Eli Hirsch

New York   Oxford
OXFORD UNIVERSITY PRESS

Oxford University Press

Oxford   New York   Toronto
Delhi   Bombay   Calcutta   Madras   Karachi
Petaling Jaya   Singapore   Hong Kong   Tokyo
Nairobi   Dar es Salaam   Cape Town
Melbourne   Auckland

and associated companies in
Berlin   Ibadan

First published by Oxford University Press, 1982
First issued as an Oxford University Presss paperback, 1992

Oxford University Press, Inc.
200 Madison Avenue, New York, New York 10016

Oxford is a registered trademark of Oxford University Press

Library of Congress Cataloging-in-Publication Data
Hirsch, Eli
The Concept of Identity
"Part One...originally published as...The
persistence of objects"—Verso of t.p.
Includes index
1. Identity. 2. Object (Philosophy) 3. Space
and time. I. title
BD236.H55 1982 111 81-9508
ISBN 0-19-502995-X AACR2
ISBN 0-19-507474-2 (pbk)

2 4 5 6 8 9 7 5 3 1

Printed in the United States of America
on acid-free paper

To the memory
of Dean Kolitch

Preface

My main concern in this book is identity through time, first with respect to ordinary bodies, then underlying matter, and eventually persons. These issues link up at various points with other aspects of identity, such as the spatial unity of things, the unity of kinds, and the unity of groups. One of my concerns is to understand how our identity concept ordinarily operates in these various respects; but I also try to understand, especially in later chapters of the book, why this concept is so central to our thinking, and whether we can justify seeing the world in terms of such a concept.

Part One, with a few minor differences (mainly in footnotes), was published several years ago as a monograph on the persistence of objects. That work, though its circulation was quite limited, did generate some interest, and this has encouraged me to present it again in a more accessible form. The views expressed in Part One are augmented, and in certain respects qualified, by the treatment in Part Two of various related themes of identity. Though both parts of this book may be said to form a single extended discussion, the chapters in Part Two can also be read as relatively self-contained essays, which is in fact the spirit in which they were written.

A number of people over the years have helped me with this book. I thank my wife Pamela, for her perceptive assistance on both matters of style and philosophy; Milton Munitz, for being a good teacher and friend; Roderick Chisholm, for his discussions of identity at an NEH-sponsored seminar I attended during a period when I wrote portions of the book; and especially Saul

Kripke, whose discussions in lectures of some of my views encouraged me to elaborate them further.

I am also much indebted to Alan Brody, Georges Dicker, William James Earle, Dean Kolitch, Joseph Margolis, and Karsten
Struhl, for their invaluable advice and comments on various portions of the book during its preparation. And Part Two, especially
Chapter 7, was substantially affected by Sydney Shoemaker's extensive criticisms, for which I am most grateful.

I have made use, with permission, of the following previously
published material:

"Physical Identity," *The Philosophical Review,* 84 (1976); portions of this paper are scattered throughout Part One.

The Persistence of Objects (Philosophical Monographs, Phila-
delphia, Pennsylvania, 1976); this corresponds to Part One.

"A Sense of Unity," *The Journal of Philosophy,* 74, no. 9 (1978);
this is Chapter 8.

New York City   E. H.
September 1981

Contents

PART ONE
THE PERSISTENCE
OF OBJECTS

Introduction to Part One

OUR CONCEPT of a physical object's persistence through time seems so fundamental and primitive that it requires a special effort to appreciate what philosophers might be after when they ask for an analysis of this concept. Traditionally the request for such an analysis might take the form of such questions as: What does the identity through time of a physical object consist in? or What is it for a physical object which exists at one time to be the same object as a physical object which exists at another time? In more recent literature one typically finds philosophers asking for an account of our "identity criteria" for objects. This new terminology, at least as I intend to employ it, still expresses very much the same traditional request for an analysis of our identity concept, except perhaps that to talk about "identity criteria" is to signal more clearly one's quite reasonable willingness to settle for an analysis which may be less than airtight and which may allow for many borderline cases.[1]

When we ask with regard to physical objects what their identity through time consists in, we are asking for an account of the unity of a physical object's career. Any physical object has a career which stretches over a period of time, a career which we can think of as comprised of a temporal succession of momentary stages. The successive parts, or stages, of an object's career must

---

1. On the meaning of "identity criteria" see Sydney Shoemaker, *Self-Knowledge and Self-Identity* (Cornell University Press, Ithaca, New York, 1963), pp. 3–5, and David Wiggins, *Identity and Spatio-Temporal Continuity* (Basil Blackwell, Oxford, 1967), p. 43.

hang together in some distinctive way; otherwise there would be nothing to prevent us from arbitrarily combining into a single career the early stages of one object with the later stages of a different object. Evidently not just any succession of object-stages corresponds to a single persisting object; some do and some do not. So in order for object-stages to add up to a single persisting object they must be related in some special way. What I am seeking in Part One is an analysis or definition of what that relationship is.

In a sense, of course, any succession of object-stages, however arbitrary, does add up to *something*: perhaps to an event, or to a state of affairs or, if nothing else, at least to a "merely arbitrary succession of object-stages." What is important, however, is that not every succession adds up to a *persisting object* or *body* (I will use these expressions interchangeably), where this fundamental category is to be understood as loosely comprising items which can straightforwardly be said to occupy space and to persist through time. Clearly only certain privileged successions are accorded the special status of uniting into a single persisting object in this sense, which gives rise to the question as to what the unity-making relationship is in virtue of which some successions enjoy this special status.

Our question, I want to stress, is primarily conceptual rather than epistemological. We are not, that is, to be thinking primarily of a situation in which someone has not seen an object for some time and a question arises as to how he can know that he has really come across the same object again. Rather we are to be thinking primarily of a situation in which someone continuously observes an object for a stretch of time, and, as I shall often put it, *traces* the object's career for that period. Our question is what criteria of identity enter into this tracing operation. How can we analyze what it means to judge in those optimal circumstances that it was a single persisting object that was being followed?

It must be emphasized, furthermore, that this is a question about our most ordinary notion of physical persistence. We want an account of what goes into our thought about the identity through time of tables, trees, and other objects that we ordinarily talk about. A philosopher may of course hold that the ordinary notion of physical persistence is not ultimately important, perhaps because ordinary physical objects are not among the "ulti-mate constituents of reality." Whatever might be the cogency of this sort of claim (and I shall have something to say about it in the course of what follows), the fact remains that we certainly do have an ordinary way of thinking about the physical world, and it must be of some philosophical interest to provide an analy-sis of that way of thinking.

Our question, then, is about as clear as the notion of giving an "analysis" (or a "definition"), which means, I think, that it is not luminously clear at all. One important difficulty with this notion has to do with deciding when an analysis is "circular," when, that is, the concepts in terms of which it is couched de-pend, in some sense, on the concept being analyzed. This diffi-culty may seem potentially devastating when the concept to be analyzed is as fundamental to our overall thought as the concept of physical persistence. But perhaps we may provisionally adopt a fairly tolerant attitude about this. If we can provide an account of our identity criteria which strikes us as at least not patently circular then we may feel that we have the kind of analytic illumination that we sought. It may turn out, of course, that granted even a reasonable measure of tolerance our concept of physical persistence, or some application of that concept, will seem to resist the sort of analysis that we are seeking. In this case we will have to say that the concept, or some application of it, is, in some important sense, ultimate and unanalyzable. Later, in Chapter 4, I will in fact defend the position that our concept of the persistence of material substance is in a sense unanalyzable. And in Chapter 5, the final chapter of this part, I will consider a bit more forthrightly some of the metaphysical issues that may revolve around the idea of giving an analysis of physical persist-ence. These issues in their full generality, however, will not be dealt with until Part Two.

The topic that I intend to focus upon in this first part is rather severely circumscribed. I want to examine our concept of per-sistence as it pertains to the seemingly most central and unex-ceptionable instances of physical objects or bodies. These would include, I assume, such things as tables and cars, mountains and stones, trees and flowers, cats and dogs, chunks of clay and bits of wood. But I shall have nothing to say in this part about the identity conditions for such nonsubstantial items as events and properties, or such corporate items as groups and forests; nor will I enter into the very special problems which seem to affect our concept of the persistence of persons. Some of these additional issues will be discussed in Part Two.

An object's unity through time is by no means the only philosophically challenging mode of object-unity. In particular one can raise questions about an object's *unity through space* which parallel in many ways questions about its unity through time. The spatial question would have to do with our basis for treating some, but not all, aggregates of matter as unitary objects. This question will eventually be addressed in Chapter 3. But in order to focus properly on the immediate question, a question essentially about identity through time, the perspective to adopt is one in which an aggregate of matter has (on whatever basis) already been delineated as a unitary object and our primary concern is to understand what it means to trace that object's career through time.

I

Continuity

I. The Simple Continuity Analysis

WE WANT to understand the nature of the unity-making relationship which binds the successive stages of the career of a single persisting object. When one first reflects upon this question, an idea which might readily come to mind is that contiguous stages of a single career must be qualitatively very similar and spatially very close. Over an extended period an object may of course significantly alter its qualitative makeup and its spatial location, but it seems that such alterations occur *continuously*, i.e., by small degrees. This may suggest the possibility of formulating a very simple kind of analysis of the unity-making relationship in terms essentially of two considerations: (1) continuity of qualitative change (which I will call, for short, "qualitative continuity"), and (2) continuity of locational change (which I will call, for short, "spatiotemporal continuity").

This very simple kind of analysis is much *too* simple, as I will explain shortly. But many philosophers of the empiricist tradition have presented accounts of the identity of objects which suggest just this simple analysis.

Certainly such an analysis seems to be suggested by the following remarks of Russell:

Given any event A it happens very frequently that, at any neighboring time, there is at some neighboring place an event very similar to A. A "thing" is a series of such events. . . . It is to be observed that in a series of events which common sense would regard as belonging to one

7

"thing," the similarity need only be between events not widely separated in space-time. There is not very much similarity between a three months' embryo and an adult human being, but they are connected by gradual transitions from next to next, and are therefore accepted as stages in the development of one "thing."[1]

I take it that by an "event" Russell means here pretty much the same as what I have been calling an "object-stage" (and what philosophers sometimes call a "temporal slice" of an object). Russell's remarks suggest that the unity-making relationship which binds a succession of object-stages ("events") into a single persisting object is essentially nothing more than spatiotemporal and qualitative continuity.[2]

A succinct formulation of what appears to be the same position is expressed by C. D. Broad. In the course of discussing "the durations of physical objects" Broad states: "A thing . . . is simply a long event, throughout the course of which there is either qualitative similarity or continuous qualitative change, together with a characteristic spatio-temporal unity."[3] Apparently Broad is saying that our criteria of identity for objects consist simply of the two considerations of qualitative and spatiotemporal continuity.

We have, then, as our first and simplest possibility, an analysis of persistence which might be formulated as follows:

The Simple Continuity Analysis. A succession S of object-stages corresponds to stages in the career of a single persisting object if and only if:

(1) S is spatiotemporally continuous; *and*
(2) S is qualitatively continuous.

I call this "the *simple* continuity analysis" because it relies exclusively on continuity considerations, whereas more compli-

1. Bertrand Russell, *Human Knowledge: Its Scope and Limits* (Simon & Schuster, New York, 1948), p. 488.
2. Russell was actually aware that this account of persistence is incomplete, as I will bring out in Chapter 4, Section I. Moreover the notion of spatio-temporal and qualitative continuity as this figures in Russell's account may imply a condition of *causal* continuity. I ignore this latter condition, but only provisionally, until Chapter 4, Section IV (see also ftn. 14 there).
3. C. D. Broad, *Scientific Thought* (Routledge & Kegan Paul, London, 1949), p. 393. See also p. 346ff.

cated analyses which will be discussed later rely on continuity considerations in conjunction with considerations of other sorts.

We might consider how the simple continuity analysis applies to a statement like "Something was a red table at time t and a green table at time t'." According to the analysis this statement is true if and only if you could trace a succession S of object-stages such that S contains a red table-stage at t and a green table-stage at t', and S is spatiotemporally and qualitatively continuous.

In the recent literature on the topic of identity the concept of a "space-time path" is frequently employed in such a way as to take over the analytic role played in the preceding discussion by the concept of a "succession of object-stages." It is useful to be able to shift freely from one idiom to the other. We may define a space-time path as a series of place-times, i.e., a series of ordered pairs (p, t), where p is a region of space and t is a moment of time. To say that the space-time path P is spatiotemporally continuous means that where (p, t) and (p', t') are place-times in P then if t is very close to t', p is very close to p'. And to say that P is qualitatively continuous means that where (p, t) and (p', t') are place-times in P then if t is very close to t', the object which occupies p at t exemplifies qualities at t which are very similar to the qualities exemplified at t' by the object which occupies p' at t'.

In the idiom of space-time paths the simple continuity analysis tells us that we can correctly trace an object's career by following a spatiotemporally and qualitatively continuous path through space-time. Hence the statement "Something was a red table at t and a green table at t'" will be true if and only if you could trace a path P through space-time such that P contains a red table at t and a green table at t', and P is spatiotemporally and qualitatively continuous.

The notion of a "succession of object-stages" could also be defined along the same general lines as a "path," though I would expect, and want, the former notion to bear some independent intuitive force. We could define an object-stage as an ordered pair (x, t), where x is an object and t a moment of time. To say that the succession S contains, say, a red table-stage at t means that some object x is a red table at t and S contains (x, t). It will be noted that a "path" and a "succession" are distinguishable in some strict abstract sense, but I shall not hesitate in what follows to use these notions interchangeably where it may seem suggestive to do so.

II. Qualitative Continuity

Before turning to a criticism of the simple continuity analysis I want to examine the two notions of continuity which occur in it. These notions of continuity will also figure as parts of other analyses which will be considered later, so it will be worth getting clearer about them.

Let me first raise a question about the notion of qualitative continuity. An object's career exhibits qualitative continuity insofar as the object either does not change qualitatively at all or undergoes qualitative changes which are continuous. An object's qualitative changes are continuous if at any given time the object is very similar to the way that it is at neighboring times. If we define a "small change" as a change which takes an object from one qualitative state to a different but very similar state then we can say that a continuous qualitative change is a change that can be thought of as divided up into a series of small changes.

But now what exactly do we mean by this? We may mean either (a) that a continuous qualitative change is a change that can be thought of as divided up into a series of changes *as small as you like*, or (b) that a continuous qualitative change is a change that can be thought of as divided up into a series of small changes, but not necessarily into a series of changes as small as you like. Let me call sense (a) the *strong sense* of "continuous qualitative change" and sense (b) the *weak sense*. My question is whether to interpret the condition of qualitative continuity in our analysis as requiring continuity of change in the strong sense or in the weak sense.

The difference between the strong and the weak sense of continuity of change can be brought out with the following example. Let us assume, as seems plausible, that if two cats are alike in every respect except that one has brown eyes and the other has green eyes then these two cats can be said to be "very similar." This implies that a change in which a cat passes from having brown eyes to having green eyes, everything else remaining exactly the same, would count as a "small change." Now suppose that we have a cat which has suffered such a small change during the time interval from t to t'; that is, the cat at t' is green-eyed whereas at t it was brown-eyed, but everything else has remained the same. If we require continuity of qualitative change in the strong sense then we would require that the small change suffered by the cat from t to t' should be further resolvable into still smaller changes; i.e., that there should be a time between t and t' such that the color of the cat's eyes at that time is intermediate between brown and green. But if we merely require continuity of change in the weak sense then it is not necessary that the small change suffered by the cat from t to t' should be further resolvable. It would be permissible for the cat's appearance to "jump" noticeably, so long as the jump is a small one.

The question that I am here raising should not be confused with a different and more famous one. A change is continuous in the strong sense if it does not involve any noticeable, albeit small, jumps like that from being a brown-eyed cat to being a green-eyed cat. By a noticeable jump I mean, intuitively, a direct transition from one qualitative state to another, where we have an idea of what it would be like for there to be a state intermediate between the two. Now the famous question is whether a change which is continuous in the strong sense, one which does not involve a noticeable jump, necessitates there being an infinite number of qualitative states intermediate between any two different qualitative states. Kant apparently thought that it does: "The question . . . arises how a thing passes from one state . . . to another. . . . Between two instants there is always a time, and between any two states in the two instants there is always a difference which has magnitude. . . . The new state of reality accordingly proceeds from the first wherein this reality was not, through all the infinite degrees."[4]

As I understand Kant, the question to which he is here addressing himself is this: Given that a particular qualitative change from the state S_1 to the state S_2 was continuous in the strong sense, i.e., that it did not involve any noticeable jumps, how are we to understand the nature of the change? Kant's answer

4. Immanuel Kant, *Critique of Pure Reason*, translated by Norman Kemp Smith (Macmillan, London, 1963), p. 231 (B253–254).

consists in positing an infinite number of states intermediate between S_1 and S_2. To Kant's question there may be other plausible answers.[5] But I am not here concerned with *this* question. I am not concerned with the question "What is the ultimate nature of a change which is continuous in the strong sense?" but rather with the question "Should we require of an object that its changes should be continuous in the strong sense?"

I think that it is a fairly common assumption among philosophers that all of the qualitative changes that are typically suffered by ordinary physical objects are continuous in the strong sense.[6] It may therefore be of some theoretical importance to show that there is a certain range of perfectly ordinary changes, generally ignored in philosophical discussions of continuity, which are not continuous in the strong sense. I have in mind cases in which an object either persists while having a part added to it, or persists while having a part subtracted from it. Frequently when an object changes in either of these two ways it suffers a qualitative change which is not continuous in the strong sense.

Consider, for example, what happens when a branch is chopped off a tree some time between t and t'. Suppose that the tree took up 30 cubic feet at t and 28 cubic feet at t', the fallen branch having taken up two cubic feet. Now we are imagining a case in which the branch was chopped off as a whole, and not demolished piece by piece. It follows that the tree suffered a noticeable jump with respect to volume. For the tree passed from taking up 30 cubic feet at t to taking up 28 cubic feet at t'. When did it take up 29 cubic feet? Obviously never.

It would be a mistake to think that a plea of vagueness could somehow be invoked to disarm this argument. Admittedly the question "When exactly did the tree lose the branch?" cannot be answered with any definiteness. Our ordinary thinking about

5. For a discussion of Kant's question see Jonathan Bennett, *Kant's Analytic* (Cambridge University Press, London, 1966), pp. 176–80.
6. Such an assumption seems implicit in Kant's discussion. Russell's attitude about this is unclear from the previously quoted passage but the strong sense seems implied in his discussion of continuity in "The Relation of Sense-Data to Physics," in *Mysticism and Logic* (George Allen & Unwin. Ltd., London, 1917), p. 170.

the case of a tree losing a branch is too vague to permit our pin-pointing the exact moment at which the branch was lost. But this is beside the point, the point being that our ordinary thinking about the case does dictate a perfectly definite answer to the question "When did the tree take up 29 cubic feet?" namely, the answer "never." And from this it follows that the change of volume was not continuous in the strong sense.

Much the same considerations serve to show that frequently in cases of part-addition and part-subtraction an object's alterations are not strongly continuous with respect to other qualities, such as color and shape. The present example is not especially well-suited to illustrate the point that a change of parts will frequently require a noticeable jump with respect to color. But to make the example work let us imagine that the bark had been stripped from that one branch before it was chopped off, so that at t every part of the tree's surface was brown except for that branch. Then at t the tree was, let us say, 90 percent brown, and at t' it was 100 percent brown. When was it 95 percent brown? Again, never.

An equally good case can be made for saying that the tree suffered a noticeable jump with respect to shape. Assuming that the tree started out at t with two branches and ended up at t' with one, the successive shapes of the tree at t and t' can be represented by Figures 1 and 2.

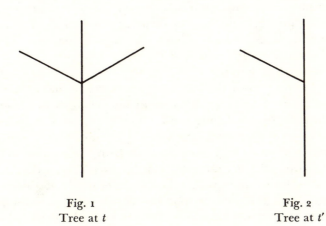

Fig. 1
Tree at t

Fig. 2
Tree at t'

Clearly there was no time between t and t' at which the tree's shape could be pictured in some way intermediate between Figure 1 and Figure 2. For example there was no time at which the tree's shape looked like Figure 3.

Fig. 3
Does not represent tree

It follows that the change from the shape pictured in Figure 1 to the shape pictured in Figure 2 was not continuous in the strong sense.

This was an example of part-subtraction. But evidently the same considerations will apply with equal force to many cases of part-addition (and also to cases of part-replacement, in which parts are both subtracted and added). If, for example, you add a wheel to a car, the car has to suffer a noticeable jump with respect to volume, weight, shape, and (generally) color distribution.

I should make it clear that I am not maintaining that *all* cases of part-addition and part-subtraction involve changes which are not continuous in the strong sense. On the contrary, it seems evident that many such cases involve no element of discontinuity. If the branch of a tree is gradually consumed by fire, without the branch splitting off from the tree, then this would typically be a case of part-subtraction in which there is no evidence of a noticeable jump; here the various qualities of the tree, its volume, shape, and so on, change in a way that can easily be regarded as continuous in the strong sense. A case of part-addition which does not apparently involve any discontinuity is that of a tooth gradually appearing and growing in a creature's mouth; here the creature suffers no noticeable jump with respect to any qualities. In these latter two cases a part is subtracted by gradually diminishing, or a part is added by gradually growing. But where a part is subtracted *as a whole*, as in the case of a branch splitting from a tree, or where a part is added *as a whole*, as in the case of adding a wheel to a car, then there is no recourse but to acknowledge a noticeable jump in an object's qualities. For an object's qualities are a function of the object's total content, of the totality of parts that make it up, and where an object gains or loses a part as a whole, then its content, and hence its qualities, must undergo some degree of discontinuous change.

The upshot of this discussion is that we must interpret the condition of qualitative continuity in the simple continuity analysis as requiring continuity in only the weak sense. According to the analysis, then, a necessary condition for a succession S of object-stages to correspond to the career of an object is that any object-stage in S should be very similar to any temporally neighboring object-stage in S. This weak requirement of continuity is *exceedingly* vague, as vague as the idea of two qualitative states being "very similar" to each other. But it does seem plausible to assert, vaguely, that in at least the most typical and standard cases of persistence some weak degree of qualitative continuity is to be expected. Whether even this weak kind of continuity is properly to be regarded as strictly necessary to an object's persistence is a question to which I will return.

III. Spatiotemporal Continuity

Much the same points as were just made with regard to qualitative continuity apply as well to the notion of spatiotemporal continuity. It may not be immediately evident that cases of part-addition and part-subtraction have any bearing on the continuity of an object's movements in space. But when one considers that an object's overall location in space is determined by the locations of its parts it becomes clear that where parts are added as a whole or subtracted as a whole the object's overall location must suffer some degree of discontinuous change. In what follows when I speak about the place which an object occupies at a given time I will always mean that overall region of space which *coincides* with the object at that time, i.e., the region which contains at that time all and only the object's parts.

An object's career exhibits spatiotemporal continuity (and corresponds, therefore, to a spatiotemporally continuous succession of object-stages, or, in the alternative idiom, to a spatiotemporally continuous space-time path) if it either does not move at all or moves continuously. If we define a "small movement" as one in which an object passes from occupying one place to occupying a different but very close place, then we can define a continuous movement as one which can be thought of as divided up into a series of small movements. And here, as before, we can distinguish between different degrees of continuity. A strong kind of spatiotemporal continuity is exhibited by an object only if its movements are divisible into movements as small as one likes. However, a weaker kind of spatiotemporal continuity would be exhibited so long as the object's movements are divisible into small movements, even if some of these movements involve a small "jump" from one place to a very close place.

One way that we might try to explicate the notion of two places being "very close" is in terms of the notion of two places *overlapping* each other, where two places are said to overlap each other if they have some part in common. In these terms we would say that x's career exhibits the weak sense of spatiotemporal continuity only if the place p which coincides with x at a given time t overlaps places which coincide with x at times slightly before and after t. This does indeed seem to be the absolutely minimal requirement for any kind of continuity of motion. Accordingly, the following definition seems reasonable.

> *Definition A.* "x's career exhibits spatiotemporal continuity in the weak sense" means: For any time t in x's career there is a time interval around t such that for any t' in that interval the place which x occupies at t overlaps the place which x occupies at t'.[7]

To explicate the strong kind of spatiotemporal continuity we have to be able to make sense out of the idea that places which

7. This definition, and the ones which follow, would have to be slightly modified in an obvious way to take account of the first and last moments of x's career.

are very close to each other (i.e., which overlap) may be *more* or *less* close. How shall we assign degrees of closeness to places which overlap each other? We may note that where p and p' are identical with each other (and are thus, in a sense, maximally close) they will overlap completely. But if p and p' are overlapping places that are not identical with each other then there must be, besides an area of overlap, an area in which they do not overlap. That is, if p is not identical with p' then there must be a part of p that is outside p', or a part of p' that is outside p, or both. Perhaps we can say, for our present purposes, that the degree of closeness between p and p' varies inversely with the extent to which they do not overlap. We might straightforwardly measure the extent of nonoverlap between p and p' by first measuring, say in cubic feet, the amount of p which is outside p', then measuring the amount of p' which is outside p, and then adding these two measures together. The strong kind of spatiotemporal continuity would then be one in which the extent of nonoverlap between x's place at t and x's place at t' can be made as small as you like by choosing t' close enough to t. This idea, or a mathematically idealized version of it, might be expressed as follows.

> *Definition B.* "x's career exhibits spatiotemporal continuity in the strong sense" means: For any time t in x's career, and for any positive number n, there is a time interval around t such that for any t' in that interval the extent of nonoverlap between the place which x occupies at t and the place which x occupies at t' is less than n.

So we have these two notions of spatiotemporal continuity, the weak notion of definition A and the strong notion of definition B. A mistake that I want to warn against, corresponding to the mistake already discussed in connection with qualitative continuity, is that of assuming that the strong notion expressed in definition B correctly characterizes, or is at least an apt idealization of, the paths typically traced by ordinary objects. The truth seems rather to be that whenever an object has a part added to it as a whole, or a part subtracted from it as a whole, then its career cannot be coherently thought of as spatiotemporally continuous in the strong sense B.

If, for example, a branch falls from a tree it seems that, at least for purposes of mathematical idealization, we must be able coherently to think of there being a final moment at which the tree included the branch. (An alternative would be to think of there being no final moment at which the tree included the branch, but there being a first moment at which it did not include the branch. My argument would work essentially the same way on that assumption.) Suppose, then, that the tree included the branch at t but not after t. Then for any time t' after t, no matter how close t' is to t, the extent of nonoverlap between the place occupied by the tree at t and the place occupied by it at t' would have to equal the extent of the fallen branch. In other words, we cannot make the extent of nonoverlap between these places as small as we like by taking t' sufficiently close to t. This means that the tree's career was not spatiotemporally continuous in sense B. On the other hand the tree's career was certainly spatiotemporally continuous in the weak sense A, because the places successively occupied by the tree did overlap to some extent.

Leaving aside for the moment the question whether even the weak degree of spatiotemporal continuity is strictly necessary for an object's persistence, it seems safe to say that this weak kind of spatiotemporal continuity is characteristic of at least the most typical and obvious cases of persistence. Now, actually, we can make a considerably stronger claim than this. Typically the successive places occupied by an object do not merely overlap to some extent or other (which is all that the weak notion of spatiotemporal continuity requires), but overlap to a relatively large extent. More specifically we may note that, at least as a general rule, an object does not persist through the addition or subtraction of a part, where the part added, or subtracted, is so large as to have the effect of precipitously doubling, or halving, the object's size. This means that, as a general rule, the places occupied by an object at neighboring times will be such that their extent of *overlap* is greater than their extent of *nonoverlap*. This suggests the possibility of formulating a definition of spatiotemporal continuity which is intermediate in strength as between the weakest sense A and the strongest sense B.

Definition C. "x's career exhibits spatiotemporal continuity in the moderate sense" means: For any time t in x's career there is a time interval around t such that for any t' in that interval the extent of overlap between the place which x occupies at t and the place which x occupies at t' is greater than their extent of nonoverlap.

Definition C is by no means the only intermediate notion of spatiotemporal continuity which could in principle be formulated. We might formulate a notion which requires that an object's successive places overlap, say, by more than two-thirds. But we can perhaps focus on definition C as presenting at least one rather reasonable-looking moderating possibility.

Now we know that the strongest sense B cannot accommodate typical cases of part-addition and part-subtraction, whereas such cases are accommodated by both the weakest sense A and the moderate sense C. Either of these latter senses may therefore be regarded prima facie as figuring in our identity criteria. Are there any considerations which might indicate that one of these senses of spatiotemporal continuity has more relevance to our identity concept than the other? I can think of one kind of case which might, with some plausibility, be interpreted as indicating a special relevance for the moderate sense C. Sometimes when an object divides into fragments the relative sizes of the fragments constitute our only apparent basis for deciding which, if any, fragment to identify with the original object. A very simple explanation of these cases can be provided if we assume that the moderate notion of spatiotemporal continuity is the operative one.

As an example of the sort of case that I have in mind imagine that at time t we have a large puddle of water, which we will call puddle 1. At time t' the puddle is split in two, so that after t' we are confronted with two puddles, puddle 2a and puddle 2b. Let us imagine that puddle 2a is considerably larger than puddle 2b. In such circumstances it would probably seem natural to identify puddle 1 with the larger fragment 2a rather than with the smaller 2b. We could, no doubt, try to account for this in a number of ways, but a very simple explanation, in terms of spatiotemporal continuity, presents itself if we adopt the moderate sense C.

This case may also help us to get clearer about the application of the three defined notions of spatiotemporal continuity. The weakest kind of spatiotemporal continuity would be satisfied whether we identified puddle 1 with the larger fragment 2a or the smaller fragment 2b. Even the latter identification would secure weak spatiotemporal continuity because any place occupied by puddle 2b immediately after the moment of split t' overlaps the place occupied by puddle 1 at t'. At the other extreme, the strongest kind of spatiotemporal continuity would *not* be satisfied whether we identified puddle 1 with the larger fragment 2a or the smaller fragment 2b. Even the former identification would fail to secure strong spatiotemporal continuity because there is an irreducible extent of nonoverlap between the places occupied by puddle 2a after t' and the place occupied by puddle 1 at t'. Thus we see that neither the weak notion nor the strong notion would prompt the seemingly natural identification of puddle 1 with 2a rather than with 2b.

But the moderate notion has precisely the effect of prompting the natural-seeming identification. The moderate kind of spatiotemporal continuity would be satisfied only if we identified puddle 1 with 2a and not with 2b. Either identification would allow us to think of the successive places occupied by the puddle as overlapping to some extent or other, but it is only the identification of the original puddle with the larger fragment which would satisfy the moderate requirement that the places successively occupied by an object should be such that their extent of overlap exceeds their extent of nonoverlap. (The identification of the original puddle with the smaller fragment fails to satisfy this requirement because we would then be thinking of the puddle as persisting through the loss of a part, where this part is so large as to have the effect of precipitously decreasing the object's size by half or more.) This sort of case might then encourage us, at least tentatively, to interpret the requirement of spatiotemporal continuity, as it figures in our analysis, in terms of some such moderate notion as that formulated in definition C.

There are two more questions about spatiotemporal continuity that I want briefly to consider. First, should we say that spatiotemporal continuity entails *temporal* continuity? This would mean that in order for an object's career to exhibit spatiotemporal continuity it would have to persist over a continuous stretch of time and not go out of existence and then come back into existence. Second, should we say that spatiotemporal continuity entails *spatial* continuity? This would mean that an object whose career is spatiotemporally continuous must, at any moment of its existence, occupy a continuous region of space and not exist in a (macroscopically) fragmented form. (We might define a continuous region of space as one in which any pair of points can be connected by a continuous curve lying wholly within the region. Thus an object with holes in it may occupy a continuous region in the sense here intended.) I do not think that the previous definitions of spatiotemporal continuity necessarily settle whether spatiotemporal continuity entails temporal or spatial continuity. Those definitions (or a slight modification of them) might be construed as satisfiable by an object irrespective of its temporal or spatial continuity, so long as the (perhaps discontinuous) regions of space which the object occupies at successive moments of its existence (moments which are perhaps separated by intervals during which the object does not exist) overlap appropriately. I think, however, that we can simplify our overall account if we make the terminological decision that both temporal and spatial continuity *are* necessary factors in spatiotemporal continuity. Of course we can always separate these factors out if it proves necessary.

So, summarily, the condition of spatiotemporal continuity in the simple continuity analysis is satisfied by a succession S of object-stages if and only if: first, each object-stage in S coincides with a continuous region of space; second, S spans a continuous stretch of time; and, third, the places which coincide with temporally neighboring stages in S overlap sufficiently (perhaps by more than half).[8]

8. Saul Kripke has pointed out that this account of spatiotemporal continuity has the counterintuitive consequence that an object can be said to move continuously if it jumps instantaneously from one place to a neighboring place in such a manner that the place it first occupies extensively overlaps the place it later occupies. This objection suggests that the account I offer may be only a first approximation, and that the notion of "sufficient overlap" may ultimately need to be refined in terms that are not purely quantitative.

The notion of spatiotemporal continuity will be taken up again in Chapter 5, Section II, and Chapter 6, Sections V and VII, where the puzzling interdependence between object-identity and place-identity will be considered.

IV. Is Continuity Necessary?

Turning now to an assessment of the simple continuity analysis I must stress again that I am going to treat this analysis, as well as the ones that will subsequently replace it, strictly from the standpoint of our most ordinary conception of physical persistence. These analyses, as I want to understand them, are attempts to describe that ordinary conception. What we are seeking at present is nothing more than an accurate description of our ordinary identity scheme. The possibility, or desirability, of revising that scheme is not now at issue, though this is a topic that I will eventually address.

According to the simple continuity analysis the two conditions of qualitative and spatiotemporal continuity are jointly necessary and sufficient for a succession of object-stages to correspond to stages in the career of a persisting object. Let us first consider the necessity part of this claim. Is it true that qualitative and spatiotemporal continuity are necessary for an object's persistence?

We should note that there is one trivial and quite irrelevant sense in which the continuity of a succession of object-stages cannot possibly be necessary for it to correspond to stages in an object's career. Suppose that S is a continuous succession which corresponds to stages in the career of some object x. Then we can certainly form a discontinuous succession S′ by picking out disjointed portions of S, e.g., all of x's Monday-stages. S′ would then be a discontinuous succession which could be said in a sense to correspond to (some) stages in the career of the single persisting object x. But this is obviouly not the sort of case we are thinking about. When we say that a succession "corresponds to stages in the career of an object" (or, for short, "corresponds to a career," or "corresponds to an object"), we are always to understand this to mean that the succession corresponds to, what might more properly be called, *the successive stages* of an object's career. This is to be understood as implying that, though the succession may not correspond to any object's *whole* career (from beginning to end), it must at least comprise *all* of the stages of an object's career from some moment to some other moment. Understood in this sense our question is not trivial: Is it true, as the analysis claims, that a succession must be continuous for it to correspond to the successive stages of an object's career?

There is at least one kind of case which seems to show rather decisively that this is not true. Many objects are thought of as retaining their identities after being taken apart and put back together again. But the careers of such objects must, it seems, be radically discontinuous.

Let us imagine, for example, that a watch w is sent to the factory for repairs. The watch is completely disassembled on the first floor of the factory and its various parts are sent to different rooms on different floors of the factory. Eventually, we will imagine, all of these same parts (perhaps oiled) are collected on the second floor where they are put together to form the watch w'. In such a case there seems to be no doubt that w' is the same watch as w.

Though there is quite definitely an outright lapse of continuity in this case it may not be entirely clear just what sort of continuity is lost. When the watch is initially disassembled and its parts are still relatively proximate (e.g., they are all lying on the same work table) there may be an inclination to say that the watch still exists but in a fragmented form. If we say this then we would so far forgo only spatial continuity but not yet temporal continuity. Eventually, though, when the watch's parts are already dispersed throughout the factory there is, I think, no serious inclination to say that the watch still exists (and that a single watch is simultaneously touching the third floor and the tenth floor of a factory). It seems that we must say that at some point the watch went out of existence, and then later it came back into existence. So temporal continuity seems certainly lost.

It might perhaps be argued that qualitative continuity is not lost in this case, on the grounds that at the moment that the watch comes back into existence it will be qualitatively very similar to the way that it was at the moment that it went out of existence. However we might settle this question about qualitative continuity (and this might depend on the details of the case), it is clear that we cannot say, in the case as I described it, that at the moment when the watch first comes back into existence it occupies a place very close to the place it occupied at the moment when it went out of existence. For the watch went out of existence on the first floor and came back into existence on the second floor. Thus spatiotemporal continuity is very definitely lost (even apart from questions about spatial and temporal continuity), because it is not true that the places successively occupied by the watch overlap.

Details aside, it seems clear enough that in a case like this, where an object is taken apart and put back together again, continuity is lost. It follows that the simple continuity analysis must be complicated at least to the extent of accommodating such cases. Actually these cases do not seem very central (standard, paradigmatic), and the complication which they introduce seems fairly superficial. Apparently the two continuity criteria mentioned in the analysis need to be supplemented by, what I will call (following Quinton),[9] a *compositional criterion*. The compositional criterion would allow us to say that x is identical with y, even if the continuity criteria do not apply, so long as all (or perhaps most) of x's parts (or perhaps x's major parts) are identical with y's.

I will discuss this compositional criterion more fully in the next chapter. For the moment I want to stress the point that the compositional criterion, as it is here being treated, is by its very nature merely a supplement to other criteria upon which it must be dependent. The compositional criterion would allow us to say that x is identical with y when we can say that the parts of x are identical with the parts of y. But then we need criteria in terms of which to analyze the latter identity judgments about the parts of x and y. Compositional considerations are thus dependent upon more primary considerations on the basis of which compositional identity can be understood. As far as our discussion now stands it may still be that these primary considerations are exhausted by qualitative and spatiotemporal continuity.

There emerges the general format of a somewhat more complicated kind of analysis than the simple one so far considered. Any analysis of persistence must start out by mentioning certain primary noncompositional criteria as being (in some specified combination) sufficient for an object's identity. Presumably

9. Anthony Quinton, *The Nature of Things* (Routledge & Kegan Paul, London and Boston, 1973), p. 69. See also p. 63ff.

these criteria will suffice for the most standard cases. The analysis must then also provide for the application of the supplementary compositional criterion in exceptional cases (such as where an object is taken apart and put back together again). The general condition which the analysis would imply to be both necessary and sufficient for an object's persistence is that either the (proper combination of) primary criteria apply or the compositional criterion applies. We have seen that the simple continuity analysis errs insofar as it ignores the compositional criterion. The more fundamental question that remains is whether that analysis at least gives a correct account of our primary criteria. To say that it does would be to imply, at the least, that qualitative and spatiotemporal continuity are jointly sufficient for an object's persistence. Whether this is so is the next question that I want to consider.

V. Is Continuity Sufficient?

According to the simple continuity analysis a sufficient condition for a succession S of object-stages to correspond to stages in the career of a single persisting object is that S be both qualitatively and spatiotemporally continuous. Is the analysis correct in this respect? Let me first briefly consider one rather obvious but, I think, relatively superficial demonstration that, contrary to the analysis, continuity is not sufficient for persistence. To say that continuity is sufficient for persistence suggests, at least on the most obvious interpretation, that the career of any given object is to be prolonged so long as tracing a continuous path allows. Now the point is often made that we sometimes judge one object to go out of existence and to turn into (to be replaced by) a second object which comes into existence. We make this sort of judgment in cases where a perfectly continuous path connects the terminal stages of the first object to the initial stages of the second object. If continuity were in fact a sufficient condition for persistence there would apparently be no basis for our making this kind of judgment.

Here is an example. There is a machine which functions to crush old cars until they turn into blocks of scrap metal. If a car undergoes this process it is presumably correct to say that, at some point in the process, the car went out of existence and was replaced by a block of scrap metal. But the transition from the car-stages to the scrap-stages was completely continuous, both qualitatively and spatiotemporally. Hence if we relied only on continuity considerations we would have to identify the car with the block of scrap metal and judge, not that the car went out of existence, but rather that it persisted in a thoroughly crushed form. This shows that continuity by itself is not sufficient for persistence.

There are many other cases like this. A log which burns in the fire may go out of existence and turn into a smoldering ash, though there was no discontinuity in the process. A gold coin may be destroyed by continuously melting it down. A table may be continuously filed down until it no longer exists and is replaced by a mere lump of wood. None of these cases can be explained by reference to continuity considerations alone. In general terms the objection is that the simple continuity analysis cannot properly account for our judgments about one object going out of existence and being replaced by another.

Now I think that this objection to the simple continuity analysis is correct so far as it goes. The trouble is that the objection does not go nearly far enough, and consequently the tendency among some philosophers to belabor it has the effect of obscuring the really fundamental difficulty with the analysis. To raise this objection gives the impression that continuity does *generally* suffice for persistence, *except* in those rather tricky and special cases in which we judge one object to go out of existence and turn into another. The mistaken view that is readily fostered (and which is, I believe, rather widely entertained) is that simple continuity criteria do in fact give us *more-or-less* all that we need for our ordinary identity judgments, but these criteria need to be supplemented in some way to deal with the tricky notion of one object turning into another. But I intend to show that simple continuity criteria *never* suffice, that these criteria do not give us even *remotely* what we need for our ordinary identity judgments.

Let me try to clarify this point by drawing a distinction between two kinds of cases in which a judgment deviates from our ordinary identity concept. (In talking of a "deviation" from the ordinary concept I leave open, for the time being, whether such deviations may be in some sense legitimate or even desirable.) I will distinguish between *drastic* and *nondrastic* deviations. An example of a nondrastic deviation would be one in which someone judged the car which entered the crushing machine to be identical with the block of scrap metal that emerges. This judgment, I assume, deviates from our ordinary conception since the car has, properly speaking, gone out of existence. Nevertheless there is a quite obvious sense in which this judgment is at least on the right track. The car is not strictly *identical* with the block of scrap metal, but the car did at least *turn into* the block of scrap metal. This deviation is somewhat subtle (not to say controversial); certainly it is by no stretch of imagination *bizarre*. A nondrastic identity-deviation is then one in which someone judges *x* to be identical with *y* where the strict truth (in ordinary terms) is that *x* went out of existence and turned into *y* (or perhaps *x* went out of existence and turned into something which went out of existence and . . . turned into *y*), or vice versa.

By a drastic identity-deviation I mean one in which *x* is judged to be identical with *y* where the truth (in ordinary terms) is that *x* did not even turn into *y* (or turn into something which turned into something which . . . turned into *y*), or vice versa. A drastic identity-deviation (when it is made in optimal conditions of observation) is likely to strike us as completely bizarre and off the track. An example would be if someone observes an ordinary moving car and judges that the car which exists at one moment is identical with the back fender that existed at a previous moment.

The earlier objection, which focused on the rather special (and perhaps controversial) cases in which one object turns into another, left the impression that, these cases aside, simple continuity criteria operate effectively. This implies that someone who relied on simple continuity considerations would thereby avoid any *drastic* deviations from our ordinary identity judgments, though he might still be led occasionally to a *nondrastic* one. But I intend to show now that someone who relied on simple continuity considerations would frequently (indeed as often as not) be led to drastic identity-deviations. This is a much deeper indictment of the simple continuity analysis, since it is tantamount to showing that continuity considerations by themselves are totally ineffective as criteria for our ordinary identity judgments.

The reason why simple continuity considerations are totally ineffective is that there are literally innumerable space-time paths (successions of object-stages), constantly encountered by us in our experience, which, though they are spatiotemporally and qualitatively continuous, do not correspond even remotely to the careers of any objects, as ordinarily conceived. This point seems completely obvious the moment it is grasped. It requires, however, thinking in unaccustomed ways about space-time paths which, from the point of view of our ordinary identity concept, seem wholly strange and unreal. But unless we can force ourselves to focus on such strange-seeming space-time paths our analysis of identity will merely presuppose what it pretends to explain.

Let me first describe schematically the sort of paths that I have in mind; then I will give examples. If you consider any object it will always be possible to trace an indefinite number of qualitatively and spatiotemporally continuous space-time paths which connect the whole object at one time to one of its parts at a later time. Furthermore if you consider any part of any object it will always be possible to trace an indefinite number of qualitatively and spatiotemporally continuous space-time paths which connect that part of the object at one time to some other part of the object at another time. Yet there will generally be no persisting objects, as ordinarily conceived, which correspond to these paths; there is, in terms of our ordinary conception, generally no persisting object which combines stages of a whole object with stages of its parts, or which combines stages of one part of an object with stages of other parts. Hence, side by side with the career of a whole and the careers of its parts the simple continuity analysis would generate a menagerie of pseudo-careers made up of scattered stages of the career of the whole and the careers of its parts. Reliance on simple continuity considerations would consequently yield the most drastic and bizarre identity-deviations.

Let me try to broach this idea by way of the following example. Imagine that a tree persists intact during the two day period from Monday to Tuesday, and that nothing out of the ordinary happens to the tree during that period. Let S_1 be the succession of object-stages corresponding to the tree's career during those two days. The tree of course will have a trunk. To be vivid about this let us in fact imagine that this is a one-branched tree consisting of nothing but a trunk and one branch. And let S_2 be the succession which corresponds to the trunk during that two day period.

Now comes the somewhat weird part. I want to consider the succession S_3 which consists of the Monday-portion of S_1 followed by the Tuesday-portion of S_2. S_3, in other words, is a succession which consists of the tree-stages of Monday followed by the trunk-stages of Tuesday.

Let us consider whether S_3 corresponds to the career of any object, as ordinarily conceived. Very evidently it does not; S_3 is in fact a mind-boggling path which we can barely get ourselves to think about. In tracing S_3 we have to follow the tree's career on Monday and then suddenly jump on Tuesday to the trunk. Remember that we are imagining a case in which nothing special happened to the tree (and, specifically, the tree did not lose its branch). In such a case there is, in terms of our ordinary conception, no persisting object remotely corresponding to S_3. If we did try to think of an object corresponding to S_3 then we would have to say that this object coincided with the whole tree on Monday and then shrunk in size so that it coincided with only the trunk on Tuesday. In the circumstances that we are imagining there is (within the limits of our ordinary identity concept) obviously no object which remotely fits this description.

But is S_3 continuous? Well, S_3 is certainly not *strongly* continuous since it involves an element of discontinuity, both qualitative and locational, in the jump from the tree on Monday to the trunk on Tuesday. But we have already seen that strong continuity is not what the simple continuity analysis requires. Moreover we saw earlier that the small element of discontinuity suffered by a tree when it loses a branch does not disqualify its career from exhibiting the degree of continuity required by the analysis. In the case we are now imagining the jump in S_3 from the one-branched tree of Monday to the trunk of Tuesday seems, on the face of it, to involve just that small and nondisqualifying element of discontinuity. So it seems that S_3 is sufficiently continuous. Hence S_3, on the simple continuity analysis, ought to correspond to the ordinary career of an object. But S_3 obviously does not correspond to the ordinary career of an object.

It is, by the way, an unimportant feature of our example that S_3 is a path which involves change, whereas S_1 and S_2 do not involve change. For we might in fact imagine that the trunk's (and tree's) color or size altered during that two day period, so that S_1 and S_2 also involve change. Indeed we might imagine that some piece of bark fell off the trunk (and tree) on Monday, so that S_1 and S_2 even involve an element of discontinuity. All that matters in our example is that the tree did not lose its branch during those two days. And the difficulty is that whereas, in terms of our ordinary identity concept, S_1 and S_2 correspond to the careers of objects, S_3 does not, though in point of continuity there seems to be no decisive difference between these paths.

Imagine someone who stands in front of a one-branched tree, to which nothing special is happening, in optimal conditions of observation, and who makes the following statement: "There is an object here that is now a trunk, and that same object was larger a moment ago when it was a whole tree." That would be what I call a drastic deviation from our ordinary identity concept. But the simple continuity analysis does not even explain why (how) this is a deviation.

We can now easily imagine even more complicated and bizarre possibilities. We can consider the succession S_4 which consists of the tree-stages of Monday, followed by the trunk-stages of Tuesday, followed by the tree-stages of Wednesday. Apparently S_4 is again sufficiently continuous, and it therefore ought, on the analysis, to correspond to an object which first got smaller and then got larger. Evidently there is no limit to the kinds of pseudo-careers that the analysis would generate in this fashion.

Someone might try to resist this point by arguing that S_3 and S_4 are somehow not sufficiently continuous. There would be no purpose in thrashing this out since we can simply change the example slightly to suit this critic. Imagine that our tree contains a very tiny twig at the end of its branch. Now consider the portion of wood W which constitutes the whole tree *except for that tiny twig*. Instead of S_2 let us now refer to the succession S_2' which consists of the stages of W on Monday and Tuesday. And instead of S_3 let us construct S_3' which consists of the

Monday-portion of S_1 (i.e., the tree-stages of Monday) followed by the Tuesday-portion of S_2'. In tracing S_3' we follow the tree's career on Monday and then jump on Tuesday to the tree minus that little twig. Certainly this minute jump is not great enough to disqualify S_3' from being sufficiently continuous. But S_3' does not correspond to a persisting object, in terms of our ordinary identity concept, any more than S_3 did. It would still be a drastic and wholly bizarre deviation from the ordinary conception if someone judged, where nothing has happened to the twig, that a tree has shrunk a little bit and no longer contains some twig which it previously contained. But it seems quite definite that the simple continuity analysis implies that S_3' does correspond to the career of a persisting object.

As before there are no limits to the complicating possibilities. If we can trace a continuous path from the whole tree to the tree minus a twig then we can trace a path back to the whole tree again. And if we can trace a continuous path from the whole tree to the tree minus *one* twig then we can surely go on from that point to trace a continuous path to the tree minus *two* twigs; and then eventually to the tree minus the branch; and then back again; and so on. The general point is that we can always move by continuous gradations from any object to any of its parts, and from any of its parts to any other part. Consequently if we relied on simple continuity considerations we would have no tracing rule at all, no basis at all for judging, in anything like ordinary terms, what is identical with what. This is the fundamental and drastic inadequacy of the simple continuity analysis, by comparison with which any other inadequacy seems scarcely worth mentioning.

I want to underscore this very central point about the insufficiency of continuity by considering another example, and in a somewhat different light. We can sometimes clarify our understanding of how our language works by finding or constructing a radically disparate language and then reflecting on what the difference is between that language and our own. In that spirit I want now to construct a language (or, really, some small segment of a language) which contains identity criteria radically different from our own. When we reflect on what the difference is between those criteria and ours we will be helped to appreciate the total ineffectiveness of simple continuity considerations.

Consider, then, a language in which the word "car" is replaced by the two words "incar" and "outcar." The criteria of identity for incars and outcars can be indicated as follows. The term "incar" will apply to any car that is entirely inside a garage, and where a car is partly inside and partly outside a garage, "incar" will apply to the segment of the car that is inside; correlatively, "outcar" will apply to any car that is entirely outside a garage, and where a car is partly inside and partly outside, "outcar" will apply to the segment outside. When (as we would say) a car moves from inside a garage to outside, the description in that other language would be: "An incar moved towards the exit whereupon it commenced to shrink in size until it eventually vanished; simultaneously with the shrinking of the incar an outcar appeared at the outside of the exit, and gradually grew until it attained the size and form of the original incar." In this description the original object inside the garage (the object which coincides with what we would call a car) is traced in such a way as to render it identical with what is later a smaller object inside the garage, and distinct from any object that is ever outside the garage.

This language strikes us as very strange. I am not at the moment concerned with the question whether this language is strange (or bad or wrong) in some absolute sense, or merely relative to our conventional way of talking. I am not, that is, concerned now with the question whether there could actually be people who spoke like that, or whether, if there were such people, their description of moving cars would be, in some sense, less correct than ours. The crucial point for my present purpose is that this language is, at the very least, strange relative to our conventional way of talking. Clearly the incar-outcar identity criteria deviate from our ordinary identity criteria. It would certainly be a mistake for someone speaking *our* language to identify what was first a whole car in a garage with what was later a small portion of that car inside the garage. It is certainly incorrect, at least in our language, to assert, in the ordinary circumstance of a car leaving a garage, that an object shrank in size and vanished.

But why would this be a mistake in our language? What ordinary criteria of identity would be violated by tracing an object's career along the path of the shrinking incar? Very evidently not *continuity* criteria. For it is strikingly obvious that if we were to trace the path of the shrinking incar we would be tracing a path that is perfectly continuous, both qualitatively and spatiotemporally. Considerations of mere continuity do not give us the slightest clue as to why it is that the path of the shrinking incar does not, in our language, correspond to the career of an object. The wrongness, indeed the strangeness, of the incar-outcar criteria, from the point of view of our ordinary identity concept, is thus a vivid indication of the ineffectiveness of simple continuity considerations to explain the nature of our identity concept.

An absolutely minimal condition of adequacy for any analysis of our identity concept is that the analysis imply that it would be wrong to trace an object in accordance with identity criteria of the incar-outcar variety. It is evident that these criteria are merely one instance of a wholly general kind of aberrant criteria (aberrant, that is, relative to our ordinary identity concept). These criteria are aberrant insofar as they would permit us to trace an object in such a way as to combine what (in our language) ought properly to be regarded as stages of the object and stages of some of its parts. A minimal condition of adequacy for any analysis of our identity concept is that it at least imply the wrongness of such drastic whole-part tracing confusions. The fundamental error of the simple continuity analysis is that it does not even satisfy this minimal condition.

2

Sortals

I. The Sortal Rule

A COMPLETELY adequate analysis of persistence would have to take account of complications involving the fact that objects can be taken apart and put back together again, and also complications involving the fact that one object sometimes turns into another. But these are relatively peripheral problems which pertain to cases that are not entirely typical. The more fundamental problem is to be able at least to characterize properly those successions which correspond to persisting objects in the most unexceptional cases. I want first to concentrate on this problem and then return to the residual complications afterwards.

We know that continuity considerations by themselves do not suffice to rule out such aberrant paths as the one which combined stages of a tree with stages of a trunk, or the one which combined stages of a car with stages of car-parts. We want to elicit some additional constraint which can be seen as operating in our ordinary identity concept to rule out such paths. Now one intuition that we may have about such paths, and why they seem aberrant from the ordinary point of view, is that tracing these paths involves some kind of illicit *shift*, some kind of rule-violating loss of constancy. How can we characterize the nature of this illicit shift?

Of course we cannot simply say that tracing an aberrant path involves shifting from *one object* to *another*, since precisely

34

what we are looking for is an analysis of what it is that constitutes staying with the same object. Nor will it do, at the present
stage of analysis, to say merely that the aberrant paths involve
shifting from a *whole* object(-stage) to a *part* of an object(-stage).
For "whole" and "part," in at least one obvious sense, are relational terms that do not necessarily exclude each other. A whole
twig may be a part of a whole branch, which may in turn be a
part of a whole tree (which may, perhaps, in turn be a part of a
whole landscape). Evidently to try to refer simply to an illicit
shift from "wholes" to "parts" would not get us very far.

When one reflects upon the problem in these terms an idea
which is likely to suggest itself, and which will in fact turn out
to be very much worth developing, is that an illicit shift occurs
in the aberrant paths insofar as these paths combine an ob-
ject(-stage) of one *sort* with an object(-stage) of another sort. An
object may of course change in the course of its career, both
qualitatively and locationally, and these changes, so long as
they are continuous, may even be quite drastic. But the present
suggestion is that it is part of our concept of object-identity that
throughout all of its changes an object must at least remain
an object of *the same sort*. The constraint, therefore, which
a succession must satisfy, in addition to the simple continuity
conditions, in order for it to correspond to the career of an
object is that it consist of object-stages of the same sort. The
idea would then be that this constraint is not satisfied by such
aberrant paths as the one which combines tree-stages with
trunk-stages, or the one which combines car-stages with stages
of car-parts.

One difficulty which this suggestion immediately faces is to
explain what is meant by saying that two objects (or two object-
stages) are of the same "sort." We want to wind up saying that
the succession which combined car-stages with stages of car-parts
does not correspond to a persisting object in our language because
it involves combining object-stages of different sorts. But consider
that from the point of view of the incar-outcar language all of
these object-stages are *incar*-stages, which would seem to imply,
perhaps, that from that point of view these stages *are* of the
same sort. Should we then say that whether or not one ob-
ject(-stage) is the same sort as another depends upon which
language we speak? This may be a helpful first move, and is

anyway quite harmless so long as we keep open, as before, the possibility that some languages may be, in some sense, "better" than others.

Recasting our earlier idea in more explicitly linguistic terms let us say that such words in our language as "car," "tree," and "trunk" are *sortal* terms. The constraint which a succession must satisfy in order for it to correspond to a persisting object (in our language) is that there be (in our language) a sortal term F such that every object-stage in the succession comes under (is an instance of) F. Hence a continuous succession of tree-stages corresponds to the career of a persisting tree, because all of the object-stages in this succession come under the sortal "tree"; and a continuous succession of trunk-stages corresponds to the career of a persisting trunk, because all of the object-stages in this succession come under the sortal "trunk"; and a continuous succession of car-stages corresponds to the career of a persisting car because all of the object-stages in this succession come under the sortal "car." But the succession which combined Monday's tree-stages with Tuesday's trunk-stages does not correspond to any persisting object because there is no single sortal term F which covers all of the object-stages in this succession. (Notice that though a trunk is part of a tree a trunk does not, in the relevant sense, *come under* the sortal "tree"). Again, the path of the shrinking incar does not correspond to a persisting object (in our language) because there is no single sortal (in our language) which covers all of the object-stages in this path.

The analysis which we are trying to develop might now be partially formulated as follows:

The Sortal Rule. A sufficient condition for the succession S of object-stages to correspond to stages in the career of a single persisting object is that:

(1) S is spatiotemporally continuous; *and*
(2) S is qualitatively continuous; *and*
(3) there is a sortal term F such that S is a succession of F-stages.

The sortal rule states only a sufficient, not a necessary, condition of persistence, because we want to leave room for the compositional criterion (and perhaps other elaborations of the rule). We may summarize the rule by saying that it permits us to trace an object's career by following a continuous space-time path *under a sortal*.[1]

We have still to clarify what it means to say that a term is a "sortal." We certainly cannot say that *every* general term in our language is a sortal since this would immediately defeat the entire rationale of the sortal rule. If we said that "brown (thing)", for example, is a sortal (so that any two brown things are, in the relevant sense, things of the same sort), then the sortal rule could no longer be relied on to disqualify the succession which combined the Monday tree-stages with the Tuesday trunk-stages. Such a succession might very well consist of only brown object-stages, and would hence qualify under the sortal rule if "brown" were a sortal. Or suppose that the term "in a garage," which applies to any object in a garage, were counted as a sortal. Then the sortal rule could no longer disqualify as aberrant the succession which combines stages of a car in a garage with stages of car-parts in a garage.

We want to be able to say that such terms as "tree," "trunk," and "car" are sortals, but that terms like "brown" and "in a garage" are not. Of course we immediately notice that the former terms are nouns and the latter are not. But this purely grammatical difference, though it may approximately coincide with the logical (conceptual) distinction which we are seeking to clarify, does not explain what that distinction is.

It is a mistake, however, to suppose that we need to be able to explain what it means for a term to be a sortal *before* we can understand the sortal rule. The proper way to look at this, rather, is that the sortal rule itself defines (constitutes) what it means for a term to be a sortal. A term is a sortal just in case the sortal rule would allow us to trace a career under the term. A sortal is thus a term which plays a distinctive role in our identity conception, and to learn to speak our language involves finding out just which terms play this role. A definition of "sortal" might then be:

"The general term F is a sortal" means: It is a conceptual truth (a rule of language) that any spatiotemporally and qualitatively

---

1. Cf. Wiggins, *Identity and Spatio-Temporal Continuity*, p. 35ff. The notion of a sortal that I intend to develop in this chapter is, I think, essentially the one employed by Wiggins.

continuous succession of F-stages corresponds to (what counts as) stages in the career of a single persisting F-thing.

Many typical nouns seem to qualify as sortals on this definition; for example, "tree," "trunk," "branch," "car," "fender," "dog," "eye," "mountain," "pebble." Many adjectives and verbs do not qualify; for example, "red," "hot," "hard," "wet," "moves," "burns," "grows." But this grammatical test is by no means decisive, even for the case of syntactically simple terms (which is the only case to which the test might reasonably apply). A rather obvious example of a noun which is not a sortal is "object," at least when we take this word in the broad sense that I have been using it. If "object" were counted as a sortal then it would follow from the sortal rule that any continuous succession of object-stages corresponds to a career, which is precisely the mistake which the rule is designed to avoid. I will consider other examples of nouns which are not sortals presently. An adjective like "canine," in the sense of "dog" (if there is such a sense), would evidently be as much a sortal as the noun form. There may even be some sortal verbs, but I do not know of any very convincing examples.

When we consider syntactically complex terms we find that any (conjunctive) combination of a sortal and a nonsortal yields a sortal. Take "brown car," which combines the sortal "car" with the nonsortal "brown." This complex term qualifies as a sortal on the definition because, if it is a conceptual truth that any continuous succession of car-stages corresponds to stages in the career of a single persisting car, then it must also be a conceptual truth that any continuous succession of brown car-stages corresponds to stages in the career of a single persisting brown car. It should be noted, however, that the sortalhood of "brown car" does not imply that the terminus of a continuous succession of brown car-stages corresponds to a brown car going out of existence, for the career of a brown car whose color changes can be prolonged under the more general sortal "car." I will return to this complication about going out of (and coming into) existence in a later section.

Many (though not all) nonsortals have an important property which may be seen as explaining why they cannot properly function as sortals. The property is that these terms apply to objects that extensively overlap each other. Consider, for example, what would happen if we tried to treat "brown (thing)" as a sortal. We would then trace the career of a brown thing by following a continuous succession of brown-stages. But this would lead to precisely the tracing chaos which showed up in connection with the simple continuity analysis.

Remember the tree whose career was traced from Monday through Tuesday. Let us imagine now that the tree is uniformly brown. S_1 was the succession of tree-stages during those two days; S_2 the succession of trunk-stages; S_2' the succession of stages of the tree minus a little twig; and S_3 was the weird succession which combined the Monday-portion of S_1 with the Tuesday-portion of S_2, while S_3' was the weird succession which combined the Monday-portion of S_1 with the Tuesday-portion of S_2'. All of these are apparently continuous successions of brown-stages. If we treated "brown" as a sortal we would have to count each of these successions as corresponding to the career of a single persisting brown thing. Moreover there is no limit to the number of different successions of this sort that could be fabricated by combining different stages of the mentioned successions.

Well, someone might ask, so what? If we *did* treat "brown" as a sortal then we simply *would* count all of those overlapping and crisscrossing successions as different careers of persisting brown objects. What would be wrong with that?

I do not want to say that there necessarily would be anything "wrong" with it. My present point is only that treating "brown" as a sortal would lead to a certain consequence which seems deeply inconsonant with the general tendency of our thought and speech about persistence, and this explains, in a sense, why "brown" is not treated as a sortal. It seems central to the way that we think and speak about persistence that we should typically be able to pick out an object and go on to trace its career unambiguously along some definite space-time path. But if we picked out a brown object, say a brown tree, and tried to trace its career under the covering concept "brown" we would not be led unambiguously along any particular path, since we could go on to trace any number of different continuous successions of brown-stages.

The property of "brown" which renders it unsuitable to play the role of a sortal is that brown objects (e.g., the brown tree and the brown trunk) may overlap extensively (where one way that objects can overlap extensively is for one of them to be a large part of the other). I will say that any such term is *dispersive,* where this is defined as follows:

"F is dispersive" means: It happens typically that different F-things overlap extensively.

I want to leave this definition quite vague. The general idea is that if F is dispersive it will frequently be possible to trace continuous paths which combine stages of one F-thing with stages of another extensively overlapping F-thing. It will frequently happen, therefore, that two continuous F-successions will *partly coincide and partly diverge,* i.e., that they will contain the same object-stages at one moment but different object-stages at another moment. In our previous example S_1 (which contains the tree-stages of Monday and Tuesday) and S_3 (which contains the tree-stages of Monday and the trunk-stages of Tuesday) coincide on Monday and diverge on Tuesday, while S_2 (which contains the trunk-stages of Monday and Tuesday) and S_3 diverge on Monday and coincide on Tuesday. It is the partial coincidence and partial divergence of continuous F-successions which makes it impossible to trace careers unambiguously under a dispersive term F.

II. The Making of a Sortal

I am suggesting, then, that nondispersiveness is a necessary condition for a term to be a sortal, but this is certainly not a sufficient condition. I am not sure whether there are any syntactically simple nondispersive terms which are not sortals, but there is no trouble concocting complex terms which are both nondispersive and nonsortals. Consider, for example, the term "largest portion of a car in a garage," where this is understood to apply to any whole car in a garage or, if the car is partly inside and partly outside, to the inside portion. This term is, in other words, the English counterpart of "incar." Evidently this term is nondispersive, and we could in principle trace perfectly unambiguous careers under it. But we do not trace such careers, which shows that the term is not a sortal.

Or consider the disjunctive term "tree that is being rained

upon or trunk that is not being rained upon," where this is to be understood as applying to an object at a given time if and only if either the object is a tree which is being rained upon at that time, or the object is a trunk which is not being rained upon at that time. This is a nondispersive term under which we could in principle trace unambiguously such weird-seeming tree-to-trunk successions as the one discussed earlier. (If it rains on Monday but not on Tuesday then we get just the path discussed.) Of course this is not a sortal and we do not trace under it.

Returning to more ordinary examples, it may not be clear how we should treat a shape word like "round" in the present connection. But I would want to count "round" as dispersive, and hence as definitely not a sortal. My reason for this judgment is that a typical round thing, say a tomato, will extensively overlap any number of round portions of matter which make it up. This judgment might be resisted on the grounds that it seems odd to apply the expression "round object" to some arbitrary portion of a tomato. Now I might agree, perhaps, that at some level, and in some sense, arbitrary round portions of tomatoes are not properly called "round objects," or even "objects." It seems reasonable, however, that at the present stage of analysis we should rely on nothing but the widest sense of the word "object," as meaning, roughly, any continuous tract of matter. To rely on any narrower sense of "object" at the present stage would be simply to assume features of our concept of an object which have yet to be explained. It seems sufficiently clear that at least in this wide sense of "object," round objects frequently overlap extensively, so that "round" is dispersive. The important point here is that our concept of "round" could not by itself provide a basis for unambiguously tracing careers.

It becomes clear why typical nouns like "tree," and "trunk," and "car" are peculiarly apt to function as sortals. These terms are nondispersive in the extreme, for there are no remotely typical cases in which two trees, or two trunks, or two cars extensively overlap. A sufficiently large portion of a tree (e.g., the tree minus a twig) is to be sure something that, as we might roughly put it, *could have been a tree* if it were separated from the rest of the tree. (That is, if you took the twig away you would be left with a tree.) None of these "potential trees," however, *are* trees. This is decisively evidenced by the fact that a term like "tree" is a paradigmatic *count noun,* which means that there is typically a completely clearcut answer to the question "How many trees are there in such and such a region?" For example, it may be a clearcut truth that there is exactly one tree in my backyard, which shows conclusively that no portion of that tree is counted as a tree. The nondispersiveness of our standard count nouns is what guarantees that we can employ them as sortals and trace unambiguous careers under them.

By contrast, the dispersiveness of such so-called *mass nouns* as "water," "wood," and "dirt" disqualifies these terms from functioning as sortals. A term like "wood" is dispersive because any stretch (quantity, bit) of wood will extensively overlap numerous other stretches of wood that make it up. The ineffectiveness of "wood" as a sortal can be brought out by considering, with respect once again to our old example, how trying to trace under "wood" would allow us to combine tree-stages and trunk-stages (or tree-stages and stages of the tree minus a twig) in an unlimited variety of ways. That mass nouns are not sortals will figure in a later chapter as posing a problem about our concept of the persistence of matter.

It may be noted, however, that mass nouns enter into various nondispersive constructions that do apparently function as sortals. Consider such expressions as "pool (or puddle) of water," "lump (or fragment) of wood," "pile (or heap) of dirt." These are, or at least can legitimately be understood as, nondispersive. If I say, "There are three pools of water on the floor," I am evidently using "pool of water" in such a way that the parts of a pool of water are not themselves pools of water. It seems rather straightforwardly correct to trace careers under these terms. If you trace a continuous succession of stages of pools of water it seems to follow that you have kept your eye on the same pool of water. Perhaps "pool of water," "lump of wood," and "pile of dirt" do not really differ much from such standard sortals as "river," "stick," and "mountain."

The sortal "pool of water" stands to the nonsortal "water" in essentially the following way: "pool of water" is equivalent, roughly, to "continuous stretch of water that is not part of any larger continuous stretch of water." Now a more difficult example to assess is a term like "continuous stretch of brown that is not part of any larger continuous stretch of brown." Is there a sortal which corresponds to this term, a sortal which stands to "brown" in the way that "pool of water" stands to "water"? Where we have a continuous stretch of brown that is not part of any larger continuous stretch of brown we have, perhaps, a *patch of brown*. Is "patch of brown" (construable as) a sortal?

Here is the sort of example to test our intuitions about this. First, as a preliminary, consider that if you add a missing drawer to your desk then something, viz. your desk, gets heavier. Anyone who knows how to speak our language knows that this is so. For anyone who knows how to speak our language implicitly knows how to operate "desk" as a sortal, and knows, therefore, that a continuous succession of desk-stages corresponds to the career of a single persisting desk. If some later member of such a succession is heavier than an earlier one it follows that a desk got heavier. Now compare this case to the following one. You have a brown desk and you place a brown ashtray on top of it. (Perhaps the ashtray even sticks a little bit to your desk.) Does anything get heavier in this process? Of course the desk does not get heavier, and the ashtray does not get heavier. But does *anything* get heavier? If "patch of brown" is a sortal then it would follow that something does get heavier, viz. a particular patch of brown. For in this example there is a continuous succession of stages of brown-stretches-not-contained-in-larger-brown-stretches, where later members of this succession are heavier than earlier ones.

It may seem outrageous in this situation to assert, without further ado, that something (let alone some *object*) got heavier. On the other hand, if it is made clear that the thing being referred to is a patch of brown, it does not seem clearly false to assert this. There may even be exceptional circumstances in which there would be a point in describing the situation in this way. Perhaps we should say that "patch of brown" is a border-line, or marginal, case of a sortal. Other examples of the same sort might be "lump of hardness" and "patch of wetness."

I bring up these borderline sortals primarily to guard against the error of construing the sortal rule as being perfectly exact. The truth, on the contrary, is that the rule, and the correlative notion of a sortal, can be no more exact than our ordinary concept of persistence. The rule is merely a framework in terms of which we can, hopefully, describe and understand the nature of our identity scheme. There is no denying, however, the marked vagueness and amorphousness of that scheme. New sortals may be brought into language, and old ones dropped out; it may remain undecided whether a given term can function as a sortal; terms may be ambiguous, in that sometimes they function as sortals and sometimes not; and makeshift sortals may be adopted to serve the needs of the moment. Indeed one positive sign of the adequacy of the sortal rule is precisely that it helps us to describe and explain the vagueness of our identity scheme.

A question which may naturally arise now is why it is that some nondispersive concepts figure as standard sortals in our language while others figure only marginally so, or not at all. This question is actually part of a much larger one, as to why our concept of persistence is what it is and not something else. I shall have considerably more to say about this question later, and in more than one context. A preliminary answer to the specific question about sortals, which may seem at least superficially satisfying, is that a nondispersive concept tends to figure as a sortal in our language insofar as this concept is important to us, from some practical or theoretical standpoint. To trace the career of a tree in the ordinary way, or a car, or a desk, seems more useful and relevant to our normal concerns than does tracing the career of a patch of brown as such, or a lump of hardness (not to mention tracing the career of an incar, or a tree-to-trunk concoction). This answer obviously needs to be elaborated, and it may actually turn out to have less explanatory value than might initially seem.

There is one complication about dispersiveness which ought to be aired before going further. I have suggested that a necessary (but not sufficient) condition for F to be a sortal is that F be nondispersive. Now it may be argued with some plausibility that a considerably stronger condition than that is in order. Consider the following definition:

"F is antidispersive" means: It cannot conceivably happen that different F-things overlap extensively.

In order for a term F to be *nondispersive* it need only be the case that F-things do not as a matter of fact typically overlap extensively. But for F to be *antidispersive* it must be that F-things never do, nor ever conceivably could, overlap extensively.

It may be argued that for F to be a sortal it is not merely necessary that F should be nondispersive, but also that F should be antidispersive. For suppose that some sortal F were merely nondispersive but not antidispersive. Then there would be a conceivable (or perhaps even an actual but atypical) situation in which two F-things extensively overlapped. It may seem to follow that in that conceivable situation there would be continuous successions which combine stages of one F-thing with stages of the other. There would then be continuous F-successions which partly coincide and partly diverge. But, if F is a sortal, we would have to judge these F-successions to correspond to F-things whose paths partly coincide and partly diverge (and hence, in a sense, to different F-things that temporarily occupy the same place). Such a judgment, it may be maintained, ought not to be admitted even as a possibility.[2] And, the argument would conclude, to rule this judgment out as a possibility we must require that sortals be antidispersive.

This argument can, I think, be questioned on several counts. For one thing it is not at all clear that wherever two F-things "extensively overlap," even if this be in some rare and idiosyncratic way, it necessarily follows that there is a "sufficiently continuous" path which combines stages of one with stages of the other. Both the notion of extensive overlap and that of continuity (especially qualitative continuity) are much too vague to allow for any such airtight connection. I did indeed assume earlier that where F is dispersive, so that the typical case is for F-things to overlap extensively, then stages of different F-things could frequently be combined continuously. And this assumption seemed completely plausible with respect to the dispersive terms which I cited (e.g., "brown," "round," "wood"). (For these terms, in fact, *perfectly* continuous paths can be traced combining stages of different objects that come under them.) But I would not necessarily assume that where F is nondispersive, and two F-things extensively overlap in some rare case, a problem would *have* to arise about continuously combining stages of these objects. On the other hand if it could be shown (which seems rather doubtful) that, for some seemingly standard sortal F, it might happen that two incontrovertibly continuous succes-

2. Wiggins accepts the principle that, where F is a sortal, it cannot conceivably happen that there are F-things whose paths partly coincide and partly diverge. See Wiggins, ibid., p. 72, ftn. 44.

sions of F-stages partly coincide and partly diverge, then I am
not convinced that we ought simply to rule out the possible judgment that these successions correspond to F-things whose paths
partly coincide and partly diverge (and hence, in a sense, to
two F-things that temporarily occupy the same place).[3]

In any case I intend to leave open this rather vexing question
as to whether sortals must be antidispersive. Perhaps the following consideration will suffice to show that this question is not
very urgent. Suppose that we have some seemingly standard
sortal F under which we apparently trace careers. But suppose
that it turns out upon reflection that F is not antidispersive. A
possible example of such a term might be "table," for it can
be argued (but not, I think, with overwhelming convincingness)
that one table might be made up of other tables in such a manner as to warrant the judgment that two different tables extensively overlap. Actually it seems rather questionable that if
two tables are put together to make a third table we can simultaneously treat as tables the composite and its components. (Do
we then have three tables at a given moment?) Furthermore
even if it is proper to count all three as tables, so that we may
in fact be said to have a composite table extensively overlapping
a large component table, it still remains questionable, as I suggested a moment ago, that we would be able to trace a (clearly)
continuous path which combined stages of the composite with
stages of its large component. But suppose even the worst possibility, that sortals must be antidispersive and that, as a consequence, "table" cannot qualify as a sortal. Would we then be
left with the problem of explaining how we ordinarily trace the
careers of tables?

Not really. For even if "table" is disqualified as a sortal,
"standard (normal) table" is not. The latter term, at any rate,
is antidispersive, since it is inconceivable that two *standard*
tables should extensively overlap. (If even this seems unacceptable then, for the purposes of this argument, replace "standard
table" by the evidently antidispersive term "table that does not

3. Note that this judgment is not ruled out by the sortal rule. The latter says
that a continuous F-succession corresponds to stages in the career of a "single
persisting object." I take this to mean that the succession corresponds to *at
least one* object, admitting the possibility that there may be more than one.
Even if this possibility cannot be realized in the kind of case under consideration it is realized in other cases, as I will show in Section IV, below.

extensively overlap any other table.") So we can say that we ordinarily trace the careers of tables under the sortal "standard table." And from this it seems a small step to saying that we ordinarily trace the careers of tables under the sortal "table" *in the sense of* "standard table." This suggests, I think—at least with respect to our most commonplace tracing procedures, which is primarily what I want to continue to focus on—that the question whether sortals need to be antidispersive, or merely nondispersive, makes no great difference. As to what tracing procedure we might follow in an atypical case like that of the allegedly overlapping tables, where arguably the sortal rule would not suffice, this difficulty will be incidentally neutralized by the discussion in the next chapter, which will suggest that our dependence upon the sortal rule is anyway less than absolute.

III. Coming into Existence and Going out of Existence

If we can assume that the sortal rule explains our primary noncompositional basis for judging of an object's identity then it should prove possible to give an account on this basis of our judgments about when objects come into existence and go out of existence (where the possibility is left open that an object which goes out of existence might, via the supplementary compositional criterion, later come back into existence). A very obvious kind of example in which an object is said to come into existence is where various bits of matter come together, either naturally or as a result of human design, to form the object. And an obvious example of an object going out of existence is where it is broken up or otherwise decomposed into fragments. Thus a table comes into existence when a carpenter puts various pieces of wood together in the appropriate form, and the table might go out of existence when it is smashed to bits. How shall we understand our thought about such cases in terms of the sortal rule?

There are several wrong answers which we might initially be tempted to give to this question. A trivial mistake would be to suggest that wherever we have a continuous succession of table-stages we can associate the beginning and end of this succession with the coming into existence and going out of existence of a table. Or, to put this in more general terms, the idea would be

(1) Where F is a sortal and S is a continuous succession of F-stages, the beginning and end of S correspond respectively to the coming into existence and going out of existence of an F-thing.

(1) is just a trivial slip because it overlooks the possibility that a continuous succession of F-stages might be merely some segment of a longer continuous succession of F-stages. Suppose that some table was created in 1910 and persisted continuously until it was destroyed in 1960. S might merely be the continuous succession of table-stages that corresponds to the segment of the table's career from 1920 to 1930. Obviously the terminal points of S do not then correspond to any table coming into existence or going out of existence. The terminal points of a continuous succession of table-stages do correspond to the coming into existence and going out of existence of a table only if the succession is a *longest* continuous succession of table-stages, i.e., it is not merely a segment of a longer continuous succession of table-stages.

A general principle which shows itself in this example is what I will call *the principle of prolongation.* This principle says that if F is a sortal and S is a continuous succession of F-stages then no (proper) segment of S is such that its terminal points correspond to the coming into existence and going out of existence of an F-thing. (For simplicity we can confine ourselves to segments of S which both begin after S begins and also end before S ends.) The principle says, in other words, that when we trace an object's career under the sortal F we must prolong the career, backwards and forwards in time, so long as tracing under F allows. So we can never say, where F is a sortal, that one F-thing went out of existence and was, without any loss of continuity, immediately replaced by another F-thing that came into existence. The principle of prolongation does not, I think, follow strictly from the sortal rule, since the latter leaves open as at least a formal possibility that one F-thing persists, corresponding to a continuous F-succession, while other F-things, corresponding to segments of that succession, come into existence and go out of existence. Be this as it may, the principle is obviously called for by the sortal rule, and seems quite plausible in its own right.

We saw that the answer to our question in the case of the table is that the coming into existence and going out of existence of a table correspond to the terminal points of a longest continuous succession of table-stages. It may seem that we can easily generalize this answer to cover all cases by emending (1) to read

(2) Where F is a sortal and S is a continuous succession of F-stages, the beginning and end of S correspond respectively to the coming into existence and going out of existence of an F-thing if and only if S is not the segment of a longer continuous succession of F-stages.

But (2) is still badly off the mark. As I pointed out earlier a term like "brown table" is a sortal, since any continuous succession of brown table-stages must correspond to stages in the career of a single persisting brown table. (2) would then have us say that the terminal points of a longest continuous succession of brown table-stages correspond to the coming into existence and going out of existence of a brown table. This implies that if you have a brown table and you paint it green the brown table goes out of existence. This *reductio ad absurdum* is not, I have found, always immediately appreciated. But surely it *is* absurd to say that the brown table went out of existence. Suppose that when the table is brown you make the prediction (vow) "That brown table will never be touched by Miriam." Could you make this prediction come true merely by painting the table green before Miriam can touch it? Evidently not; evidently if Miriam touches the table after it is painted green your prediction turns out false, because the brown table that you referred to still persists, though it is now the green table. An even more obvious example, if one is needed, is the term "table in the living room," which is as much a sortal as "brown table." (2) would imply the patent absurdity that if the table in the living room is about to be moved into the dining room then the table in the living room is about to go out of existence.

Moreover, in implying these absurdities (2) turns out to be internally incoherent since (2) would lead us to violate the very principle of prolongation which it expresses. If we had to say, as (2) implies, that a *brown table* goes out of existence when it is painted we would also have to say then that a *table* goes out of existence (since it seems undeniable that "A brown table went out of existence" entails "A table went out of existence"). But

to say that a table goes out of existence when it is painted vio-
lates the principle of prolongation which (2) expresses, insofar as
the table's career, which is traced under the sortal "table," can
be further prolonged under that sortal.

It might now be suggested that the difference between the case
of painting a table, where nothing goes out of existence, and
the case of smashing it to pieces, where the table does go out
of existence, is that in the former case we can continuously prolong the career of the brown table by shifting from the sortal
"brown table" to the sortal "green table," whereas in the latter
case we simply lose the ability to prolong continuously the path
we are tracing, no matter how we might try to shift sortals.
That we cannot in any manner continuously prolong the path
of the table after it is smashed to pieces does seem a rather
plausible assessment, especially if we adopt my suggestion in the
last chapter that spatiotemporal continuity be interpreted in
the moderate sense. The principle of prolongation, as defined
earlier, required that a career which is traced under a sortal F
should not be terminated when it can be continuously prolonged
under F. The present suggestion is that the principle be strength-
ened to require that a career which is traced under a sortal F
should not be terminated when it can be continuously prolonged under any other sortal. The rule for terminating a career
would then be

(3) Where F is a sortal and S is a continuous succession of F-
stages, the beginning and end of S correspond respectively
to the coming into existence and going out of existence of
an F-thing if and only if S is not the segment of a longer
continuous succession of object-stages (where these object-
stages may come under various sortals).

(3) gets considerably closer to the truth than either (1) or (2),
and does perhaps accommodate the majority of typical cases
in which we distinguish between an object persisting through
change and an object going out of (or coming into) existence.
But (3) is still not correct. Whereas (1) and (2) were wrong in
ignoring, or not giving sufficient scope to, the principle of prolongation, (3) goes wrong in exaggerating this principle. It is
not true, as (3) implies, that we are always permitted to prolong
an object's career by shifting to a sortal other than the one

under which we were tracing. Sometimes this is so but sometimes it is not. The sorts of cases that need to be taken into account are those that were mentioned in the last chapter to show that an object can sometimes go out of existence only to be continuously replaced by another object. When a car is subjected to the crushing machine it goes out of existence and is replaced by a block of scrap metal. (3) would imply, however, that the car's career ought to be prolonged by shifting from the sortal "car" to the sortal "block of scrap metal."

There may in fact be some considerable resistance to admitting that the car has to go out of existence just because it turns into a block of scrap metal, and one important possible source of this resistance will emerge in the next chapter. When we soberly reflect upon this case, however, and keep in mind that we are talking about the car and not about the material components that make it up, it becomes sufficiently clear, I think, that the car does go out of existence (though the material components that make it up may of course persist). If you predict "That car will never be touched by Miriam" then you can presumably make this prediction come true by immediately putting the car into the crushing machine. It will not matter if Miriam later touches the block of scrap metal that comes out of the machine because she would not be touching the car that you referred to.

What is evidently required, and what (3) does not accomplish, is to explicate the rule on the basis of which it is legitimate to prolong the career of a brown table by shifting to the sortal "green table," where it is not legitimate to prolong the career of a car by shifting to the sortal "block of scrap metal." We want to understand the conceptual difference between the legitimate shift from "brown table" to "green table" and the illegitimate shift from "car" to "block of scrap metal." When our question is put in these terms the correct answer fairly leaps to the eye. There is after all a very obvious and special relationship between "brown table" and "green table" that does not obtain between "car" and "block of scrap metal." The former pair of sortals, but not the latter, are qualifications or restrictions of a common sortal. "Brown table" and "green table" are, as I will say, *subordinate to* "table." To say that the term F is subordinate to the term G means that F's being truly predicable of an object analytically entails G's being truly predicable of it.

(This implies, as a degenerate case, that any term is subordinate to itself.) The rule which has now emerged is that when an object's career is traced under the sortal F its career is to be prolonged by shifting to the sortal F' just in case F and F' are both subordinate to some common sortal G. Thus:

> *The Sortal Rule Addendum.* Where F is a sortal and S is a continuous succession of F-stages, the beginning and end of S correspond respectively to the coming into existence and going out of existence of an F-thing if and only if S is not the segment of a longer continuous succession of G-stages, for any sortal G to which F is subordinate.

The sortal rule addendum properly explicates the principle of prolongation which was already implicit in the original sortal rule. The basic idea here is really quite simple. Any object's career, from the moment of its coming into existence to the moment of its going out of existence, must correspond to a continuous succession of F-stages, where F is some highly general sortal like "table," "car," or "tree." In the course of its career, however, the object will pass through various transitory phases that are marked off by such less general sortals as "brown table," "car in a garage," or "tree with snow on it." The gaining and losing of these less general sortals do not affect the continuance of the object's career so long as its career remains traceable under the more general sortal. The object goes out of existence, however, when its career can no longer be prolonged under the general sortal.

It will be noted that insofar as spatial continuity is regarded as an ingredient of spatiotemporal continuity the sortal rule addendum implies that an object can never persist in a spatially discontinuous form (though, again, the rule allows for the possibility that an object which goes out of existence because of fragmentation may later come back into existence when its parts are reassembled). As such the rule seems to provide one reasonable, and especially simple, way of describing our ordinary thought about what happens when objects are fragmentized. A possible alternative, however, would be to suppose that there are circumstances in which an ordinary object like a table might be said to persist in a spatially discontinuous form (perhaps, for example, where the table is only momentarily dismantled and then immediately reassembled). Presumably this supposition would imply that the table might persist *as a table* in a spatially discontinuous form. The idea, generally, would be that, for some sortals F, there are special circumstances in which it is proper to speak of there existing a spatially discontinuous F-thing. If this alternative is favored all that is required is that for the purposes of the sortal rule and addendum spatial continuity *not* be regarded as an ingredient of spatiotemporal continuity. The rule would then imply that the career of a table be prolonged so long as we can trace a temporally and qualitatively continuous succession S of (perhaps spatially discontinuous) table-stages such that the (perhaps spatially discontinuous) places which coincide with temporally neighboring stages in S overlap appropriately.

Wiggins draws a distinction, which is relevant to the present discussion, between what he calls "substance sortals" and "phase (or restricted) sortals."[4] This distinction, along the general lines that he explains it, might be defined as follows:

> "F is a substance sortal" means: F is a sortal, and it is a conceptual truth that if S is a continuous succession of F-stages, and S is not a segment of a longer continuous succession of F-stages, then the beginning and end of S correspond respectively to the coming into existence and going out of existence of an F-thing.

> "F is a phase sortal" means: F is a sortal and F is not a substance sortal.

A highly general sortal like "table" seems to qualify as a substance sortal on this definition because, as we said before, it seems to be a conceptual truth that the terminal points of a longest continuous succession of table-stages correspond to the coming into existence and going out of existence of a table. A less general sortal like "brown table" would be a phase sortal, since it is not a conceptual truth that the terminal points of a longest continuous succession of brown table-stages correspond to the coming into existence and going out of existence of a brown table. Phase sortals will typically be complex expressions constructed from a substance sortal and a qualifying adjectival expression. Hence "brown table," "car in the garage," and "tree with snow on it."

4. Wiggins, *Identity and Spatio-Temporal Continuity*, pp. 7, 29–30.

There are, however, some clearcut examples of syntactically simple phase sortals. One example is "kitten." It is clearly not a conceptual truth that a kitten goes out of existence whenever a continuous succession of kitten-stages terminates. This is because "kitten" (roughly, "young cat") is subordinate to "cat," so the principle of prolongation expressed by the addendum requires us to prolong the kitten's career by shifting from "kitten" to "(older) cat."

It is easy to see that if F is a sortal and F is not subordinate to any other sortal then F must be a substance sortal. The sortal rule addendum says in effect that the terminal points of a longest continuous F-succession (i.e., a continuous succession of F-stages that is not a segment of a longer continuous succession of F-stages) correspond to the coming into existence and going out of existence of an F-thing *unless* the F-succession is a segment of a longer continuous G-succession, for some sortal G to which F is subordinate. But if F is not subordinate to any other sortal then there can be no such sortal G. Hence the terminal points of a longest continuous F-succession must correspond to the coming into existence and going out of existence of an F-thing, which qualifies F as a substance sortal.

Someone might want to argue for the converse principle as well, viz. if F is a substance sortal then F cannot be subordinate to any other sortal. Instead of displaying this argument in general terms I will illustrate it for the case of "dog" and "animal." Assume that "dog" is a substance sortal and that "dog" is subordinate to "animal." It might then be argued as follows that "animal" cannot be a sortal. We can conceive of a continuous succession S of animal-stages such that an initial segment of S contains dog-stages and a later segment of S contains nondog-stages. S might correspond, for example, to the imaginable situation of a dog gradually changing into a cat. Since "dog" is assumed to be a substance sortal we would have to say that the end point of the segment of dog-stages in S corresponds to a dog going out of existence (i.e., that the dog goes out of existence when it turns into the cat). Since necessarily any dog is an animal ("dog" being assumed subordinate to "animal") whenever a dog goes out of existence an animal must go out of existence. We would then be saying that it is possible for there to be a continuous succession S of animal-stages which contains a segment the end point of which corresponds to the going out of existence of an animal. (We would be saying, in other words, that it is possible for there to be a situation in which one animal went out of existence and was continuously replaced by another animal.) But if "animal" were a sortal the principle of prolongation expressed by the sortal rule addendum would prevent us from admitting this as a possibility. Hence "animal" cannot be a sortal.[5]

One rather serious defect of this argument, I think, is the controversial status of the initial assumption that we can conceive of a continuous succession of animal-stages which contains dog-stages followed by nondog-stages. If a dog changed *gradually* into a cat is it clear that we would have an *animal* during the intermediary stage of this process (an animal that is, perhaps, no particular sort of animal)? On the other hand if the dog changed *instantaneously* into a cat it may certainly be doubted that we have the requisite degree of qualitative continuity.

Even if this objection strikes someone as not very pressing with respect to the case of "dog" and "animal," it would certainly have to be taken seriously if the argument is to be generalized to cover all cases. Another, somewhat more pedestrian, case that we might consider is that of "shirt" and "article of clothing." Certainly a shirt might be cut and resewn to form an article of clothing of a different sort, e.g., a scarf. Here we would presumably want to treat "shirt" as a substance sortal and say that one article of clothing (i.e., the shirt) went out of existence and another article of clothing (i.e., the scarf) came into existence. But it is doubtful that this sort of possibility proves "article of clothing" to be a nonsortal, since we might certainly question whether we have in this case a continuous succession of stages of articles of clothing, whether, that is, the tattered bit of cloth found in the transition stage from the shirt to the scarf counts as an article of clothing.

If we countenanced the principle that a substance sortal cannot be subordinate to any other sortal then we might be left floundering over which terms to count as sortals, and which of these to count as substance sortals. If counting "dog" as a substance sortal actually forced us not to count "animal" as a sortal

5. Wiggins holds that "animal" is not a proper sortal, but his reasons may not depend on the sort of argument just given. Cf. Wiggins, ibid., pp. 61–63.

it is not at all clear what we want to say. For that matter we might begin to wonder whether even "dog" is a sortal, since it seems not implausible to treat terms like "terrier" and "spaniel," which are subordinate to "dog," as substance sortals. The doubts over which terms to reckon as substance sortals do not trouble me too much, since this notion does not figure in the sortal rule or its addendum, as I formulated these. But it would certainly be discomfiting to the present analysis if we had constantly to hesitate over reckoning any term a sortal on the grounds that some other term subordinate to it might plausibly be reckoned a substance sortal.

My suggestion would be to avoid this situation by rejecting the problematical principle that substance sortals cannot be subordinate to other sortals. We can, I think, reasonably adopt a more permissive policy towards the application of "sortal" and "substance sortal." A term can be reckoned a sortal, or substance sortal, so long as there is no conceivable situation which would constitute a relatively *clearcut* (i.e., nonborderline) case in which the term fails to function as a sortal, or substance sortal. Thus I would want to count all of the terms "terrier," "dog," and "animal" as sortals on the grounds that there is, so far as I can tell, no conceivable situation which would constitute a relatively clearcut case in which a continuous succession of terrier-stages (dog-stages, animal-stages) failed to correspond to the career of a single persisting terrier (dog, animal). And I would also count all of these terms as substance sortals on the grounds that there is no conceivable situation which would constitute a relatively clearcut case in which the terminal points of a longest continuous succession of terrier-stages (dog-stages, animal-stages) failed to correspond to the coming into existence and going out of existence of a terrier (dog, animal). We can conceive of borderline cases (e.g., a dog changing into a cat) which, if they were to occur, might possibly force us (perhaps on theoretical grounds) to make new decisions as to which terms are sortals and which terms are substance sortals (or even as to which terms are subordinate to which). But until such decisions need to be made we can reasonably adhere to the permissive policy of counting all of these terms as substance sortals. Other sortals such as "fat dog," "white dog," "dog in the yard," and "puppy" remain as clearcut phase sortals.

IV. Identity, Predication, and Constitution

Earlier in the course of discussing the question whether sortals need to be antidispersive I mentioned, and left open, the question whether there could conceivably be, for sortal F, F-things whose space-time paths partly coincide and partly diverge. Though this question will remain open the following related proposition is quite definitely true: For different sortals F and G it may happen that the path of an F-thing and the path of a G-thing partly coincide and partly diverge.

Consider again our one-branched tree on Monday. But this time imagine that at the beginning of Tuesday the tree's branch is actually chopped off, so that all that remains of the tree on Tuesday is its trunk. We might certainly want to say in such a case, especially if the branch was fairly negligible, that the tree still persists on Tuesday, though it has been reduced to a trunk. If S is the succession which corresponds to the tree's career from Monday through Tuesday and S′ corresponds to the trunk's career during those two days, then S and S′ diverge on Monday and coincide on Tuesday. S, it may be noted, is similar in a way to the weird concoction of tree-stages and trunk-stages discussed in the earlier example, except that in the present case, where the branch was actually chopped off, there is nothing weird about S, since S is just the path of the tree. So here we seem to have a rather clear case in which the path of an F-thing and the path of a G-thing partly coincide and partly diverge (where F is the sortal "tree" and G is the sortal "trunk").

This kind of case, however, gives rise to a certain difficulty. It may seem perfectly legitimate in the case just imagined to make each of the following three assertions on Tuesday:

(a) This tree is identical with (is one and the same object as) this trunk.
(b) This tree was bigger yesterday.
(c) This trunk was not bigger yesterday.

The difficulty is that these three apparently true propositions seem to be logically incompatible with each other. If it is true, as (a) asserts, that the tree and trunk are one and the same object, then it seems to follow that there is that one object which we can refer to both as "this tree" and "this trunk." Well, was that object bigger yesterday or not? If it was bigger then (c) must be false in asserting that it was not, and if it was not bigger then (b) must be false in asserting that it was.

If the identity claim made by (a) does in fact commit us to holding that there is some object on Tuesday which we can refer to both as "this tree" and "this trunk" then there seems to be no satisfactory way around this difficulty. It would not help us to "relativize" our remarks about the object in question (i.e., the object that can be referred to as both "this tree" and "this trunk") by saying, for example, that the object was a *bigger tree* yesterday but was not a *bigger trunk* yesterday, or that the object was *the same tree* yesterday as a bigger object but was not *the same trunk* yesterday as a bigger object.[6] These maneuvers, whatever their precise import might be, do not apparently help us at all to answer the question "What was the object's size yesterday?" It seems certain that this question must have an answer. If there is that particular object which we can refer to today as both "this tree" and "this trunk" then that object must have had some definite size yesterday, and that size was either bigger or not bigger than the size of the tree (the trunk) that is now presented to us. We cannot possibly have it both ways. But if there is some single object to which we intend to refer when we say both "This tree was bigger" and "This trunk was not bigger" then we would be trying to have it both ways.

Our difficulty is obviously not just with respect to the size of the tree and the trunk. The general problem is that there may be various properties which the tree had prior to Tuesday but which the trunk did not have. It may be, for example, that the trunk was never touched by human hands whereas somebody did touch the tree by touching its branch. Or it may be that yesterday, on Monday, the tree was partly white (the branch having been white) but the trunk was completely brown. But if there is some single object which we can refer to on Tuesday as both "this tree" and "this trunk" then clearly that object was either once touched

6. Such relativizing maneuvers are suggested in P. T. Geach, *Reference and Generality* (Cornell University Press, Ithaca, N.Y., 1962), p. 39ff.; and are criticized in Wiggins, *Identity and Spatio-Temporal Continuity*, part one, and in Sydney Shoemaker, "Wiggins on Identity," *Philosophical Review*, 79 (1970), 530–35.

by human hands or not, and it was either once partly white or not.

The only sensible move to make here, I think, is to deny that there is some single object which we can refer to on Tuesday as both "this tree" and "this trunk." And to deny this is quite certainly to assert, on the contrary, that there is one object which we can refer to as "this tree" and *another* object which we can refer to as "this trunk." We must assert, in other words, that the tree and the trunk are, at least in some important sense, *not* identical with each other, that the tree is one thing and the trunk is another thing. We can also acknowledge, however, that there is a sense in which, as (a) correctly asserts, the tree and the trunk *are* identical with each other. In a sense they are not identical, but in a sense they are.

In line with a good deal of recent literature I will distinguish these senses as "strict identity" and "constitutive identity."[7] We might define "x is constitutively identical with y" (or "x and y constitute each other") as meaning "x and y occupy the same place." It is in this sense that we can say that the tree and the trunk are identical on Tuesday, for the tree and the trunk occupy the same place on Tuesday. There is, at least with respect to the most obvious cases, a rather straightforward connection between "constitutive identity," in the defined sense of spatial coincidence, and the intuitive notion of constitution (composition). Roughly put, if two things are constitutively identical, in the sense of occupying the same place, then they must be composed of the same matter. But I do not want to enter into a discussion of material composition until a later stage. For my immediate purposes the definition of "constitutive identity," in terms of spatial coincidence, suffices to draw the required contrast with "strict identity."

I will not attempt to define "x is strictly identical with y," as it is highly doubtful that this notion can be defined in any useful way. But the meaning of strict identity, and its contrast with constitutive identity, can be indicated in two related ways.

First, where a and b are singular terms which refer to individ-

7. See Wiggins, *Identity and Spatio-Temporal Continuity*, p. 10ff.; R. M. Chisholm, "Parts as Essential to Their Wholes," *Review of Metaphysics*, 26 (1973), 587ff.; and Shoemaker, "Wiggins on Identity," 531ff.

ual objects the statement "a is strictly identical with b" implies that there is some single object to which both a and b refer. On the other hand, "a is constitutively identical with b" does not imply this. We cannot say that the tree is identical with the trunk in the strict sense because, as we saw, we cannot coherently suppose that there is some object to which both "the tree" and "the trunk" refer.

Second, it is strict identity, but not constitutive identity, which satisfies the logical principle of substitutivity ("Leibniz's Law"), according to which if x is identical with y all of x's properties, past, present, and future, must be the same as y's. It seems self-evident that we have a concept of identity which satisfies this principle. It was this principle which I tacitly employed when I argued in effect that the tree and the trunk cannot be strictly identical since they have different past histories. We can say, however, that the tree and the trunk are constitutively identical, that they occupy the same place, without implying that their past (or future) properties are the same.

If we conceive of the relationship between the tree and the trunk in terms of the successions or space-time paths associated with them it becomes very easy (in a sense, perhaps, too easy) to understand how the difference between strict and constitutive identity arises. There is certainly nothing difficult in the abstract about the "Y"-shaped configuration of two successions of items which differ up to a point but then share some segment in common. Looked at in this way the tree and the trunk are two successions which share their post-Tuesday segment. This way of thinking about the matter helps to relieve the sense of paradox in saying that objects that are not strictly identical may occupy the same place at once. The commonsense dictum that two things cannot occupy the same place at the same time remains correct, however, on the interpretation that if x and y occupy the same place then x and y must be identical in at least the constitutive sense.

If x and y are constitutively identical at a given time t then their properties may differ radically both before and after t. This is the essential contrast with strict identity. On the other hand, if we consider only time t, since at that time x and y occupy the same place (and are composed of the same matter), they will evidently have to share their properties at that time (or, at least, they will have to share at that time such straightforward properties as size, shape, color, location). Hence constitutive identity is, so to speak, a weakened version of strict identity, which may explain why the ordinary locution "x is (one and the same as, identical with) y" can be used in both senses.

It will be seen that constitutive identity requires a temporal qualification. The tree and the trunk are constitutively identical on Tuesday but not on Monday. On the other hand it seems evident (though I will not attempt to prove this) that an ascription of strict identity cannot be temporally qualified. It would make no sense to say that x and y existed on Monday and Tuesday, that x and y were strictly one and the same on Monday, but that x and y were not strictly one and the same on Tuesday. This would make as little sense as saying that there was an object that existed on Monday and Tuesday, and it was identical with itself on Monday but not on Tuesday.

When the space-time paths associated with objects partly coincide and partly diverge we have a case in which two (strictly) different objects occupy the same place at one time, and do not occupy the same place at another time when both of them exist. Thus the tree and the trunk occupy the same place on Tuesday and do not occupy the same place on Monday, though both objects exist on Monday. There is, however, another kind of case in which different objects occupy the same place. It may happen that the path associated with the object x is a segment of the longer path associated with the object y. In this case x and y will occupy the same place at every moment that x exists, but x and y are not strictly identical since y exists at times when x does not exist.

A possible example of such a case is the following. Suppose that a lump of gold is made into a coin in 1940, and that the coin persists until 1960 at which time it is melted down into a lump of gold. In such a case we might certainly want to say that the coin came into existence in 1940 and went out of existence in 1960. We may also want to say that a single lump of gold persisted throughout this entire period. The space-time path associated with the coin is then a segment of the longer path associated with the lump of gold.

If I held the coin in my hand in 1950 I might want to assert the following three propositions:

(d) The coin in my hand is identical with the lump of gold in my hand.

(e) The coin in my hand did not exist before 1940.

(f) The lump of gold in my hand existed before 1940.

If we did not already have available the distinction between strict and constitutive identity we might perhaps have been tempted to maneuver around this case by denying either (e) or (f). (To deny (e) would be to deny that "coin" is a substance sortal, while to deny (f) would be to deny that "lump of gold" is a sortal.) Given the distinction, however, it seems that the most plausible expedient is to maintain both (e) and (f), but to interpret (d) as asserting, not strict, but mere constitutive identity. The coin and the lump of gold are strictly two objects, but they occupy the same place at every moment that the coin exists.

I have presented two examples, of slightly different sorts, in which we need to say that two strictly distinct objects occupy the same place at once. Other examples of both sorts could evidently be found. It is not entirely clear, however, just how common we ought to consider such cases to be. This will depend, in part, on how broadly we employ the notion of an "object." A point which must, I think, remain valid is that such cases occur in a severely circumscribed and tightly controlled fashion, and are in an important sense exceptions to the rule. It still remains correct to say, as I did earlier, that it would seem deeply inconsonant with our intuitive notion of persistence to conceive of the careers of objects as crisscrossing and overlapping in an endless and unmanageably complicated variety of ways.

The distinction between strict and constitutive identity implies a correlative distinction between two senses in which a sortal may be said to apply to an object. When I hold the coin in my hand in the previous example I might certainly want to say "This lump of gold is a coin" (and, also, "This coin is a lump of gold"). But there is obviously a difficulty about saying this. For if the lump of gold *is* a coin, then it seems that it should be correct to *call* it "a coin." It should therefore be correct to say, in virtue of the fact that the lump of gold existed before 1940, "A coin which is now in my hand existed before 1940," or "There is now a coin in my hand which existed before 1940," or "This coin existed before 1940." But this is precisely what we cannot say, for the coin did not exist until 1940.

What is evidently required here is a distinction between two senses of the sentence-form "*x* is a coin," corresponding to the two senses of identity. In order for it to be correct to say "*x* is a coin" in the strict *predicative* sense it must also be correct to say "*x* is strictly identical with a coin." Since the lump of gold is not strictly identical with any coin we cannot say that the lump of gold is a coin, in the predicative sense. There is however another sense of "*x* is a coin" which implies merely "*x* is constitutively identical with a coin." It is only in this weaker *constitutive* sense that we can correctly say that the lump of gold is a coin. The constitutive, but nonpredicative, application of the term "coin" to the lump of gold does not permit us to refer to the lump of gold as "the (some, a) coin."

This distinction between the predicative and constitutive application of a sortal to an object affects the earlier characterization of what it means for one sortal to be subordinate to another. The sortal F is subordinate to the sortal G if the predicative application of F to an object entails the predicative application of G to the object. Hence "dog" is subordinate to "animal" because if something is, in the predicative sense, a dog (and can be referred to as "the dog") it must be, in the predicative sense, an animal (and can be referred to as "the animal"). But it is not sufficient for F to be subordinate to G that the constitutive application of F should entail the constitutive application of G. "Gold coin" is not subordinate to "lump of gold" even though "*x* is (constitutively) a gold coin" entails "*x* is (constitutively) a lump of gold." This point is essential to our account, for if "gold coin" were reckoned as subordinate to "lump of gold" the principle of prolongation would prevent us from saying that a gold coin goes out of existence when it is melted down into a lump of gold that is not a coin. (So I would say that part of knowing our language consists in having in effect learned which sortals are subordinate to which, and resultantly which sortals can be predicatively tied to each other, and which sorts of objects can be strictly identical with each other.)

It is now possible to characterize substance sortals in a manner which might earlier have been open to misunderstanding. F is a substance sortal if the terminal points of a longest continuous F-succession correspond to the coming into existence and going out of existence of a single persisting F-thing. This implies the important principle that, where F is a substance sortal, if F is predicatively true of an object at any moment then F must remain predicatively true of the object until it goes out of existence. Hence a coin (i.e., something which is, in the predicative sense, a coin) must continue to be a coin until it ceases to exist. This valid principle about substance sortals must, however, be properly distinguished from the false statement that, where F is a substance sortal, if F is constitutively true of an object at any moment then F must remain constitutively true of the object until it goes out of existence. A lump of gold might be (constitutively) a coin at one moment but not be a coin at a later moment that it exists.

V. The Compositional Criterion

The sortal rule tells us that spatiotemporal and qualitative continuity under a sortal is a sufficient condition for an object's persistence. We want now to formulate a supplementary condition which would allow us to judge, for example, that a watch which is taken apart and goes out of existence may retain its identity when it is later put back together. One important feature of this sought after condition is that if x and y are judged to be identical on the basis of compositional considerations then there must presumably be some sortal F which is predicatively true of both x and y. We want to allow for the possibility of a watch being taken apart and later coming back into existence *as a watch,* or a car being completely dismantled and later coming back into existence *as a car,* but not that the watch should come back into existence as a car, or vice versa. A moment ago I mentioned the principle that if F is a substance sortal (like "watch" or "car") then if F is ever predicatively true of the object x, F must remain true of x *until x goes out of existence.* But it seems that we should now strengthen this principle to read: If F is a substance sortal then if F is ever predicatively true of x, F must remain true of x *at any moment when x exists* (even if x should perhaps come back into existence after going out of existence).

A first approximation to the compositional criterion might be:

(1) Where x is an object that exists at time t_1 and y is an object that exists at a later time t_2, a sufficient condition for x to be identical with y is that some sortal is predicatively true of both x at t_1 and y at t_2, and some set of objects exhaustively comprises both x at t_1 and y at t_2.

To apply the compositional criterion we pick out the F-thing x at some early time t_1 and the F-thing y at some later time t_2 (where F is a sortal). We then consider whether x's parts at t_1 are identical with y's parts at t_2. This judgment about the identity through time of the parts is made on the basis of the sortal rule, upon which the compositional criterion is dependent.

The criterion as thus formulated, however, is too stringent in one respect and too lax in another. We certainly want to be able to say that if a watch is taken apart it can retain its identity even if some small number of parts are replaced when it is put back together. In this case there would be no single set of objects which exhaustively comprises the watch before and after it is repaired. We need to relax the condition to require of x at t_1 and y at t_2 not compositional *identity*, but merely compositional *similarity*. This latter requirement is roughly that some single set of objects should comprise a *major portion* of both x at t_1 and y at t_2.

On the other hand even if some single set of objects does exhaustively comprise x at t_1 and y at t_2 it is not clear that this would be sufficient to induce us to say that x is identical with y. We may require that the set of objects that comprises x at t_1 and y at t_2 should be similarly arranged in x at t_1 and y at t_2. If a sweater is completely unravelled and the wool used to make a sweater again then, unless we somehow had reason to think that the wool was arranged the second time like the first, I think we should not be much inclined to say that we had the same sweater.

A better formulation might then be:

(2) Where x is an object that exists at time t_1 and y is an object that exists at a later time t_2, a sufficient condition for x to be identical with y is that some sortal is predicatively true of both x at t_1 and y at t_2, and some set of objects comprises a major portion of both x at t_1 and y at t_2, and this set of objects is similarly arranged in both x at t_1 and y at t_2.

What counts as a "major portion" of an object is evidently quite vague, and many borderline cases can, and actually do, arise in this connection. Brute considerations of bulk or volume will certainly matter considerably in determining what is a major portion, but it may also matter whether the portion contains parts that seem especially relevant to the object's being (called) the sort that it is. If the car x is dismantled at t_1 and some of its parts are used to construct the car y at t_2, then x's having the same engine at t_1 as y has at t_2 would seem to count more in favor of saying that x is identical with y than would the fact that x has the same airconditioner at t_1 as y has at t_2.

If compositional similarity under a sortal, as expressed in (2), is sufficient for identity then it follows immediately that so is *compositional continuity* under a sortal. Suppose that x is a car which is dismantled on Monday and a major portion of its parts, in similar arrangement, are used on Tuesday to construct the car y. Suppose, further, that y is dismantled Tuesday night and a major portion of its parts, in similar arrangement, are used on Wednesday to construct the car z. It may of course happen that no set of parts comprises a major portion of both x on Monday and z on Wednesday. (This possibility might be schematically represented as follows. On Monday x is comprised of the parts A, B, and C; on Tuesday y is comprised of the parts A, B, and C′; and on Wednesday z is comprised of the parts A, B′, and C′. If two parts in common counts as a major portion we get the mentioned possibility.) But it would still follow from (2) that x and z are identical. For it follows from (2) that x and y are identical and that y and z are identical, and (by the "transitivity of identity") if x and y are identical and y and z are identical it must follow that x and z are identical. This case could obviously be elaborated in such a way that (2) forces us to judge that an object x, which is picked out at t_1, is identical with an object y, which is picked out at t_2, even where *no* parts are common to x at t_1 and y at t_2. It is a quite unavoidable and generally satisfactory corollary of (2) that an object may retain its identity through a drastic or even total alteration of its parts, so long as this alteration takes place by a continuous sequence of small changes, each small change leaving the object with a major portion of the similarly arranged parts that it had prior to the change. This condition of "compositional continuity," it should be noted, may be satisfied by an object even when its career is not *temporally* continuous, as in the case just discussed, in which an object goes out of existence and comes back into existence.

It seems perfectly evident that the condition of compositional similarity defined in (2), and the correlative condition of compositional continuity, depend outright on some prior notion of persistence in terms of which we can understand what it means to talk about the persistence of the parts which make up an object. This is why I urged earlier that compositional considerations must be construed as merely supplemental to more primary criteria. There seems however to be a rather deeply rooted tendency among philosophers to treat compositional considerations as primary. Often, as in the case of Locke's treatment of the identity of organic bodies, this tendency takes the form of the suggestion that our concept of the persistence of familiar observable objects is to be understood in terms of the idea that the *atomic particles* which compose these objects are replaced only gradually.[8] Apart from leaving unanswered the question "And what does the persistence of an atom consist in?" the glaring difficulty with any such account is that our everyday concept of familiar and observable cases of persistence cannot plausibly be regarded as analyzable in terms of the highly theoretical concept of the persistence of atoms. It cannot be that what I judge (and *observe*) to be the case when I assert, for example, "This car has persisted for the past few moments" is some theoretical fact about the comings and goings of invisible atoms.

Once it is conceded that our concept of the car's persistence is not primarily to be understood, via the compositional criterion, in terms of the persistence of exotic atomic particles, there seems little temptation to suggest instead that this concept is primarily to be understood, via the compositional criterion, in terms of the persistence of such smaller familiar objects as engines, fenders, wheels, etc., where the persistence of these smaller objects is then explained in the noncompositional terms of the sortal rule. Admittedly in order for something to be (called) a car it must presumably stand in various typical compositional relations to some of these smaller objects. But if our concept of the persistence of

8. John Locke, *An Essay Concerning Human Understanding*, book 2, chapter 27, sections 3–6.

an engine (fender, wheel, etc.) is primarily to be understood, via the sortal rule, in terms of the idea of a spatiotemporally and qualitatively continuous succession of engine-stages (fender-stages, wheel-stages, etc.), then it seems equally correct to say that our concept of the persistence of a car is also primarily to be understood, via the sortal rule, in terms of the idea of a spatiotemporally and qualitatively continuous succession of car-stages. There would seem to be no point in treating our concept of the persistence of a relatively larger familiar object like a car in some fundamentally different way from our concept of the persistence of a relatively smaller familiar object like an engine or a fender. Whether an object is large or small the sortal rule is to be regarded as defining its primary identity condition, and the compositional criterion is merely supplementary.

Nor is there any mystery as to why, given the primacy of the sortal rule, we should allow compositional considerations to function as a supplement. Looked at in a certain way an object at any particular moment is nothing over and above the parts that make it up, arranged in a distinctive way. It seems therefore entirely natural, if not inevitable, that when we come across those same parts, or most of them, similarly arranged we should be inclined to say that we have the same object again. This inclination, however, is coherent only against the background of a more primary notion of persistence.

I want to consider now a certain rather intriguing difficulty which besets the compositional criterion when it is formulated in some such manner as (2) above. The criterion, thus formulated, implies that compositional similarity, and hence compositional continuity, is sufficient for an object's identity in all cases. The difficulty is that in some cases considerations of compositional similarity or continuity yield incompatible identity judgments. A famous case of this sort is that of "the ship of Theseus."[9] Suppose that we start out in January with the ship x, which, let us imagine, is made up entirely of wooden planks. We proceed gradually to replace x's planks one by one until by December, perhaps, we wind up with a ship y, such that none of the planks which composed x in January compose y in December. Our criterion dictates that x and y are identical on the grounds of com-

9. See Thomas Hobbes, *Concerning Body*, chapter 11, section 7.

positional continuity, on the grounds, that is, that the original ship retains its identity through each small compositional change. But suppose now that someone collected together all of the planks that were removed from the ship during that year, and he used those planks in December to construct the ship z, arranging the planks in just the way they were originally arranged in x in January. Our criterion obviously dictates that the original ship x is identical with z. In this imaginable case, then, our criterion yields the incoherent judgment that the original ship x is identical with the two different ships y and z.

My own somewhat ambivalent inclination when reflecting upon this case is to judge that x is identical with y and not with z.[10] If this intuition is generally shared there would be two related ways to explain it. It will be noted that the judgment that x is identical with y follows from the sortal rule as well as from the compositional criterion, whereas the judgment that x is identical with z follows only from the compositional criterion. This is because if we start out with the original ship x in January and trace a spatiotemporally and qualitatively continuous succession of ship-stages we wind up with y in December. Hence we might say that x is identical with y and not with z because where the sortal rule conflicts with the compositional criterion the former rule, which we know to be primary, takes precedence. Or, forgetting about primacy, we might simply say that the sortal rule in conjunction with the compositional criterion outweighs the latter standing alone, and this is what favors x's being identical with y rather than with z.

The potential conflict between the sortal rule and the compositional criterion might induce someone to suggest that the sortal rule ought to be weakened. Instead of expressing a logically sufficient condition of identity, as it does in its present formulation, the suggestion would be that it ought to express only a condition which counts logically in favor of identity, but which might in principle be defeated by competing compositional considerations, or perhaps by other kinds of overriding considerations as well. This suggestion for weakening the sortal rule certainly deserves to be taken seriously. So long as the considerations which might

10. Wiggins, *Identity and Spatio-Temporal Continuity*, p. 37, shares this intuition.

override the sortal rule could be loosely specified in advance, and seen as built a priori into our identity concept, we would still have an acceptable kind of analysis of what our concept of identity consists in. Nevertheless I am inclined to resist any such weakening of the sortal rule. I think it is reasonable, barring some relatively clearcut counterexample, more simply to regard the condition expressed by the sortal rule, that of spatiotemporal and qualitative continuity under a sortal, as no less than logically sufficient for identity. Certainly we seem to have no convincing counterexample in cases like that of the ship of Theseus, at least if we agree that in such cases it is plausible to make the judgment which accords with the sortal rule.[11]

We might indeed wish to reformulate the compositional criterion so as to accommodate cases like that of the ship of Theseus, and to provide that in such cases the favored identity judgment is the one that accords with the sortal rule. One rather straightforward way of accomplishing this, I suggest, is explicitly to limit the application of the compositional criterion to just those situations for which we had originally invoked the criterion, i.e., to situations in which an object goes out of existence and comes back into existence. Looked at in this way, the compositional criterion has no bearing on the case of the ship of Theseus, since in that case when we trace the original ship according to the sortal rule we have no occasion to judge that the ship went out of existence.

Perhaps, then, the compositional criterion (clearly) applies only in a case in which x goes out of existence at t_1 and y comes into existence at t_2, and x's composition at t_1 is appropriately similar to y's composition at t_2. This still does not get it quite right, though. We need to rule out a more complicated variant of the ship of Theseus case. Suppose that the ship x is completely dismantled early in January, and that the ship y is constructed later in January out of all of x's parts (say, wooden planks again), arranged in the same order. Then x is identical with y. But now suppose that y undergoes the process described earlier, in which all of its planks are gradually replaced, and in December a ship z is constructed out of those planks, arranged in the same old order. Then we do not want to say that x is identical with z, even

11. Several other possible counterexamples will be discussed in Chapter 7.

though x's composition when it went out of existence was appropriately similar to z's composition when it came into existence. Here y's prior coming into existence with x's old parts already preempted x's identity and left no room for a compositional claim in behalf of z for x's identity.

Taking these points into account, and making explicit now the dependence of the compositional criterion upon the sortal rule (including the addendum), a formulation of the criterion might be:

> *The Compositional Criterion.* Where (the sortal rule would have us judge that) an object x goes out of existence at t_1 and an object y comes into existence at a later time t_2, a sufficient condition for x to be identical with y is that (the sortal rule would also have us judge that):
>
> (1) Some sortal F is such that F is predicatively true of x at t_1 and F is predicatively true of y at t_2; *and*
>
> (2) Some objects are such that they comprise a major portion of x at t_1 and they comprise a major portion of y at t_2, and they are similarly arranged in x at t_1 and y at t_2; *and*
>
> (3) There is no object z such that z comes into existence at a time t' between t_1 and t_2, and conditions (1) and (2) (substituting "z" for "y" and "t'" for "t_2" in these conditions) would have us judge that x is identical with z.

This completes my formulation of the sortal analysis of physical persistence. The overall analysis is to be understood as implying that a necessary and sufficient condition for an object's persistence is that the object's career exemplify either the primary criterion specified by the sortal rule or the supplementary compositional criterion. In the next two chapters I will raise two rather different kinds of questions about the adequacy of this analysis. My general assessment of it, however, is highly favorable. It is not easy to conceive of any situation, actual or imaginary, involving standard physical objects, which would constitute a relatively clearcut counterexample to this analysis.

3
The Basic Idea
of Persistence

I. A Question about Sortal-Relativity

ONE IMPORTANT difference between the simple continuity analysis (discussed in Chapter 1) and the sortal analysis (discussed in Chapter 2) comes out when we consider the following question: Can we analyze our concept of a physical object's identity through time without taking cognizance of what sort of object we are dealing with? Obviously the simple continuity analysis, which makes no reference to sortal differentiations, implies an affirmative answer to this question. That analysis attempts a wholly general and sortal-neutral account of physical persistence, and, as we saw, fails drastically in so doing. A negative answer to the question seems, on the other hand, indicated by the sortal analysis. The latter analysis is, to be sure, quite general in a sense, since the sortal rule is a single comprehensive formula which is intended to apply to physical objects of all sorts. Evidently, however, we can apply the rule to an object only insofar as we do take cognizance of what sort of object it is, for it is only then that we can properly trace the object under a sortal. Indeed the essential idea behind the sortal rule was that we need to divide objects into different sorts before we can adequately analyze our identity concept.

In the present chapter I intend to argue that there is an important, albeit limited, extent to which we *can* analyze our concept of an object's identity without taking cognizance of what sort of object it is. Though the simple continuity analysis was shown to be totally ineffective I will propose a modification of that analysis which preserves its sortal-neutral character. This proposal will not, however, imply a repudiation of the sortal analysis. For it is only the latter analysis which, I will maintain, can provide a relatively complete and accurate account of our fully elaborated concept of persistence. The proposed sortal-neutral analysis, on the other hand, will be able to provide no more than a partial account of our concept of persistence, but one which can plausibly be regarded as capturing the basic kernel of that concept. Thus, on the view which I am now going to develop, it will be equally important to appreciate both the scope and the limits of a sortal-neutral account of persistence.

One extreme position which I want to contest is that our concept of persistence is at its very roots dependent upon sortal differentiations. It is this extreme idea which Wiggins seems to be expressing when he says that there could not be "any usable account of what it is, in general, to make a mistake or avoid a mistake in tracing [an object] a. . . . To trace a I must know what a is."[1] He then explains that to know "what an object is" in the relevant sense is to be able to apply a special kind of term to the object, viz. a sortal. It is only by reference to an applicable sortal that we can understand what it means to trace the object.

Wiggins is apparently claiming that our identity criteria are dependent upon sortals in a very radical way. When he says that we can give no *usable* account of our identity criteria in sortal-neutral terms, this seems to imply something much stronger than simply that we could give no *completely accurate* account in such terms. He seems to be implying that we could not even formulate a usefully close approximation to our identity criteria without appealing to sortals, that we could not even formulate an account which works for the most part.[2]

This position strikes me as intuitively quite implausible. I am prepared to believe that our sortal classifications affect our identity criteria in various significant respects. But should it not also be possible to formulate some underlying general rule of identity which cuts through those sortal classifications, a rule which it

1. Wiggins, *Identity and Spatio-Temporal Continuity*, p. 35.
2. It may possibly be that Wiggins does not mean to imply this extreme position, but the fact that his account of persistence is from start to finish inextricably tied to sortals leaves the strong impression that he does.

would be correct to follow, if not always, at least almost always? When we consider what it means to trace the careers of such sortally diverse objects as, for example, trees, apples, cars, and the wheels of cars, certainly our intuitive impression is that, though there might be certain nuances of difference between the tracing rules which we follow in these cases, there must also be a significant common denominator running through all these cases, one which could supply a usable, even if not absolutely accurate, handle on all of them.

The implausibility of the extreme contention that our identity criteria are totally dependent upon sortal differentiations can be brought out by reflecting upon the following obvious fact. A person will frequently be able correctly to trace the career of a new sort of object without requiring any information as to what the identity criteria are for that new sort. Certainly the simplest (though, perhaps, not the only possible) explanation of this fact is that the person is applying the same criteria to the new case that he has already learned to use in the old cases. But this implies that, contrary to the extreme position, there are usable general criteria which cut through sortal divisions.

We can, for example, easily imagine a child raised on a farm who knows a substantial amount of English but who has never seen or heard of a car, or, to make the case even purer, has never seen or heard of *any* transporting vehicle. He is now shown a car for the first time in his life, say, a blue and white car moving across an open field. There is no doubt that he is immediately in the position to say such things as "That big blue and white thing (with the four round black things on the bottom) is moving across the field." In these circumstances it would seem natural to assume that the child is using the expression "that big blue and white thing (with the four round black things on the bottom)" to refer to the same object that we might refer to as "that car." And, what is critical in the present connection, having referred (in his way) to the car he seems perfectly competent to trace the car as it moves across the field. Moreover there seem to be no very obvious limitations on his ability to reidentify the car over longer periods or in more complicated circumstances. It seems quite certain that his ability to reidentify the car would not be in the least stymied by such typical alterations of the car as its doors opening and shutting, its wheels turning, or its windshield wipers starting to move. He seems, in short, capable of getting on quite well without the allegedly special identity criteria relativized to the sortal "car." This is evidence that in fact no such radical sortal-relativization is necessary, that in fact the general concept of the identity of an object provides, if not all, at least a significant part of the identity criteria that we ordinarily need.

Or consider another example. Suppose that you know of someone, say an Eskimo, who has never before seen a tree. Imagine that you bring this person to a tree and say to him (in his language), "Keep your eye on that object." If when you say this you move your hands and eyes in the appropriately suggestive way, if you make the appropriate "sweeping gesture of ostension," as Quine calls it,[3] there is every likelihood that you can get your Eskimo friend to focus on the tree, rather than on one of its parts or on some larger portion of the landscape. On the other hand there is no reason to expect that by focusing on one isolated tree he would thereby immediately come to understand the general sortal concept of a tree, a general concept, that is, which he would apply to all and only trees. Presumably he may remain quite ignorant of that sortal concept until he is shown some fair selection of trees and, perhaps, hears some single word applied to them. But would his ignorance of the sortal prevent him from tracing the tree, from "keeping his eye on it" in an essentially normal way? This seems wholly implausible. Even if you proceeded to break a leaf off the tree, or rub some dirt on it, or bend one of its branches, there seems little doubt that your Eskimo friend, despite his sortal ignorance, would correctly reidentify the tree through these changes. (This could be shown by the answers he gives, or the pictures he draws, in response to the question "What happened to the object I asked you to keep your eye on?") Again, the simplest explanation of what is going on here is that he is employing a concept of identity which does not, at least in any radical way, depend upon sortals.

3. W. V. Quine, *The Roots of Reference* (Open Court Publishing Co., Illinois, 1974), p. 53.

I am not suggesting that someone's sortal ignorance is likely to have no effect at all on his identity judgments. It may seem immediately plausible to expect that sortal ignorance might sometimes generate what I earlier called *nondrastic* identity-deviations, i.e., conflations of cases in which x and y are identical with cases in which x goes out of existence and turns into y. The child who does not know the sortal "car" might very well judge that the blue and white object which he picked out persists in a flattened form after it is subjected to the crushing machine. And there may even be some rather special cases, as I will show shortly, in which sortal ignorance can lead to *drastic* identity-deviations. What seems quite incontrovertible, however, is that someone who is presented with a new sort of object will by and large be able to trace the object in an essentially correct manner, even though he knows of no sortal under which to trace the object.

Certainly there is no serious possibility that someone's sortal ignorance could lead him to trace any of the completely aberrant-seeming paths which showed up in earlier discussions. We are entirely confident, for example, that the child who has never before heard of a car would undoubtedly describe the scene of a car moving out of a garage in terms of the essentially correct idea of an object maintaining its size while moving from inside to outside, and would not, in those circumstances, trace a shrinking object along the path of an "incar." Nor could we seriously wonder whether the Eskimo's ignorance of the sortal "tree" might perhaps lead him to trace an object along a path which combines tree-stages and trunk-stages (where we are imagining, of course, that the tree was not actually reduced to its trunk). The path of the shrinking incar, and the path which combines tree-stages and trunk-stages, evidently clash with our ordinary identity concept in some general way which does not depend upon the role of sortals. This is presumably why we are confident that no one (or, perhaps more cautiously, no one who operates with our ordinary concept of identity), regardless of his sortal ignorance, would trace an object along those aberrant paths. It must then be possible to formulate an analysis of our identity concept which is independent of sortal differentiations at least to the extent of enabling us to explain, in sortal-neutral terms, why such paths are aberrant.

II. The Basic Rule

We are essentially back at the problem that we faced at the beginning of Chapter 2, but with a new twist. At that point we realized that simple continuity considerations could not even exclude the obvious kinds of aberrant paths just mentioned, and we sought some other considerations which would accomplish this. The solution which then suggested itself was the sortal rule, i.e., that an object's career must be continuously traced under a sortal. At present, however, we have found reason to impose an additional constraint on our problem, a constraint that was not satisfied by the previous solution. We now need to elicit some rule of identity which is independent of sortal differentiations but which is nevertheless adequate at least to exclude the most obvious kinds of aberrant paths, so that someone could rely on this rule to judge correctly of an object's identity in most ordinary circumstances without having to apply any sortal to the object.

It is not to be anticipated, however, that the sortal-neutral rule now being sought will supersede the sortal rule, for it seems rather clear already, and will become more clear as we go along, that only the latter rule can adequately explain various nuances of our identity judgments. The relationship to anticipate between the sortal-neutral rule and the sortal rule is rather that of the basic core of a concept to its more fully sophisticated elaboration. The former rule must capture, in a way that the latter does not, that most basic and elementary idea of persistence which we confidently expect anyone to employ regardless of his sortal ignorance.

Let us consider again the Eskimo looking at the tree, which we will now imagine undergoes no qualitative change at all during this stretch of observation. Suddenly he turns to us and says, "The object I was looking at was first rather wide and very oddly shaped, but then it changed and now it is much thinner and cylindrically shaped." As he says this perhaps he also gestures with his hands in a way which suggests first the outline of a whole tree and then the outline of a tree trunk. In other words, he has in effect judged that the original tree is now identical with the trunk. This, we are quite certain, could never happen. But our question now is why not? What is the rule of identity which we expect him to be following, and which would preclude that incredible judgment? It cannot be a rule so simple as to be definable purely in terms of continuity considerations, since we know that any number of perfectly continuous paths could in fact be traced from the tree at one moment to the trunk at a later moment. Nor, on the other hand, can it be anything as sophisticated as the sortal rule which we expect him to follow, since by hypothesis he lacks the conceptual resources for the application of that rule. That is our puzzle.

When we reflect on this puzzle we might initially be inclined to respond like this: "Why would he judge that the object changed in size and shape when *nothing happened*?" This response is, I think, essentially on the right track, but it is not helpful as it stands. For if what is meant is that "nothing happened *to the tree*," well, then that just begs the question outright, since precisely what we want to understand is how the Eskimo is in the position to make any correct judgments about what happened or did not happen to that persisting object. And if what is meant is that "nothing happened *period*," this is just wrong, since doubtless many things happened of which the Eskimo was aware when he watched the tree, e.g., a cloud may have moved behind the tree.

What we intuitively want to say, I think, is: "But nothing happened to make him judge that the object changed in those ways." The key words here are "to *make* him judge." Our intuition seems to be that when someone traces the career of an object he will not countenance a change in the object unless he *has* to. We imagine that the Eskimo fixes his attention on that tall oddly shaped object and then traces its career by following a continuous space-time path that is as stable, as unchanging, as he can get it to be. Perhaps he did see a cloud move behind the tree. But there was nothing in that, or in anything else, which would force him to give up the stabilizing judgment "The object is still the same size and shape" in favor of the change-countenancing judgment "The object changed its size and shape." This is why we are certain that he would make the former judgment and not the latter.

The basic sortal-neutral identity rule which we confidently expect to govern the Eskimo's thought might then be put roughly: Trace an object's career by following a spatiotemporally and qualitatively continuous path which minimizes changes as far as possible.

We just saw how this rule explains the Eskimo's judgment in the case where the tree actually suffers no qualitative change while it is being observed. But the same explanation is also straightforwardly applicable to many cases in which the tree does change. Suppose that while the Eskimo watches, a leaf is broken off the tree. We are certain that this change in the tree could not induce the Eskimo to judge that the tree has turned into the trunk. The change-minimizing condition immediately explains this. For the condition requires that the Eskimo's identity judgments should minimize change *as far as possible*. What must be assessed, therefore, are *degrees* of change, and this assessment is at least quite often perfectly clearcut. When the leaf is broken off the tree the Eskimo has no choice but to countenance some degree of change in the tree, a change which we can perhaps loosely characterize as involving an element of size and shape. But he is in no way forced to countenance the relatively greater change in size and shape that would be entailed by judging that the tree has turned into the trunk. This is why he would never make that judgment.

When we try to apply the change-minimizing condition to the other aberrant path we needed to exclude, the path of the shrinking incar, we come up against a fairly serious complication. We would like to be able to say that anyone, no matter what his sortal ignorance, would trace a car leaving a garage in the ordinary way, and not in the incar-outcar way, because the ordinary way involves countenancing less change. This may seem obviously correct on the grounds that tracing the car in the ordinary way does not involve countenancing any such alterations in size and shape as is suffered by the shrinking incar. But what should we say about the fact that the incar is relatively more stable than the car in the following respect: the incar remains wholly inside a garage whereas the car does not? Since the path of the incar minimizes change in at least this respect how exactly does the change-minimizing condition dictate that the car be traced in the ordinary way?

A somewhat ad hoc answer to this question, which seems nevertheless to ring true, is that stability with respect to a merely locational property like *being wholly in a garage* simply does not count in assessing which of two paths minimizes change. This answer would seem considerably less ad hoc if it could be generalized to read: None of an object's relational properties (i.e., no facts about how an object is related to other objects) count in applying the change-minimizing condition. We might then even try to explain why an object's relational properties do not count by connecting this proviso to the intuitive idea that an object must be in some sense *self-complete,* which implies, perhaps, that an object's (rule of) identity must not depend upon how it is related to other objects. The generalized proviso, however, despite its element of attraction, is too problematical. For one thing it is not sufficiently clear in practice where to draw the line between relational and nonrelational properties, since the ascription of almost any property might plausibly be regarded as entailing a comparison between objects. Furthermore, we will see in the next section that some rather special properties which are pretty clearly relational do apparently count significantly in making a change-minimizing judgment.

I think, therefore, that our most promising approach is simply to lay down the more specific proviso that locational properties do not count in applying the change-minimizing condition. We might define a locational property as one which can be signified by an expression of the form "being in such and such a spatial relation to such and such an object." Thus: "being inside (on top of, to the left of, in contact with) a (the) garage (roof, red thing)." This notion might be further clarified by reference to specific cases, as the need arises. We can say, perhaps, that an object's locational properties constitute at any moment the object's most obvious and direct relations to other objects. Hence a loose connection might still be upheld between the intuitive idea that an object must be self-complete, that its identity cannot depend upon any other object, and the proviso that when we trace an object's career along a change-minimizing path we discount mere locational changes.

My proposal, then, is that our most basic idea of the persistence of an object (which coincides approximately, but not exactly, with the more fully developed idea) can be analyzed in terms of the following sortal-neutral rule of identity.

The Basic (Change-Minimizing) Rule. A sufficient condition for a succession S of object-stages to correspond to stages in the career of a single persisting object is that:

(1) S is spatiotemporally continuous; *and*
(2) S is qualitatively continuous; *and*
(3) S minimizes change (discounting mere change of location).

The basic rule might also be supplemented by a suitable version of the compositional criterion. I will not work out this detail.

Let us try to get clearer as to what the change-minimizing condition (3) amounts to when we consider this in terms of successions of object-stages. A succession S minimizes change if, roughly, any divergence from S would involve more change than S does. That is, S minimizes change if, for any succession S′ which is such that S and S′ partly coincide and partly diverge, S′ contains more change at the time of divergence than S does. Suppose S is the succession corresponding to the tree from 3:00 to 3:10, and S′ is the aberrant succession which combines the tree-stages from 3:00 to 3:05 with the trunk-stages from 3:05 to 3:10. Then S and S′ coincide from 3:00 to 3:05 and diverge from 3:05 to 3:10. The "time of divergence" would then be 3:05. We want to say that S′ is aberrant because it contains more change at the time of divergence 3:05 than S does. What this means is that if we compare S's object-stages at times very close to 3:05 we find that they are more similar to each other than are the object-stages of S′ around 3:05.

It should be noted that it is only comparisons around the time of divergence that matter. S′ would obviously still be aberrant even if it should seem reasonable to judge that over the entire interval from 3:00 to 3:10 S′ contains on the whole less change than S does. This might happen if the tree undergoes various changes from 3:05 to 3:10 whereas the trunk is relatively unchanging during that five minutes. Then S′ would contain a relatively larger change than S at 3:05 but relatively less change after 3:05. Still S′ is aberrant and S is change-minimizing, because at 3:05, the time of their divergence, S contains less change. Intuitively put, the idea is that when we trace an object's career we evidently do not countenance a needless change at a given moment just to assure greater stability at later moments. (The implications of such a tracing strategy are completely alien to us; e.g., if there were a very stable object in the neighborhood we would try to trace all paths to that object.)

The change-minimizing condition (3) of the basic rule might then be put somewhat more strictly as:

(3′) For any succession S′, if S and S′ partly coincide and partly diverge and t is their time of divergence, then object-stages in S at times very close to t are more similar to each other than are object-stages in S′ at times very close to t (discounting mere locational similarity).

III. Limitations of the Basic Rule

The basic rule does, I think, adequately accomplish the task originally set for it, viz. to express in sortal-neutral terms that most elementary conception of persistence which anyone can rely on regardless of his sortal ignorance. We have seen how the basic rule yields (what we ordinarily regard as) correct identity judgments in several specific cases, and these cases could obviously be multiplied without difficulty. It seems fairly clear, in fact, that these cases are representative of the vast majority. The application of the basic rule yields identity judgments which coincide for the most part with the ones which we actually make, and this is why we confidently expect anyone to trace an object in an essentially ordinary way even if he is unable to apply any sortals to the object. It is now necessary to appreciate the important correlative point, that the basic rule provides only a good approximation to our operative identity scheme, but not a wholly accurate account of it. There is in fact a certain general disparity between the judgments of identity which we would make if we relied entirely on the basic rule and the judgments we actually make relying on sortal-relativized criteria. This is why the basic rule represents only a partial analysis of our identity concept, and needs to be completed by reference to the sortal rule.

The most obvious disparity between the basic rule and our actual identity judgments shows up in connection with some of the cases in which objects are said to come into existence or go out of existence. The rule that is evidently suggested (if not

entailed outright) by the basic rule is that we should prolong
an object's career, backwards and forwards in time, so long as
tracing a continuous and change-minimizing path allows. Or,
to put this in a form corresponding to the sortal rule addendum,[4] the basic rule suggests that, where S is a continuous and
change-minimizing succession, the beginning and end of S correspond respectively to the coming into existence and going out
of existence of an object if and only if S is not the segment of a
longer continuous and change-minimizing succession.

Evidently this rule will not explain the kinds of judgments
that we make about objects going out of existence and continuously turning into other objects. The basic rule would yield
the (conceptually) incorrect judgment that a car persists in flattened form when it passes through the crushing machine, because we can trace a continuous and change-minimizing path
from the original car to the block of scrap that emerges. Or, to
take another case, if a table is gradually whittled away so that
it eventually goes out of existence and turns into a small lump
of wood, the basic rule would have us judge instead that the
table persisted through a decrease of size.

Though there seems quite definitely to be a disparity between
the basic rule and the judgments that we actually make in these
kinds of cases (i.e., cases in which an object goes out of existence
by continuously turning into another object), it should be noted
that in many (perhaps in most) cases the basic rule yields the
correct judgments about objects coming into existence and going
out of existence. Suppose, for example, that a table is precipitously smashed to pieces. In such a case it is plausible to judge, as
I earlier maintained, that there is no way at all to prolong the
table's career along a continuous path. Here the basic rule would
correctly enjoin us to judge that the object has gone out of
existence.

Another kind of case in which the basic rule would lead to
our judging correctly about an object going out of existence is
if the object vanishes by merging indiscriminately into its environment. In such a case we cannot continuously trace the object
along a path which has any claim to being change-minimizing.
If, for example, a number of cars are melted down into a single

4. See Chapter 2 above, p. 52.

indiscriminate mass then, though we could preserve continuity by arbitrarily identifying each car with some specified portion of the mass, there would be no plausible way to regard these identifications as change-minimizing since any number of other arbitrary identifications would be on an equal footing. Thus, in general, if there is no path which can be plausibly regarded as the distinctive change-minimizing one we can only say that the object has vanished and no longer exists. We might regard as a special case of this sort one in which an object continuously diminishes until there is nothing left of it, e.g., where an ice cube melts away.

At the level of the basic rule, then, objects go out of existence (by breakage, burning, etc.) either when they are precipitously rendered into fragments or when they vanish by merging into their environments. These ways of ceasing to exist do represent, I think, the most fundamental sense in which an object might be said to go out of existence. But then there are also the other kinds of cases mentioned, where an object is said to go out of existence and continuously turn into another object, which the basic rule cannot apparently explain. Now this limitation of the basic rule seems fairly marginal, and would in any case merely lead to nondrastic identity-deviations (i.e., judging that x is identical with y when the strict truth, in ordinary terms, is that x went out of existence and turned into y). There is, however, a far more fundamental limitation of the basic rule which I now want to explain.

Though the rule would enable us successfully to trace objects, parts as well as wholes, in a wide variety of circumstances, it suffers from a general, and ultimately destructive, kind of vagueness. For there will be too many circumstances in which the rule will not clearly guide us in choosing which of a number of paths is to be treated as minimizing change. The kind of case which gives rise to this problem can be characterized generally as one in which, starting from a given object, we can trace continuous paths in different directions each of which minimizes change in a different respect. The few rather simple problem cases which I will now examine in order to illustrate this point are not intended merely to defeat the letter of the basic rule as formulated. For there would be nothing to prevent us from trying to retain the essential sortal-neutral character of the rule while emending it with various additional provisos (indeed the exclusion of locational properties is already such a proviso). But I think these examples will show that any attempt to force the basic rule to work leads to indefinitely mounting complications, and there is finally no indication that we can formulate for even the most common cases a sortal-neutral procedure, accurately matching our actual identifying practices, for unambiguously choosing between conflicting paths which minimize change in different respects. This is the fundamental limitation of the basic rule and the essential reason why we eventually need to invoke the sortal rule.

To begin with a very simple example, imagine that you have a red table and you decide to paint half of it black (perhaps intending to finish the job later). As you apply the black paint the red expanse which initially coincides with the full extent of the table gradually diminishes in size as it is encroached upon by a widening black expanse. Now if you tried to trace the table according to the basic rule you would be faced with the following choice. You might decide that the way to minimize change is to preserve as far as possible stability of *color*. You would then judge that the original wholly red table remained wholly red while gradually diminishing in size until it is now only half of a table. Or you might decide that the correct way to minimize change is to preserve as far as possible stability of *size*. You would then make the ordinary judgment that the table's color has altered.

Perhaps it will be suggested that this is not really a hard conflict since in tracing the table in the ordinary way we preserve not only stability of size but also stability of shape, so that we thereby minimize change in the greatest number of respects. We might then consider adding to the basic rule the proviso that where two paths minimize change in different respects we must choose the path which minimizes change in more respects. But it seems doubtful that this proviso could really even cope with the present simple case, let alone more complicated ones. For suppose that the black paint significantly alters the texture and temperature of the surface to which it is applied. How should we then weigh up all the stabilities preserved by one possible path against all those preserved by its competitor?

This might still be dismissed as too easy a case since I have

omitted a possibly crucial stability which we preserve in the ordinary way of tracing the table, viz. its stability as a *separately
movable* thing (that is, roughly, a detached thing that tends to
move together with its parts). The property of being separately
movable does, I think, strike us as possibly deserving to bear
some special weight in tracing an object's career. We might then
consider adding to the basic rule the proviso that stability of
separate movability outweighs any other stability in making a
change-minimizing judgment. Note, incidentally, that separate
movability seems a pretty clearcut relational property. This is
one of the properties that I had in mind earlier when I said
that we do not want simply to exclude all relational properties
from being taken into account in change-minimizing judgments.

But, aside from the fact that we will soon come across cases
in which stability of separate movability is not favored in tracing
an object, it is immediately obvious that any special appeal to
this specific stability could not possibly provide a general solution to our difficulty. For we would still have no way of dealing with a large variety of objects that are not, at least in any
perfectly straightforward way, separately movable: for example,
a fence, or a radiator, or a tree, or the wheel of a car, or, for that
matter, a table that is securely fastened to something else (e.g., to
the floor). We certainly cannot rely on any general presumption
that objects either are, or must remain, detached from other
objects.

It might still be suggested that the kind of change-minimizing
conflict which could arise in the case of painting an object can
easily be resolved by simply adding a proviso to the basic rule
that minimizing change in size and shape weighs more than minimizing change in other respects. However, this suggestion will
again fall far short of providing a generally applicable interpretation of the basic rule, since the mentioned proviso could
certainly not qualify as a general principle, even if it works well
enough for the specific kind of example just considered. There
are many other examples in which our ordinary tracing procedure shows no bias toward preserving size or shape. Consider,
for example, what happens when you add bumpers to a car
which previously had none. To make this vivid suppose that the
bumpers are imposingly large, prominently curvacious, and
colored conspicuously different from the rest of the car. Here our

ordinary identity criteria determine the judgment that the car which was orginally bumperless is now bebumpered, with the necessary implication that the car has altered somewhat in size, shape, and color distribution. But at the level of the basic rule we could just as well have traced the original car along a path which perfectly preserved size and shape, as well as color distribution. We could have done this simply by judging that the original car is now sandwiched between the bumpers but does not contain them as parts. Our operative identity criteria, which are relativized to the sortal "car," determine us to trace a path which might be said, in crudely unanalyzed terms, to preserve the object's stability as a whole car. However, from the sortal-neutral point of view of the basic rule there could be no decisive reason to favor this stability over all the others that could be preserved in the alternative way of tracing.

It is this last sort of case, in which objects are attached to each other, that presents what is perhaps the most serious difficulty for the basic rule.[5] If the small object y is attached to the larger object x to yield the composite object x-with-y the basic rule will not clearly instruct us whether or not we are entitled to trace a continuous path which would identify x-with-y with the original x. (Presumably the identification of x-with-y with the smaller y can be ruled out on grounds of insufficient continuity.) Whether this identification of the composite object with the larger original component is permissible can only be determined by reference to the sortal under which we are tracing the object: it will depend upon whether we can treat both x and x-with-y as coming under the same sortal. Though there is unquestionably a great degree of potential latitude in this decision, and we can think up any number of borderline cases, at least with respect to many typical and obvious cases a sortal concept will provide a basis for deciding about the composition of an object that is brought under the sortal. Thus we identify the car-with-bumpers with the original car-without-bumpers, and accordingly judge the car to have altered in size and shape, because we treat both the object-with-bumpers and the object-without-bumpers as coming under the sortal "car"; but we would almost

5. Actually an exactly parallel difficulty arises when objects are detached from each other. Cf. the discussion later about the trunk-tree.

certainly not say that the car altered in size and shape if, say, a small trailer or sled was attached to it, since we would not normally think of a trailer or sled as entering into the composition of a car. Nor, pretty obviously, would we say that a tree has altered in size or shape if some car bumpers are nailed onto it, since the car bumpers would not naturally be treated as part of the tree's composition. Here, at least, are judgments of identity that are in a fairly compelling sense sortal-relative.

It might be urged that these latter cases actually suggest a more severe and perhaps fatally ubiquitous limitation of the basic rule. For should we not say that even where the small object y is merely brought into contact with the larger object x but not attached to it (e.g., an ashtray is placed on a table) the basic rule will not clearly instruct us whether or not we should identify the composite x-with-y with the original x (e.g., whether or not we should judge that a table gets bigger when an ashtray is placed on it)? But this difficulty is, I think, not really serious. To deal with cases in which y is merely brought into contact with x but not attached to it we can safely lay down the general proviso (which may no doubt admit of a few exceptions) that tracing a change-minimizing path should not involve identifying the cohesive x with the fragmented x-with-y. The property of cohesiveness, by which I mean roughly being able to withstand various typical strains without coming apart, may seem intuitively quite important in tracing an object's career (though this too is apparently a relational property). But in cases where y is attached to x there is apparently no property which we could properly single out to resolve the change-minimizing conflicts which would typically arise.

I suggested earlier that someone, perhaps a child, who did not know the sortal "car" could still pick out a car as, e.g., "the big blue and white thing," and successfully trace its career in many ordinary circumstances. We are now in the position to understand why this is so. In many ordinary circumstances all that the child will need to trace the car is the basic rule. But we can now also take note of the kind of limitation which his ignorance of the sortal will impose upon the child's tracing ability.

Imagine indeed that for the winter a small yellow sled is attached to the back of the car. (It will not, I think, necessarily matter whether or not the child knows the sortal "sled," but to simplify let us assume that he does not.) How will the child see this? Will he see it, in the way we do, as the original blue and white thing maintaining its size and color but being attached to the yellow thing? Or will he see it as the original blue and white thing *becoming bigger and partly yellow,* i.e., as now containing the yellow thing as a part? The basic rule provides no definite guidance. Tracing the first way, as we do, preserves stability of size and color, but tracing the second way preserves (what may seem important) stability of separate movability. (Note that this is a kind of case in which the ordinary way of tracing does not favor separate movability.) Which of these two ways of reidentifying the object might strike the child as most natural is *unclear.* There is here a genuine *illusion* of clarity because the grip of the sortal on our thought prevents us from experiencing the conflict which could be generated in such a case at the level of the basic rule. But that a real potential for conflict does exist can scarcely be questioned once one stops to compare this case, of attaching a sled to the car, with the case of attaching bumpers. Our sortal-relative criteria determine a relatively clear (though not, certainly, an absolutely exact) basis for making discrepant identity judgments in these cases, but it seems evident that from the child's sortal-neutral vantage point there can be no relatively clear difference between the cases (though there may be any number of obscure differences which might point him in one direction or the other). Both cases essentially leave the child with an option that is only properly resolved by appealing to sortal-relative criteria.

It is worth noting that some cases of change-minimizing conflict correspond to, and in a way explain, a feature of our ordinary identity criteria which was discussed in the last chapter, viz. that sometimes in tracing an object we will branch off in two different directions under two different sortals. These kinds of cases were described as involving (strictly) two objects of different sorts occupying the same place at once. If you chop off all of a tree's branches so that all that is left of it is its trunk, then, as we saw, in a sense the tree and the trunk are now one, but in a strict sense they are not since they have different histories, the tree having once been larger and the trunk never having been larger than it is. If we trace the trunk-tree backwards in time in order to determine its past we reach a conflict point where we can trace along different paths in order to preserve different stabilities. These different paths in fact correspond to tracing under the sortal "trunk" and tracing under the sortal "tree." Tracing under the first sortal (i.e., determining the history of the trunk) allows us to preserve stability of size, whereas tracing under the second sortal (i.e., determining the history of the tree) allows us to preserve, roughly, boundary sharpness (i.e., the tree, as compared with the trunk, always has a boundary which is relatively more sharply discriminated from its environment).

In the last case our sortal-relative criteria resolve the conflict in a compromise fashion, by allowing us to trace both paths under different sortals. In other (perhaps in most) cases (e.g., the case of painting the table and the cases of attaching the bumpers or the sled to the car) the sortal criteria resolve the conflict by choosing one path and discarding the other. But the basic rule would leave us essentially stranded in all of these cases.

And that, I suggest, is the primary reason why we ultimately need the sortal criteria properly to fill out our identity conception. What we have seen in the few cases examined, and could see in any number of other cases, is that the sortal rule enables us to trace objects through those junctures at which the basic rule is helplessly vague. My view is that the sortal rule is in essence nothing more than a clarification, a refinement, of the basic rule. The excessively vague idea of tracing a continuous path *that minimizes change* now gives way to the relatively clearer idea of tracing a continuous path *under a sortal concept*. But these two ideas are not logically independent. When we trace under a sortal we are ordinarily tracing a path which incontrovertibly minimizes change; and even when we allow the sortal to guide us through points of change-minimizing conflict we nevertheless continue to trace a path which minimizes change *in a certain respect* (i.e., in respect of satisfying the sortal concept). The sortal, we might say, orients us toward an object in terms of a specific viewpoint that clarifies for that object which stabilities count, and which do not, in minimizing change.

IV. Refining the Basic Rule

I remarked a moment ago that in many cases the sortal rule resolves change-minimizing conflict by choosing one path and dis-

carding the other. Now this assessment seems evidently correct
at least if we limit ourselves to tracing under such standard
and relatively unquestionable sortals as "table" and "car." But
it might be suggested that the situation would be considerably
altered, in the direction of possibly expanding the legitimate
scope of the basic rule, if we allowed into play such marginal or
borderline sortals as "patch of red." For we might then construe
the basic rule as implying that in cases of change-minimizing
conflict we are allowed to trace paths in *both* directions, and
associate with these paths (strictly) different objects that temporarily occupy the same place. And if we are sufficiently permissive in counting terms as sortals might it not turn out that
the basic rule, thus construed, yields judgments that conform
even in many cases of change-minimizing conflict with our
sortal-relative judgments? It will be instructive to examine the
implications of this suggestion.

If we interpret the basic rule in the manner just suggested then
in the case of painting the black table red we would be allowed
to trace both a path which preserves size and shape and a path
which preserves color. The first of these corresponds to tracing
an object under the standard sortal "table" and the second, it
is now being suggested, might be said to correspond to tracing
an object under the borderline sortal "patch of red." So it looks
as if the basic rule is working well.

In the case of adding bumpers to the car the basic rule, as now
construed, would allow us to trace both a path which preserves
size and shape and a path which preserves separate movability.
The second of these corresponds, we know, to tracing under the
standard sortal "car." Can we find some sortal, even a marginal
one, which would allow us, in terms of the sortal rule, to trace
the first path? This is not easy to answer. *Possibly* the term
"portion of a car other than the bumpers" might qualify. If we
did treat this term as a sortal then we could say that when we
add bumpers to a car some persisting object, viz. the portion of
the car other than the bumpers, maintains its size and shape
while being sandwiched in between the bumpers.

It must be noted (and this is a point to which I will return in
the next chapter) that if we do treat "portion of a car other
than the bumpers" as a sortal, then we have to be prepared to
allow that the "object" which we trace under this term can

retain its identity while altering its material composition. (We would have to distinguish, then, between that portion of the car and the matter which, at a given moment, makes it up.) Suppose, for example, that after you add the bumpers to the car you also add a door that was missing. If you trace an object under "portion of a car other than the bumpers" you would have to say that this object (in contrast with the car) did not gain any parts when the bumpers were added to the car, but that (like the car) it did gain a part when the door was added. This sounds *very* dubious, but is perhaps not entirely out of the question.

In general it seems difficult to evaluate the possible sortalhood of various constructions involving words like "portion" and "part." Consider, e.g., "crumpled part of a shirt," "corner (portion) of a table," "top (part) of a tree," "thin part of a piece of clay." If we do trace persisting items under such terms we are certainly not intuitively inclined to think of these items as persisting *objects,* perhaps because their identities depend too blatantly on their relations to the objects of which they are parts. Some of these items we are inclined to treat as *places* on objects, especially those whose identities depend on where they are located in objects (e.g., the top of a tree is a place on the tree). But the logic and status of these constructions out of "portion" and "part" would have to be examined more closely than I can now undertake.

If "portion of a car other than the bumpers" is allowed as a marginal sortal we might go on to consider whether we can find marginal sortals to cover the various other paths which showed up in change-minimizing conflict (e.g., the path of the car-*cum*-sled). Instead of pursuing the point in that direction, however, I want to explain the decisive and important reason why this attempt to enhance the scope of the basic rule is unsuccessful. Imagine now the following variation of the case of painting the table. On Monday you have a wholly red table. On Tuesday you paint half of it black. Then on Wednesday you change your mind and repaint it all red. And then, finally, on Thursday you change your mind again and paint it half black. Consider the following statements:

(a) Throughout these operations, some object maintained a constant size from Monday through Thursday.

(b) Throughout these operations some object got smaller on Tuesday, and then it got larger on Wednesday, and then it got smaller on Thursday.

(c) Throughout these operations some object got smaller on Tuesday, and then it got larger on Wednesday, and then it maintained a constant size on Thursday.

(a) is the standardly correct description of what happened to the table. (b), it is being suggested, is a marginally correct description of what happened to the patch of red. But (c) is very definitely not a correct description of any object of any sort whatever.

If, however, we construed the basic rule as allowing us to trace both paths in any change-minimizing conflict (c) *would* be a correct description. For there would then be nothing to prevent us from resolving our conflict on Tuesday by choosing the path which stabilizes color, and then resolving our conflict on Thursday by choosing the path which stabilizes size. The reason why we cannot do this is decisively beyond the scope of the basic rule. The only way that we might try to emend the rule to deal with this point is to assume that we have initially specified some relatively clear list of distinguishable properties, and the rule tells us that when we trace a given object's career we must consistently resolve change-minimizing conflict for that object by stabilizing the object with respect to some particular one of those properties (and that we are not allowed to shift from one property to another in the course of tracing that object's career). But that is in all essentials the *sortal rule*. For the essence of the sortal rule, and its definitive refinement of the basic rule, is that we associate with any object some specifiable sortal-property under which its career is consistently traced. Hence this effort to force a more accurate fit between the basic rule and our ordinary identity judgments in effect transforms the basic rule into the sortal rule. Insofar as the basic rule is allowed to retain its elementary sortal-neutral character we must conceive of it as not containing anything so elaborate as a specifiable list of properties under some one of which any object must be consistently traced. In whatever way we might then try to conceive of the rule's application to change-minimizing conflict (either as requiring us to choose one path or as allowing us to trace both paths) the rule surely cannot provide a reasonably accurate account of our ordinary judgments in such cases.

The primary disparity between the sortal rule and the basic rule, then, is that these rules yield different results in cases of change-minimizing conflict. This disparity, however, carries with it the derivative and somewhat more obvious one discussed earlier. The sortal rule implies that an object goes out of existence at the moment when we can no longer apply to it the sortal under which its whole career is traced. We can, admittedly, shift from one *phase* (restricted) sortal to another (e.g., from "red car" to "green car") as an object passes through different phases, but the object's whole career, from beginning to end, must be traced under one *substance* (unrestricted) sortal (e.g., "car"), and the moment this sortal can no longer be applied the object's career must be extended no further. But this, as we noted earlier, can easily happen in such a way that, from the point of view of the basic rule, there is no reason at all to judge that the object has gone out of existence. If a car, for example, is crushed into a block of scrap metal, but suffers no discontinuous breakage in the process, then the basic rule would have us say that it still exists in a different form, whereas the sortal rule forces us to say that, if it is no longer a car, it no longer exists.

The sortal rule is the operative one, but we can still quite definitely sense in such a case the latent pull of the basic conception. For one thing, people (philosophers not excluded) are simply not that quick to admit (if they ever do) that the car has to go out of existence just because it ceases to be a car. Furthermore we feel distinctly inclined in cases like that of the crushed car to *stretch* the sortal as far as possible to keep our identity judgment in line with the basic conception. ("Well, it's still a car *in some sense.*") Eventually though, despite the *understandably* opposite inclination, I think we must yield to the pressure of the operative sortal criteria and say that we are no longer presented with a car and therefore the car no longer exists.

A tendency to avoid in discussing these matters is that of implying that the central role of our sortal criteria is precisely this, to have us judge that an object ceases to exist when it ceases to be the same sort. This makes it sound as if the sortal rule strikes like an arbitrary bolt from above to drive objects to an early doom. That an object ceases to exist at all is only a depressing corollary of the logical conditions of its persistence through change. And the central role of our sortal criteria is to clarify and complete those conditions, which are only vaguely and partially given by the basic rule. A somewhat earlier demise is only the necessary price which an object sometimes pays for having enjoyed a logically more refined mode of persistence.

The upshot of this discussion is that while the sortal rule provides a relatively more accurate account of our fully developed identity concept, it is the basic rule which ought to be seen as providing our most fundamental standard of what the persistence of an object consists in. This interplay between the two rules does not, perhaps, imply any rigid consequences, but does suggest certain general tendencies, which are readily apparent in our language. It suggests, for one thing, a general restriction on the range of concepts which are apt to figure as sortals. In order for a concept to be apt for sortalhood it must be, as we already know, nondispersive.[6] But it must also be such that when we typically trace a continuous path under it we are tracing a path which, at least from some intelligible viewpoint, minimizes nonlocational changes. This is why the introduction into our language of a sortal like "incar" (or, even worse, a sortal like "tree that is being rained upon or trunk that is not being rained upon") would be, if not outright incoherent, at least conceptually jarring in the extreme. The reason is that a shrinking path traced under "incar" fails to minimize nonlocational change in any respect which seems remotely conceivable. Terms like "top of a tree" or "middle of a table," which include a locational element, may perhaps qualify as exceptions to this general tendency, though, as noted earlier, such terms are at best marginal sortals, and the items traced under them are not naturally regarded as proper objects.

Another general tendency implied by the latent presence of the

6. Cf. above, p. 40ff.

basic rule is the logical pressure, mentioned earlier, for us to keep our sortal-level judgments about "going out of existence" more or less in line with the basic-level ones. It certainly strikes us as being a rather fundamental feature of our conceptual scheme to think of objects as persisting through far and away the large majority of changes that they can suffer. Our language does not proliferate highly specific substance sortals in a manner which would force us to judge objects to go out of existence whenever they change slightly. This is why even if someone has no idea what sortal applies to an object he can, for the most part, confidently trace it in accordance with the basic rule. So long as he traces a path which unambiguously minimizes change he need not be overly concerned with the merely remote possibility that what he identifies as a persisting thing has, according to the operative sortal criteria, gone out of existence and been replaced by something else.

In explaining that the basic rule is fundamentally limited with respect to cases of change-minimizing conflict, I have in effect been suggesting two rather different kinds of points. The clearest sense in which the rule is limited is that it cannot be made to coincide exactly with our actual identity judgments. But the rule seems also limited in the sense that if we did actually base our identity judgments on it, these judgments would be considerably more vague and unwieldy than the judgments that we actually base on the sortal rule. This is because the basic rule, even when buttressed with additional provisos, must remain relatively problematical in its application to cases of change-minimizing conflict. Now such cases may be in one sense rare, since they perhaps occur in only a small proportion of the times that make up an object's duration. (Consider the small proportion of times in a car's total duration that the car is painted, or a sled is attached to it, or a bumper is changed, or anything else happens which might plausibly be regarded as giving rise to change-minimizing conflict.) In another sense, however, such cases are common, since they occur repeatedly and regularly. If we tried to rely entirely on the basic rule these cases would regularly infect our thought and communication about the identity of objects with a far greater degree of obscurity and indefiniteness than our ordinary identity criteria tolerate.

V. Unity through Time and Space

In developing the several foregoing analyses of persistence I was always imagining a situation in which an object has already been picked out at a given moment, and what we wanted was an explanation of the identity rule in terms of which the object's career is traced through time. But another question that we might ask is what the rule is for picking out objects at a given moment. When does an aggregate (or collection) of matter presented at a given moment count as a unitary object? This is a question about an object's *unity through space* which might be seen as paralleling, at least to an extent, the question about unity through time which has so far concerned us.

The question about spatial unity naturally leads to distinguishing several senses of "(physical) object" ("body," "thing," "entity"). There may possibly be a completely permissive sense of the word "object" which applies in fact to *any* aggregate of matter, however spatially discontinuous, and our question about the nature of an object's spatial unity would evidently not arise with respect to this sense (if there is such a sense). A criterion of spatial unity first comes into play with respect to the less permissive, but still very broad, sense of "object" that applies to any continuous portion (mass, bit) of matter. Hence:

(1) An aggregate of matter constitutes a single object, in the sense of a single *portion (mass, bit) of matter*, if and only if the aggregate is spatially continuous.

(1) explains how the parts of an aggregate or collection of matter must hang together in order to comprise a single object, in one sense of that word. If we assume the geometrical notion of a continuous curve we can define spatial continuity as follows: x is spatially continuous if and only if any two parts of x can be connected by a continuous curve every point of which touches x. A somewhat simpler definition to the same effect is: x is spatially continuous if and only if x is not exhaustively comprised of two parts that neither touch nor overlap each other.

I am inclined to think that the broad sense of "object" defined by (1) deserves to be called an *ordinary* sense of that word. On the other hand there is no doubt that the word is standardly employed in a considerably narrower sense. Imagine that a child sees two socks tied together and asks, "What is that thing?" We would no doubt want to correct him by showing him that "it is really *two* things, and not *one* thing." The way to understand this, perhaps, is that though the two connected socks do constitute one thing in a sense (i.e., in the sense of (1)), they do not constitute one thing in the sense which allows for an answer to the question "What is that thing?" since to answer this question ordinarily involves telling what sortal applies to the thing. We might say, therefore, that the socks do not constitute a *standard object*, where this notion is explained as follows:

(2) An aggregate of matter constitutes a single object, in the standard sense of the word, if and only if the aggregate is spatially continuous, and some sortal applies to it.

I want to understand (2) in such a way that something is a standard object only if some relatively clearcut sortal applies to it. Hence cars, tables, and trees are standard objects, as are the trunks and branches of trees. Perhaps we can also allow such things as pools of water and splinters of wood. But I would not count something as a standard object just because of the application of some such highly questionable sortal as "patch of brown" or "portion of car between the bumpers."

That some reidentifiable aggregates of matter may not be standard objects (may not have any sortals apply to them) forebodes a difficulty, viz. if no sortals apply to them how are their careers traced under the sortal rule? I shall return to this question in the next chapter.

It might now occur to someone to suggest that given the concept of a standard object the simple continuity analysis can be resurrected as at least an approximately correct analysis. That analysis stated that any continuous succession of object-stages corresponds to the career of a single object. We know that this is completely wrong if we take "object" in the broad sense which applies to any spatially continuous portion of matter. On the other hand it may seem approximately correct to say that any continuous succession of standard object-stages (i.e., stages of standard objects) corresponds to the career of a single standard object. Apart from the special case of one object turning into another, exceptions to this principle may be fairly rare, e.g., in the case of a tree with one small branch where an aberrantly continuous succession can be traced combining stages of the tree, which is one standard object, with stages of the trunk, which is another standard object.

But this suggestion does not really show that the simple continuity analysis can give us any independent insight into the concept of object-identity. For the idea of a standard object must be explained (as in (2)) in terms of the idea of a sortal. Consequently the simple continuity analysis, insofar as it aspires to operate independently of the idea of a sortal, cannot avail itself of the idea of a standard object. It can only be understood as making the drastically mistaken claim that, in the broad sense of "object," any continuous succession of object-stages corresponds to a single object.

It is perhaps worth noting that there seems to be a sense of the word "object" even narrower than "standard object." We may be inclined to say that the trunk of a tree, and even perhaps the attached bumper of a car, are in some sense not (whole) objects but "merely parts of objects." Here we seem to be using "(whole) object" to mean something like "standard object that is not part of any standard object."

I want to turn now to a consideration of various similarities and differences between the unity through time of a standard object and its unity through space. Both modes of unity seem to involve (a) an element of continuity, and (b) an element of sortal-coverage. The temporal unity of a standard object, as explained by the sortal rule, is constituted by spatiotemporal and qualitative continuity under a single sortal. And the spatial unity of a standard object, as explained by (2), might be said to consist in spatial continuity under a sortal.

One difference that immediately meets the eye is that, given what I just said, there seems to be nothing corresponding to qualitative continuity in the case of an object's unity through space. Now this point is actually quite tricky since it is by no means clear what *could* be the spatial analogue of qualitative continuity (i.e., continuity of qualitative change). Instead of trying to work this analogy out I will simply make a few observations about an object's qualitative makeup.

Certainly an object need not be homogeneous with respect to such qualities as color or texture. The cushion of a chair may be soft and white while the legs of the chair are hard and black. Nor does such qualitative heterogeneity require that some portion of the chair exemplify qualitative states intermediate between the contrasting ones, in the sense in which grey is intermediate between white and black. It may, of course, be that no portion of the chair is semi-hard or grey. But notice, and here is one tricky point, that obviously many portions of the chair, like the chair itself, would have to be partly hard and partly not hard, and partly black and partly not black. (So perhaps we would have, as a necessary corollary of spatial continuity, something analogous to qualitative continuity.)

The possible disanalogies between the continuity elements of the definitions of temporal and spatial unity concern me less than the fundamental difference in the sense in which these two modes of unity involve sortal-coverage. The role played by sortals in a standard object's unity through time turns out, when one considers it carefully, to be quite different from the role played by sortals in a standard object's unity through space. (2) says that a continuous aggregate x constitutes a single standard object if some sortal applies to x. But the sortal rule does not say that a continuous succession S corresponds to a career if some sortal applies to S *as a whole*. Rather the rule imposes a condition on *all of the object-stages in S*, viz. that they must all be F-stages, for some sortal F. Now an object-stage is a (temporal) part of an object's career, and the spatial analogue of an object-stage would evidently be a (spatial) part of an object. The sortal rule says that, where F is a sortal, any continuous succession of F-stages (i.e., any continuous succession each of whose members is a stage of some F-thing or other) constitutes stages of a single persisting F-thing. The proper spatial analogue of this claim would have to be something like:

(3) Where F is a sortal, any spatially continuous set of F-parts (i.e., any spatially continuous set each of whose members is a part of some F-thing or other) constitutes parts of a single F-thing.

(3), however, is clearly false. Consider, for example, what (3) implies if we take "car" as the sortal F: "Any spatially continuous set of car-parts constitutes parts of a single car." This is false since the set in question might contain the parts of two cars that touch each other (or that are even attached to each other). Then the set would be spatially continuous, and each of its members would be part of a car, but the set would certainly not constitute parts of any single car.

The reason why (3) is false is that the spatial analogue of the principle of prolongation does not generally hold. The principle of prolongation said that, where F is a sortal, one F-thing cannot go out of existence just to be replaced, without any loss of spatiotemporal or qualitative continuity, by another F-thing. The spatial analogue to this (if we may ignore qualitative factors) is the false principle that one F-thing cannot spatially begin where another F-thing ends off. But certainly one car can begin where another car ends off. In general where F is a sortal, two F-things might certainly touch each other. (3) implies that this can never happen (or, more strictly, that if it does happen then the two F-things would have to be parts of some single F-thing). There may perhaps be certain special sortals with respect to which the principle expressed by (3) does hold. It may be, for example, that if two pools of water come into contact they necessarily form a single pool of water. But the principle certainly does not hold with respect to most sortals.

The reason why the principle fails for most sortals is fairly obvious. A typical sortal F is associated with the idea of a certain kind of size, or a certain kind of shape, or a certain kind of internal makeup which an object must exemplify in order to qualify as an F-thing. There is therefore no reason to suppose that when two F-things are brought into contact they will add up to something which has that kind of size or shape or makeup. On the other hand there seems typically to be no temporal analogue of size or shape or makeup which is conceptually required of the career of an F-thing, at least none such as to allow us to think of one F-thing being continuously replaced by another F-thing.

This difference between a standard object's temporal unity and its spatial unity is closely related to another one, which Quinton expresses as follows: "The temporal parts of an enduring thing would have been a perfectly good thing of that kind if they had existed on their own, without the other phases which in fact preceded and followed them, while this is very seldom true in the analogous spatial case: the spatial parts of a thing, conceived as existing in spatial disconnection from each other, are not things of the same kind."[7]

Let me try to clarify Quinton's point by reformulating it in slightly different terms. To begin with, I will use the expression "part of an F-thing" (e.g., "part of a car") in such a way as to apply also to a whole F-thing (so that, e.g., a whole car is part of a car). And, similarly, I will use the expression "stage in the career of an F-thing" (e.g., "stage in the career of a car") to apply also to the whole career of an F-thing (so that, e.g., the whole career of a car is a stage in the career of a car). Now where p is part of an F-thing (at a given moment) I will say that p is an *intrinsic F-part* (at that moment) if what qualifies p as part of an F-thing does not depend upon p's relationship to other F-parts outside it. A whole car is an intrinsic car-part because what qualifies it as a car (and hence as a car-part) does not depend upon its relationships to car-parts outside of it (though it would depend upon its part-whole relationships to car-parts *inside* it). Similarly, where s is a stage in the career of an F-thing s is an *intrinsic F-stage* if what qualifies s as a stage in the career of an F-thing does not depend upon s's relationships to F-stages at earlier and later times. The contrast between an object's spatial unity and temporal unity might now be expressed by saying that whereas typically a part of an F-thing will not be an intrinsic F-part, typically a stage in the career of an F-thing will be an intrinsic F-stage.

This contrast is perhaps best regarded as one of degree. Certainly many *large* parts of an F-thing will qualify as intrinsic F-parts. The portion of a car between the bumpers, for example, is certainly an intrinsic car-part, since this portion would constitute a car-part no matter how it was related to other car-parts outside it. (If it were *spatially disconnected* from any car-parts outside it, it would qualify as a whole car, and hence as a car-part.) On the other side it seems not entirely clear that *every* stage in the career of an F-thing will be an intrinsic F-stage. It would seem at least arguable that in some cases an F-stage qualifies as an F-stage only because it is suitably connected to F-stages at other times. Indeed this point seems trivially correct if we

7. Quinton, *The Nature of Things*, p. 77. Compare with Whitehead's notion of a "uniform object" in *The Concept of Nature* (Cambridge University Press, London, 1920), p. 162.

take into account such *phase* sortals as "car which is in the process of moving from New York to California." Taking "H" as the abbreviation for this sortal, it seems clear that some hour long H-stage qualifies as an H-stage only insofar as it is suitably related to earlier and later H-stages.

Even if we focus entirely on high-level substance sortals like "car" and "tree," which is the more important case, it is perhaps still possible to maintain that the application of such a sortal to an object may depend in part on the object's behaving in certain ways distinctive of that sort of thing (or, perhaps more plausibly, on the object's *not* behaving in ways incompatible with that sort of thing), so that to qualify under the sortal an object-stage might have to be suitably related to other object-stages in such a manner as to add up to the required form of (non-)behavior. On the other hand it seems quite unclear to what extent such criteria of behavior are absolutely essential to the application of a typical substance sortal. Perhaps we can say, at any rate, that the application of a typical substance sortal depends for the most part on features of an object (indeed on "features" in something like Strawson's sense)[8] which could in principle be exemplified by an object in any duration no matter how short. It would seem therefore no great distortion to say that, for a typical substance sortal F, an F-stage of even minute duration can more or less qualify as an F-stage (can qualify at least as a prima facie F-stage) quite independently of its relationships to earlier and later F-stages.

The contrast that we then have is this. Where F is a typical substance sortal, the only parts of an F-thing which can qualify as intrinsic F-parts are those which are relatively large as compared to the (whole) F-things of which they are parts. In contrast, many intrinsic F-stages will be of relatively short durations as compared to the (whole) careers of which they are stages; and there seems indeed to be no definite lower limit on how brief an intrinsic F-stage might be.

That an object-stage of relatively minute duration might plausibly be regarded as (more or less) intrinsically qualifying as an F-stage, quite independently of its relationships to earlier and later F-stages, seems rather essential to the whole enterprise of

8. P. F. Strawson, *Individuals* (Methuen & Co. Ltd., London, 1959), p. 202ff.

the sortal analysis. Surely the underlying point of that analysis is that we can regard the concept of the unity through time of an F-thing as in principle constructible out of the concept of the interconnections between *momentary* F-stages, i.e., F-stages which do not themselves depend upon any principle of unity through time. But the analysis would seem rather blatantly circular if the momentary F-stages in terms of which it is couched could not be regarded as essentially *intrinsic* F-stages, for then these F-stages would qualify as such only in virtue of their standing to each other in just the unity-making relationship which the analysis is supposed to explain. The analysis does in fact seem illuminating because we apparently can regard the unity through time of an F-thing in terms of the interconnections between momentary intrinsic F-stages, in terms, that is, of the interconnections between intrinsic F-stages that are, if not literally instantaneous, at least so brief that their durations can plausibly be disregarded within the context of the analysis.

We saw before (*vis-à-vis* the falsity of (3)) that there is no general formula, analogous to the sortal rule, which would express the unity through space of an F-thing (for some typical sortal F) in terms of the continuity connections between F-parts. An additional point which has now emerged is this. Even if we could somehow express the unity through space of an F-thing in terms of the idea of some more complicated connections between F-parts (e.g., in terms of the *overlap* relations between F-parts) such an exercise would be quite unilluminating as an explanation of an F-thing's unity through space. Since relatively minute F-parts will generally not qualify as intrinsic F-parts any reference to minute F-parts as such would already presuppose that those parts stand to each other in just the spatial unity-making relationship which needs to be explained. If, on the other hand, the explanation took the form of merely expressing the unity through space of an F-thing in terms of the interconnections between relatively large intrinsic F-parts, the question would remain glaringly left over as to what the unity through space of a large intrinsic F-part consists in. It therefore seems quite hopeless to seek a general sortal-relative analysis, modelled on the sortal rule, of a standard object's unity through space in terms of how its parts are interconnected. Here we seem to be left with saying (as in (2)) that we have a unified standard object wherever we have, for some sortal F, a unified F-thing, i.e., wherever we have a unified table, or a unified tree, or a unified car, etc., etc. Of course we might then go on and try to give an analysis, on a case-by-case basis, of what the spatial unity of a table consists in, of a tree, of a car, etc., etc.

VI. Articulation

This leads to one final question that I want to raise about the similarities and differences between the spatial and temporal unity of a standard object. In the case of temporal unity we have in the form of the basic rule an elementary sortal-neutral conception which approximates at least fairly well to our full-blown conception. Is there something comparable for the case of spatial unity? Can we also provide an approximately correct general account of when an aggregate of matter constitutes a standard object, without presupposing the notion of a sortal?

That any such account is likely to be not a very *close* approximation may seem pretty clear at the start. We imagined before that a child might want to treat a pair of socks that are knotted together as a unitary object. It seems unlikely that, without relying on the notion of sortal coverage, we could formulate any general rule which would exclude such a case, and many others like it.

On the other hand the general consideration which initially led us to search for the basic rule, as a sortal-neutral account of unity through time, seems to bear at least to some extent on the case of spatial unity as well. Perhaps any continuous portion of matter is a unitary object in some very broad sense, and could reasonably be treated as such in some suitable circumstance (i.e., could be picked out and described as having a shape, size, location, duration, etc.). But it seems certain that anyone, regardless of his sortal ignorance, would be far more likely to treat some portions of matter as units than others. Moreover we would expect that the portions of matter which are especially apt to be treated as units in sortal ignorance would coincide at least roughly to those which we treat as standard (sortal-covered) objects. So it appears that there is some sortal-neutral principle of unit-selection which approximates in some rough manner to our fully developed concept of the spatial unity of a standard object.

This point can be illustrated by reference to the example we once considered in which a child who does not have the sortal concept "car" observes a car moving across a field. It seemed perfectly natural to imagine that the child would pick the car out as a unitary object. We would certainly not, however, imagine that he would pick out some arbitrary portion of the car as an object. If the car is anything like ordinary looking, he could not be imagined to pick out the front and back halves of the car as units (and to judge, "Two objects of roughly equal size and shape and color are attached to each other and moving across the field").

It seems, intuitively, that the car *stands out* from its surroundings in a way that its front and back halves do not, and this is why the car, rather than either of its halves, is likely to be picked out as a unitary object even by someone who cannot apply any relevant sortals. The car, I will say, is *articulated* in a way (or to a degree) that its front and back halves are not. Articulation, as I want to try to understand this, is an elementary sortal-neutral idea. If we can give an account of what makes for articulation we may have at least some rough sortal-neutral approximation to our concept of a standard object's unity through space.

The notion of articulation is closely related to a view that has been developed by a number of psychologists, for example, Köhler and Koffka.[9] According to these theorists our sensory fields tend "naturally" and "spontaneously" to be broken down (articulated) into unitary objects in accordance with certain general principles of "sensory organization." (These principles are also alleged to explain why we tend to see objects as forming distinctive kinds of groups or clusters, but this part of the theory is not directly relevant.) From my present point of view the only sense in which these principles of articulation (as I would call them) need to be regarded as "natural" or "spontaneous" is that they can operate at a relatively elementary level of knowledge, and particularly at a level of sortal ignorance. What seems completely plausible intuitively, and is perhaps also confirmed by experimental evidence, is that anyone (or, more cautiously perhaps, anyone who speaks our kind of language) will tend, even

9. Wolfgang Köhler, *Gestalt Psychology* (Liveright Publishing Corporation, N.Y., 1947), chaps. 5–6; K. Koffka, *Principles of Gestalt Psychology* (Harcourt, Brace & World, Inc., N.Y., 1935), chaps. 3–7.

in a state of sortal ignorance, to see as unitary objects only a select few continuous portions of matter, of the unlimited number potentially present to him. Why this is so (whether it is "learned" or "innate") may at present be left open.

I should emphasize that what I call a "state of sortal ignorance" in no way implies a lack of general concepts (e.g., of color, shape, size). I am certainly not referring to a "preconceptual level," if such an idea makes sense. Someone is in a state of sortal ignorance with respect to a given object so long as none of the (perhaps diverse and even sophisticated) general concepts that he can apply to the object have the special status of sortalhood, as this status was earlier characterized. (Roughly this would mean that he can apply no ordinary nouns to the object, other than such nonsortals as "object," "body," "thing.") What seems intuitively plausible, I am suggesting, is that someone's sortal ignorance with respect to a given object will typically not prevent the object from presenting itself as an articulated unity, as something that stands out from its surroundings.

Articulation is actually a large and intricate topic in its own right, and I will confine myself here to the barest intuitive sketch, drawing in part from Köhler and Koffka. Some of my remarks in this section may be rather speculative, and of a psychological nature. At the very end of the section, however, I will draw certain philosophical conclusions which seem fairly straightforward.

A leading articulation-making factor is *boundary contrast*. A portion of matter seems to impress itself upon us as a unit insofar as it is segregated, bound off, from its surrounding. This segregation is accomplished primarily by the fact that there is a qualitative contrast between points on the object's surface and points in the surrounding medium. We might consider as a maximally articulated object a black billiard ball rolling across a green felt table. Every point on the ball's surface contrasts dramatically with either the air around it or the felt beneath it. Boundary contrast, it should be noted, is a matter of degree, as will be the case with every other articulation-making factor. The ball contrasts sharply with its surroundings, both visually and tactually, whereas in other cases the contrast may be less sharp, or in only one modality. The factor of boundary contrast is sufficient to explain why the car stands out in a way that its halves do not, since the halves have no contrast at the boundary where they meet.

The *qualitative homogeneity* of the surface of the billiard ball strikes us as enhancing its presence as a unit. Perhaps this is because homogeneity of surface highlights boundary contrast. In any case it is clear that homogeneity without contrast amounts to nothing in the way of articulation, as is evidenced by arbitrary portions of the billiard ball, which are as homogeneous as the whole ball but not therefore articulated. Homogeneity, it will easily be seen, is a matter of degree, and many objects may have relatively little of it.

An object seems evidently to stand out more dramatically if it is observed to move as a unit, i.e., to move together with its parts but not together with anything else in its immediate vicinity. Even if an object is stationary its articulation is seemingly enhanced insofar as we can think of it as tending readily (which is a matter of degree) to move as a unit. Hence I will call this articulation-making factor *separate movability*.

A closely related factor is *dynamic cohesiveness*, which is the object's capacity (again a matter of degree) to hang together when subjected to various strains. This factor seems intuitively important. Someone in a state of relevant sortal ignorance might be initially inclined to treat as a unit a table together with the identically colored ashtray that rests on it, but this inclination would probably be dispelled as soon as he discovered how easily the ashtray separates from the table. Perhaps dynamic cohesiveness ought to be regarded as a necessary condition for separate movability, but certainly not conversely. A tree has virtually no movability but it is highly cohesive.

Köhler and Koffka mention as another articulation-making factor *regularity* (or *simplicity* or *symmetry*) *of shape*. This condition is not very easy to define or to assess. A possible example of its application is the fact that some trunks of trees (e.g., trunks of evergreens) seem to stand out rather prominently, perhaps because their cylindrical shapes are in some sense simple.

There is one other rather obscure articulation-making factor that I want to indicate, but not attempt to define. Certainly a whole branch of a tree stands out as a unit much more than some arbitrary portion of it, e.g., its outer half. But why is this? Both the whole branch and its outer half enjoy boundary contrast except, respectively, where the branch meets the trunk and where the outer half meets the inner half. And with respect to every other articulation-making factor they are evidently the same. Why then the drastic difference in their articulation?

Intuitively the answer has something to do with the fact that where the whole branch touches the trunk there is a joint, whereas there is no joint, but rather a smooth continuation, where the front half of the branch meets the back half. To explain properly what this means would, if I am not mistaken, require a quite elaborate account. I will limit myself here merely to naming this articulation-making factor. I will say that the whole branch *forms a joint* where it lacks boundary contrast, whereas half the branch does not form a joint where it lacks boundary contrast.

The articulation-making factors that I have mentioned are: (a) boundary contrast, (b) qualitative homogeneity, (c) separate movability, (d) dynamic cohesiveness, (e) regularity of shape, and (f) joint-formation at boundaries lacking contrast.

Of these articulation-making factors the boundary requirements (a) and (f) seem most fundamental, at least in the sense of defining the bare minimal conditions of articulation. It seems reasonable to say that in general an object has virtually no articulation at all unless most of its boundary exhibits some degree of boundary contrast and it forms a joint wherever it completely lacks boundary contrast. Certainly some arbitrary portion of a branch, for example, does not stand out as a unit at all, despite its perhaps being to a high degree homogeneous, cohesive, and of regular shape. Perhaps (though this is almost certainly something of an oversimplification) we can regard the two boundary requirements (i.e., boundary contrast and joint formation) as by themselves determining the difference between an (at least somewhat) articulated object and a (wholly) non-articulated object, and bring in the other articulation-making factors only for the purpose of determining degrees of articulation. Looked at in this way, a rough preliminary sketch of articulation might be summed up in the following two propositions:

(1) A continuous portion of matter is articulated—i.e., stands out as something apt to be treated as a unit—insofar as most of its boundary exhibits some degree of boundary contrast and it forms a joint wherever it completely lacks boundary contrast.

(2) An articulated object's degree of articulation is determined by its degree of boundary contrast, qualitative homogeneity, separate movability, dynamic cohesiveness, and regularity of shape.

The sought after sortal-neutral approximation to our concept of the unity through space of a standard object might now be expressed in terms of the following principle.

The Principle of Articulation. In the vast majority of cases a continuous portion of matter constitutes a unified standard object if and only if it has a relatively high degree of articulation.

How much a "relatively high" degree of articulation is can perhaps be roughly indicated by reference to some well-chosen examples which exemplify different combinations of the articulation-making factors. But this too might eventually be worked out more carefully in the context of a fuller treatment of articulation.

The principle of articulation can give us at best a rough approximation to our concept of the unity through space of a standard object. There are any number of cases in which objects are attached to each other to form a continuous portion of matter which seems sufficiently articulated but is nevertheless not a standard object. The two attached socks is one example. Another possible example that came up earlier is a car-*cum*-sled, which is not a standard object despite being perhaps as articulated as many (ill-shaped) cars. Examples like these could be multiplied indefinitely. Besides such examples of problematically over-articulated nonstandard objects there will also be cases of problematically under-articulated standard objects, most obviously where a standard object suffers a temporary lapse of articulation because of being in some special setting (e.g., where a sock is tied to another one just like it).

On the other hand, I think that the principle of articulation can fairly be regarded as providing an importantly viable sortal-neutral perspective on the basic outlines of the standard objects that figure in our identity scheme. The principle at least rules out that vast ubiquitous background of continuous portions of matter that seem straightforwardly lacking in sufficient articulation. These would include, most obviously, arbitrary portions of

standard objects (e.g., half of a table), and continuous summations of such portions (e.g., half of a table-*cum*-half of an ashtray),
which lack the essential boundary requirements, and are therefore not articulated at all. The principle would also rather definitely rule out as insufficiently articulated typical summations of
whole standard objects (e.g., a table-*cum*-ashtray) which, though
they satisfy the minimal boundary requirements, are lacking in
any high degree of homogeneity, movability, cohesiveness, or
shape-regularity. In general the principal of articulation might
be said to draw the outlines of our standard objects in exceedingly broad strokes, but these are still recognizably the essential
outlines of our standard objects.

The overall position which has now emerged is that our most
basic conception of the spatial and temporal unity of an object,
a conception which is refined and clarified by our sortals, is that
of a relatively articulated object whose career unfolds along a
continuous change-minimizing path. Now it will probably have
been noticed that several of the articulation-making factors had
already shown up earlier in the quite different connection of
change-minimizing conflict. There were a number of examples
in which it seemed intuitively important to stabilize these factors
when tracing a change-minimizing path. (In the case of painting
the table it seemed that it might be important to stabilize the
table's separate movability; in the case of placing the ashtray
on the table it seemed that it might be important to stabilize the
table's dynamic cohesiveness; in the trunk-tree case it seemed that
it might be important to stabilize the tree's sharpness of boundary contrast.) This suggests the intriguing conjecture that there
may possibly be a deeper connection between articulation and
the change-minimizing condition, in that there may be some
general tendency to resolve change-minimizing conflict by stabilizing articulation-making factors. I shall not here attempt to
develop this suggestion, though it may be, I am led to believe,
consonant with a number of principles enunciated by psychologists.[10]

I stated earlier that for my immediate purposes the question
could be left open whether we are innately disposed to pick out
objects which satisfy the articulation-making factors or learn to

10. See Koffka's comments on Von Schiller's experiments and Metzger's experiments, *Principles of Gestalt Psychology*, pp. 300–303.

do so. The same question could be raised about our disposition to trace objects along continuous change-minimizing paths. This issue is notoriously difficult to clarify, and many questions converge on it, particularly questions about the relationship between thinking and speaking. My tentative opinion (in general agreement with that of Köhler and Koffka) is that there probably is some important sense in which human beings are innately disposed both to pick out articulated objects within their sensory fields and to trace those objects along continuous change-minimizing paths.[11] One relatively clearcut consequence of this hypothesis is that there probably never has been, or will be, a natural (first) language spoken by humans which contains an identity scheme whose basic structure could not be captured in terms of the principle of articulation for spatial unity, and the rule of change-minimizing continuity for temporal unity. Cultural divergence is to be looked for at the level of sortal refinement but the basic structure of human thought about identity is universal. That, at any rate, seems to me a highly plausible hypothesis.

But it is, as far as I am concerned, essentially an *empirical* hypothesis, to be dealt with in an empirically scientific manner. The only a priori philosophical doctrines to which I want to be committed, and for which I have tried to present arguments, are these:

(i)   We can provide a relatively accurate account of our (English speaker's) concept of the unity through time and unity through space of a standard object only by taking cognizance of what sort of object we are dealing with, since sortal-coverage (though in two rather different senses) figures in both modes of unity;

(ii) However, a significant approximation to this account can be presented without taking cognizance of what sort of object we are dealing with, and this sortal-neutral approximation might be regarded as capturing our most basic conception of an object's unity through time and space.

11. Compare with Quine, who suggests that the unity of a body is something that we are "innately predisposed to appreciate" (*The Roots of Reference*, p. 54), and that "body-unifying considerations . . . are rooted in instinct" (ibid., p. 55). The innateness question will be considered at length in Chapter 8.

4

The Persistence of Matter

I. A Puzzle about Matter

EARLIER I expressed the opinion that any continuous portion of matter, even one which does not come under any sortal (and which does not, therefore, constitute a standard object), can perhaps be called an "object" in one very broad, ordinary sense of that word. This is certainly a debatable point, and I do not intend to presuppose it in anything that follows. What seems less debatable, however, and more important, is the following proposition. Our ordinary concept of identity through time applies, in at least many typical cases, to portions of matter (whether or not these be called "objects") that do not come under any sortals. And this immediately presents a difficulty, since sortal-coverage is, according to the foregoing account, an operative condition for the application of our full-blown identity concept.

Suppose, for example, that I specify some portion of wood which partially makes up the uniform wooden table in front of me. I might do this by momentarily laying my hand on the surface of the table and thereafter referring to the hand-shaped portion of wood which had momentarily extended directly downwards beneath my hand. Now that portion of wood is quite definitely not covered by any sortal, since we know that the dispersive term "wood" is not a sortal,[1] and there is evidently no other possible sortal which applies to the wood. Yet there seems no

1. Cf. above, p. 42.

doubt that (whether or not we call it an "object") we do think of that wood, of the particular portion of wood that was directly under my hand, as having an identity of its own, as being spatially related to other portions of wood that surround it, and as in fact having almost certainly persisted for a longer time than the table has. But what does this concept of persistence mean if it cannot be understood in terms of the idea of a sortal-covered path?

It will of course be tempting to suggest that the basic rule can help us here. Can we not perhaps say that with respect to a portion of matter which is not sortal-covered our only relevant concept of persistence is the relatively primitive one provided by change-minimizing considerations? However, this answer will not work. We can indeed conceive of the basic rule as straightforwardly applicable to non-sortal-covered portions of matter (to nonstandard "objects") wherever these portions of matter are at least to some extent *articulated*. For example, the portion of matter which constitutes two socks that are tied together could typically be traced along a continuous change-minimizing path. But there is something especially problematical about the sort of case that I am considering in which a wholly non-articulated portion of matter is referred to. It would seem that in many (though perhaps not all) such cases the change-minimizing condition is thoroughly inapplicable. Where a portion of matter is wholly non-articulated it will often be the case that we could trace continuous paths from the portion in any and all directions, none of which could straightforwardly claim the unique status of minimizing change in any relevant (i.e., nonlocational) respect. This point seems rather clear in the particular case under consideration. Since we are imagining that the hand-shaped portion of wood being referred to is merely a wholly indistinct portion of a larger uniform mass of wood, we cannot possibly trace that portion along a change-minimizing path, for there will be an indefinite number of paths extending away from that portion, all of which contain qualitatively indistinguishable hand-shaped portions of wood.

I do not wish to base my argument on the overly problematical (though possibly defensible) general principle that the change-minimizing condition can *never* straightforwardly apply to cases of non-articulated portions of matter. All that I require for my present purposes is the limited point that the change-minimizing condition seems quite helpless at least with respect to *some* cases of non-articulated portions, i.e., cases like the one under consideration, involving some wholly undifferentiated portion of a larger uniform mass.

It might still be urged, however, that even in the latter cases change-minimizing considerations can work effectively so long as we allow ourselves to take into account the location of a portion of matter within the object that it partially constitutes. Perhaps this should be treated as a special kind of locational consideration, which does in fact count in tracing a career. The suggestion would be, in effect, that we can state identity criteria for the specified hand-shaped portion of wood in terms of its location relative to the outlines of the table. Our concept of the identity of that portion of wood would then be criterially determined by the rule that you are referring to the same wood so long as you are referring to the wood which occupies the same place on the table (i.e., the same place relative to the outlines of the table).

But this is unquestionably wrong, because it is certainly not the case that the same wood cannot alter its location on the table. Suppose that yesterday I had filed the table down to make it several inches shorter. Certainly this would warrant my now saying, "The hand-shaped portion of wood which was directly under my hand a moment ago was closer to the outlines of the table yesterday than it was a day before yesterday." And quite apart from anything akin to filing, it must surely be admitted that it is at least *conceptually coherent* to suppose that my table suffered from some chemical quirk which made some of its wood regularly contract while the rest expanded, in which case *possibly* that portion of wood which was momentarily under my hand regularly altered its size and its place on the table. No, the location of the wood on the table quite definitely does not criterially define its identity. It seems sufficiently clear, therefore, that the change-minimizing condition will not explain the wood's identity, even if we allow locational considerations into play. And this leaves us with the puzzle as to what does explain the wood's identity.

Perhaps this puzzle can be made a bit more stark by slightly altering the image. Suppose that I break the table to pieces so that I am left with a large number of wooden fragments. Holding one of these fragments in my hand I certainly want to say, "This fragment of wood came out of the table." Now this is, so far, no problem since we can in principle trace the fragment backwards in time to some portion of the table, tracing, that is, along a change-minimizing path or, if necessary, a path covered by the nondispersive concept "fragment of wood."[2] There is no problem here because, first, a fragment of wood is articulated, which immediately invites a straightforward application of the change-minimizing condition, and, second, "fragment of wood" can function in a straightforward way as a sortal which covers a tracing path. There is indeed the possible complication that, depending on how the table broke, we might have to say that the fragment is traceable back to some portion of a larger fragment, which is in turn traceable back to some portion of a still larger fragment, which is in turn . . . , which is in turn traceable back to some portion of the table. Still, so long as "coming out of" is transitive, there should be no major problem in explaining at least what it means to say that the fragment came out of the table.

The problem arises insofar as I also want to say *something else*, viz. "This wood used to make up part of the table." (Not, strictly, "This *fragment* of wood used to make up part of the table," since my table was not made up of articulated *fragments*.) But what can I possibly mean by this? What can I mean by saying that *this wood* was in my table yesterday though it was then merely a wholly indistinct portion of some larger uniform mass? If I want to talk about that selfsame wood persisting from yesterday to today I should, it seems, have criteria of identity which explain what this means, which explain what the unity-making relationship is that binds together the stages of that persisting wood. But it seems that I have no such criteria of identity, at least none provided by the idea of a change-minimizing or sortal-covered path.

Now the very natural first impulse upon hearing this puzzle is to protest that the whole thing is really very obvious. (It is a philosophically important feature of this puzzle that we find it extremely difficult to take it seriously.) "Look, that wood that you're holding in your hand came out of the table, right? If it

2. Cf. above, p. 42.

came out of the table it had to be *in* the table. Now it certainly didn't jump into the table when we weren't looking. So it's been in there all the time."

This seems like an outright evasion, for I was not asking for a *justification* (for *evidence*) but for an *analysis* (for *criteria*). I was not asking, "*How do we know* that the wood persisted before it came out of the table?" which would imply that I already understand what that state of affairs amounts to, but rather "*What can we mean* by speaking of the persistence of the wood before it came out of the table?" The challenge is to show me the criteria of identity. (But we will see shortly that this natural response, which apparently ignores the request for criteria, may be in a certain sense quite apt.)

It is interesting to note that Russell was consistently sensitive to the puzzle about the identity of matter which I am now discussing, even though he formulated it in the context of his previously mentioned inaccurate account of the identity of standard objects. At one point Russell explains that ". . . continuity is not a sufficient criterion of material identity. It is true that in many cases, such as rocks, mountains, tables, chairs, etc., where the appearances change slowly, continuity is sufficient, but in other cases, such as the parts of an approximately homogeneous fluid, it fails us utterly. We can travel by sensibly continuous gradations from any one drop of the sea at any one time to any other drop at any other time."[3]

Russell is wrong (or misleading) in stating that continuity is a sufficient condition of identity for standard objects like tables and chairs, since (as shown in Chapter 1) even in such cases continuity considerations by themselves do not exclude aberrant paths which combine stages of a whole with stages of its parts. Yet Russell correctly perceives that there is an important difference between cases involving standard objects like chairs and tables, and cases involving a merely undifferentiated portion of some larger uniform mass, like a drop of water in the sea. The difference, which Russell however never makes explicit, is that considerations of sortal-covered (or change-minimizing) continuity suffice for the former cases but not for the latter.

A problem about the identity of matter is most immediately

3. Russell, "The Relation of Sense-Data to Physics," p. 171.

apparent in the sort of case that I considered, or the one that Russell considers, involving a portion of matter which is neither sortal-covered nor articulated, and which is evidently amenable to neither the sortal rule nor the change-minimizing rule. But the problem is actually a more general one, and pertains even to portions of matter that are, at a given moment, both fully articulated and sortal-covered. This is because it is always necessary to distinguish between the identity through time of a portion of matter and the identity through time of the articulated object which, at a given moment, it makes up. Suppose that the portion of wood x composes the whole table y today. Though the table y's career can be traced along a path covered by the sortal "table" (or along a change-minimizing path), x's career cannot be traced in this manner, since x's career may not be the same as y's. If, for example, a piece of wood chipped off the table yesterday then, whereas the table y was larger yesterday, x was the same size but composed only part of the table. (Hence the relationship between x and y today is only one of *constitution*, but not *strict identity*.)[4] This shows that even where a portion of wood is covered by the sortal "table" (in the sense that "table" constitutively applies to it), its career cannot properly be traced along a sortal-covered (or change-minimizing) path.

A distinction between the identity of a portion of matter and the identity of the articulated object which it makes up must be acknowledged even in those cases where the only sortal under which we can trace the articulated object that the matter makes up is some term with roughly the force "articulated bit of such and such matter" (e.g., "puddle of water," "fragment of wood"). Thus we have to distinguish between the identity of a puddle of water (fragment of wood) and the identity of the water (wood) which makes it up. This distinction is very obviously required whenever a smaller articulated bit of matter is separated from, or joined to, the larger articulated bit which we are tracing. For example, we would not necessarily expect that in tracing a puddle (or pool or expanse) of water we are thereby tracing the *very same water*, since someone may have removed a glass of water from the puddle, or added one. Or if a splinter of wood is separated from a larger fragment (or lump or chunk) of wood then

4. Cf. above, p. 59ff.

of course we no longer have the *very same wood*. But, to take this point one step further, even where no smaller articulated bit separates from, or joins, the larger articulated bit which we are tracing this still does not give us a *criterial guarantee* that we are tracing the very same matter. This is perfectly obvious in the case of the puddle of water since we know that water may evaporate out of, or condense into, the puddle. And a moment's thought should convince us that even in tracing an apparently intact fragment of wood it must always remain a conceptually coherent possibility that some of the wood is vanishing (changing) into thin air while some other wood is materializing into the fragment. (Consider that a tree is in a way just a big chunk of wood, whose matter is continuously changing.) So it seems that the idea of a change-minimizing or sortal-covered path gives us no criteria for the concept of the persistence of matter under any circumstances. How then does this concept operate?

II. An "Ultimate" Kind of Persistence

It might be suggested that the appropriate move at this point would be to search diligently for some perhaps complicated and ingenious formulation of our identity criteria for matter (where these criteria might vary significantly from one sort of stuff to another). Before directly addressing this suggestion I want to explain an alternative approach, which is the one that I hold to be correct. My position, to put it somewhat incautiously at first, is that we do not have any identity criteria for matter. But this idea needs to be explained.

To begin with, it should be clear that the sort of identity criteria that I have been discussing in this book are *observational* criteria. We have observational criteria for an identity judgment if we are able to explain these criteria by reference exclusively to conditions of a straightforwardly observable sort. This seems tantamount to saying that observational criteria must not go beyond the ordinary manifest properties of things (e.g., something's being a table or something's being red) and the ordinary manifest relations between things (e.g., spatial and temporal).

Now for the case of the persistence of an ordinary articulated object we can draw a fairly clear distinction between *criteria of*

identity and *evidence of identity*. The criteria are those observational considerations in terms of which we can, at least roughly,
analyze or define what our concept of the object's persistence
consists in. Identity criteria, on my understanding, may be exceedingly vague and allow for any number of borderline possibilities. But we have criteria of identity for ordinary objects
insofar as in the most typical nonborderline cases our judgments
of identity about these objects are analytically entailed by
straightforwardly observable conditions. These conditions, I have
argued, basically amount to the requirement that an object's
career be traceable along a change-minimizing or sortal-covered
path. Evidence of identity, on the other hand, comprises facts
from which we can inductively conclude that the criteria are
satisfied. On the basis of directly tracing various objects along
change-minimizing or sortal-covered paths we arrive inductively
at generalizations (e.g., that a table tends, when left alone, to
remain qualitatively and locationally stable) which allow us to
judge that the identity criteria were satisfied in those cases where
we could not directly observe this. (So the fact that the table
which is present when we return to a room is qualitatively and
locationally similar to the one that we saw before leaving provides evidence that probably the criteria of sortal-coverage and
continuity were satisfied, and that we have the same table.)

But for the case of the persistence of matter I think we can
draw no such distinction between criteria and evidence of identity: here, in a sense, we have only evidence and no criteria. By
this I mean that the only way to characterize our general procedure for judging of the identity of matter is to say that we
reidentify matter in such a way as to arrive at the most coherent
and theoretically satisfying account of what we observe. In this
way we arrive at various principles which, both at the commonsense level and at scientific levels, specify how bits of matter of
various sorts may be presumed to behave under different observable circumstances. (For example, one such principle might
be that, other things being equal, a non-articulated bit of wood
is presumed to maintain a constant location within a table.) But
these principles are both partial and provisional, and may, within
broad limits, be supplemented or revised in the light of scientific
progress. These principles cannot therefore provide an analysis
or definition of our concept of persisting matter.

This account implies that our concept of persisting matter, even at the most commonsense level, incorporates something in the way of a theoretical-explanatory posit of an underlying mode of physical persistence which ultimately accounts for the observed behavior of ordinary articulated objects. Even the most limited level of common sense contains an abundance of relatively secure and well-founded views about that underlying domain, though it is ultimately for science to fill in the details. But no belief about the observable manifestations of matter, however well founded, is analytic of our concept of persisting matter. It must always remain a conceptually coherent possibility that our explanations have been faulty and that matter behaves differently from the way that we think.

Though I am maintaining that we have no ordinary observational criteria of identity for matter it might still be possible to provide some level of analysis or explanation of our concept of persisting matter. We can, in fact, broadly distinguish between two philosophical (and scientific) approaches to such an explanation.

a. It might be held that the persistence of matter is ultimately to be understood in terms of the persistence of particles such as atoms, molecules, or electrons. These particles might be said, in a somewhat extended sense, to be articulated by various unobservable properties in terms of which a sortal such as "atom" can be defined. The persistence of an atom is then analyzed in the standard way as depending upon the continuity of the atom's path under the sortal "atom." (Alternatively we can say that the atom's path minimizes change with respect to its unobservable properties.) The persistence of a bit of matter is thus ultimately analyzed in terms of the sortal-covered persistence of the particles which make it up. (We can then say, if we like, that we have "theoretical identity criteria" for matter since we can give an analysis of the persistence of matter in theoretical terms.)

b. If we want to avoid a commitment to atomism we might say simply that the persistence of matter depends upon some unobservable relationship which binds the successive stages of a single bit of matter. This relationship has sometimes been called "genidentity."[5] So we can, in a sense, explain the identity

5. See Rudolph Carnap, *Introduction to Symbolic Logic* (Dover Publications, N.Y., 1958), p. 198. See also the remarks about genidentity in Hans Reichen-

of matter by reference to that relationship. (Though this "explanation" seems very thin indeed, there is still nothing to prevent
us from saying that in terms of the unobservable relationship of
genidentity we can state "theoretical identity criteria" for matter.)

The (b)-approach seems to me on the whole the more sensible
one. The (a)-approach does admittedly have the advantage of
allowing a closer analogy between the persistence of matter and
the ordinary sortal-covered persistence of familiar articulated objects. The (b)-approach, on the other hand, at least maintains a
formal analogy between these two modes of persistence, insofar
as in both cases a unity-making relationship (sortal-covered continuity for ordinary objects and genidentity for matter) can be
thought of as binding object-stages into successions which do not
generally crisscross or overlap. And the (b)-approach has the
decisive-seeming advantage of not forcing us to wed the concept
of persisting matter a priori to atomism. (The (b)-approach does
not *exclude* atomism since there is nothing to prevent the relationship of genidentity from turning out to depend upon the
sortal-covered persistence of atoms.) The a priori atomistic position implied by the (a)-approach would have us reject on a priori
(conceptual) grounds various anti-atomic theories of matter that
have been influentially maintained in the history of science.[6]
This seems implausibly overbearing. It seems that our concept
of the persistence of matter ought to be seen as a priori accommodating the possibility that, even from the deepest theoretical
vantage point, portions of matter might persist as merely non-
differentiated parts of larger masses.

The contrast that I am trying to develop here between the
persistence of standard objects and the persistence of (portions
of) matter seems the more compelling, certainly, if one agrees
with me in rejecting an a priori atomistic analysis of our concept
of the persistence of matter. But I think that the point remains
essentially intact even if one opts for a priori atomism. There is
surely an important sense in which the persistence of such par-

---

bach, *The Philosophy of Space and Time* (Dover Publications, N.Y., 1958),
p. 270ff.
6. See the conflict between atomic theories and "continuum" theories as discussed in Stephen Toulmin and June Goodfield, *The Architecture of Matter*
(Harper & Row, N.Y., 1962), p. 64ff. and p. 158ff.

ticles as atoms, molecules, and electrons cannot be understood in straightforwardly observational terms. Obviously these particles cannot be observed except perhaps by way of highly technical and theory-imbedded apparatus. Moreover it would seem that we cannot even soberly visualize such particles in terms of ordinary qualities like color or texture. The conclusion seems therefore warranted that if the only account that we can give of our concept of the persistence of matter is in terms either of atomism or genidentity, then our concept of this mode of persistence is not properly regarded as analyzable in terms of ordinary observational identity criteria.

There is a philosophical tradition, loosely associated with the word "substance," to the general effect that our concept of the persistence of matter points to something beyond the reach of what can be straightforwardly observed. (This is the gist of Descartes's discussion of the wax in Meditation 2.) This seems closely akin to the position which I am here advancing. My position would also entitle us, I think, to say something else which is close to the heart of the substance tradition, and this is that the unity through time of matter, in contrast to that of familiar articulated objects, is in a sense *ultimate*. This sense of ultimacy derives from the two related points that the unity through time of matter goes deeper than (because it is not analyzable in terms of) the ordinary manifest properties and relations of things, and this unity is posited as playing a central role in the ideally most complete explanation of physical phenomena.[7]

III. Searching for Identity Criteria

This, then, is my view on the identity of matter. Let me return now to the previously postponed suggestion that perhaps, contrary to my view, there really are observational identity criteria for matter and we ought to look harder for them. I would not expect this suggestion to induce a great deal of enthusiasm at the present stage of the discussion. For we now have before us two possible accounts, two possible models, for understanding the nature of our judgments about the identity of matter. According

7. Cf. Shoemaker's discussion of the connection between the substance tradition and the analyzability of identity judgments, in *Self-Knowledge and Self-Identity*, pp. 57–63 and pp. 254–60.

to the criterial model these judgments are to be seen as analytically entailed by some complex conjunction of straightforwardly observable conditions. The model that I propose denies that any such analytic entailments apply to these judgments. The latter model must seem far more promising than the former in light of the cases considered earlier (the hand-shaped bit of wood in the table, the fragment of wood, the puddle, the tree). For these cases certainly did not make it appear remotely hopeful that we could specify even vaguely some observable conditions which analytically entail the relevant judgments about the identity of matter.

To recapitulate briefly, we recall that the identity of the non-(observably)articulated bit of wood in the table could evidently not be analyzed in terms of any straightforward considerations of sortal-covered or change-minimizing continuity. Nor, we saw, did the wood's location in the table afford a criterial basis for judging of its identity. And notice now the more general point that our ability conceptually to divide an object like a table top into such parts or portions as *the part in the middle, the curved part, that corner, that edge,* and so on, will never give us the sought-after criterial basis for the identity of the bits of matter which compose the object, since it is by no means an analytic truth that the same parts, in this sense, must be composed of the same matter. Or, to consider a slightly different sort of case, when a piece of clay is deformed we may be able straightforwardly to observe the differing movements of such parts as, for example, the top part, the middle part, the thin part, the bumpy part. But none of this gives us a criterial basis for judging of the identity of the matter which makes up these parts.

This point reverts back to my observation in the preceding chapter that if we want to trace a career under a term like "portion of a car between the bumpers" then we must be careful to distinguish between the item thus traced and the matter which, at any given moment, makes it up. I noted then the apparent difficulty in assessing the status as sortals of various constructions out of "part" and "portion," and the correlative difficulty in assessing the status as objects of the items traced under such constructions. What seems sufficiently clear, however, is that these items, whatever their precise status, cannot provide us with identity criteria for the bits of matter which partially compose an object. And once this is clear I think it is immediately apparent that there are no remotely plausible candidates for such a criterial basis.

The reasonable conclusion seems to be that we simply do not rely on observational criteria when we judge of the identity of some matter which partially composes an object. In a case like that of the wood in the table what we do rely on (at a common-sense level) is the *simplifying assumption* that the wood's location in the table probably remains fairly constant. That is, we rely on some such general simplifying principle as this: Other things being equal the location of a non-articulated bit of matter within an articulated object may be presumed to remain fairly constant. But this principle provides nothing like a criterial guarantee, and there is no saying a priori in how many different ways the principle might have to be augmented and reshaped both by common sense and science. (There is no saying a priori in how many different ways the "other things being equal" clause would have to be filled in to yield the simplest and most coherent account of the careers of different bits of matter.) In those various cases where we judge that some non-articulated matter has altered its location within an object (e.g., in the case of a piece of clay that is being deformed, or in the case of a tree, or in the case of a river) we rely on the most diverse evidential considerations and ultimately on the best theory of matter we have available.

Even when we turn to the much simpler kind of situation, in which the quantity of matter under consideration is fully articulated, we find nothing like a criterial guarantee of our identity judgments about the matter. Suppose, for example, that I am holding a perfectly solid block of wood in my hand, stationary, not squeezing it too hard, in ordinary atmospheric conditions, with nothing observably weird going on (for example, there are no observable changes in either the size or shape of the block). In such circumstances I might venture the following identity judgment: "The wood which now makes up this block is identical with the wood which made up this block a moment ago." We are searching for some observable conditions which might criterially (analytically) entail the truth of this judgment. What needs to be ruled out, among other things, is the possibility that some of the wood vanished (changed) into air (or into the flesh of my hand) and/or that some additional wood materialized out of the air (or out of my flesh) into the block.

What observable conditions could conceivably be such as to entail analytically that this has not happened? Surely not the conditions mentioned earlier (that the block was not squeezed, that its size and shape remained constant, etc.). It might be startling, but certainly not incoherent, for scientists to tell us that under just those conditions some bit of wood turns into air and vice versa. (The constancy of the block's size and shape might be accounted for by positing suitable expansions and contractions of the wood inside the block.) Is it not clearly hopeless to seek some *other* observable conditions which somehow *would* analytically entail the identity judgment?

If someone is not convinced that this is hopeless then let him reflect upon the following point (which seems to me fairly decisive). In order for it to be true to say "The wood which now makes up this block is identical with the wood which made up this block a moment ago" it must be the case that *all* the original wood of the block is still in the block. This means that even if some minute and possibly invisible speck of wood in the block turned into air the identity judgment in question is, strictly speaking, false. But it seems obvious beyond the need for further argument that no straightforwardly observable conditions (no facts about the ordinary properties and relations of things), however complex, could analytically guarantee that no such minute speck turned into air. And since the identity judgment requires just this guarantee it follows immediately that no observable conditions can criterially guarantee the identity judgment.

Indeed the position that I am here defending seems evident almost to the point of triviality the moment we remind ourselves that the proposition "x (which exists now) is the same wood as y (which existed before)" entails "Every (wooden) part of x, no matter how minute, was a part of y." This entailment seems immediately to render unobservable the identity through time of matter. And, I might add, one can apparently say this without being committed to any special views about the much debated nature of the "observational"-"theoretical" distinction. Whatever might be the ultimate epistemological status of the "straightforwardly observable" it seems sufficiently clear that in the sense in which the persistence of a table, or a block of wood, is straight-forwardly observable, the persistence of a portion of matter is not, since the latter mode of persistence depends upon the clearly unobservable condition that every minute part of the matter remain the same.

We are perhaps inclined to ignore considerations about minute and possibly invisible specks of matter in the context of a discussion of our most commonsense concept of persisting matter. But such considerations, once we are reminded of them, seem quite definitely to have a legitimate bearing on the meaning of that commonsense concept, and indeed to be in a way definitive of it. If someone, say a child, could not appreciate the relevance, with respect to his judgments about "same wood," of scientific theories about minute and invisible specks of matter, this would seem to be grounds for saying that he was not really employing the concept of the identity of matter but was instead still at the more elementary level of thinking only about, e.g., "same block," "same stick."

Admittedly a commonsense judgment about the identity of some matter is not likely to stickle over details about minute parts. From a commonsense point of view perhaps what I would really want to say about the block of wood is that the wood which makes it up now is *more or less* the same as before, but not necessarily *exactly* the same. Be this as it may it would certainly seem a mistake to try to suggest that though we have no observational criteria for the judgment "x (which exists now) is the same matter as y (which existed before)" we do nevertheless have such criteria for the judgment "Some large portion of x is the same matter as some large portion of y," or, colloquially, "x is more or less the same matter as y." Surely our understanding of these latter judgments presupposes our understanding of the former, presupposes, that is, our understanding of what it means to say of a particular bit of matter that it has persisted over some period of time. And since, by hypothesis, we have no observational criteria in terms of which to analyze or define what is meant by the former judgment it follows that we cannot have observational criteria in terms of which to analyze or define what is meant by the latter judgments.

The inescapable conclusion seems to be that in judging of the identity of matter, even in those cases where the matter happens to be articulated (e.g., in judging of the identity of the wood in the block), we do not rely on identity criteria, but we rely instead on some such simplifying principle as the following: Other things being equal an intact articulated object (like an intact block of wood) may be presumed to alter its material composition, if at all, only partially and very slowly. Common sense and science augment this principle (fill in the "other things being equal" clause) not on the basis of some a priori criterial strictures but on the basis rather of the widest and in principle most unlimited variety of facts about how things alter in size and weight, decompose, mix together, and so on. The proper model here is not that of criteria application but rather that of working towards the most coherent theory of an underlying level of persisting matter.

IV. Matter and Common Sense

That our commonsense concept of persisting matter involves the positing of an underlying reality may seem unbelievable because the concept strikes us as absolutely obvious and inevitable. Indeed the premise that the concept is not criterially definable in conjunction with the recognition of its utter obviousness could naturally lead to the surmise that the concept must be in some sense a priori. But I think that a more straightforward explanation of why the concept is so obvious is that our experience with ordinary articulated objects provides us incessantly with a literally overwhelming barrage of evidence that there exists underlying matter. That is, our most immediate and surface-level observations of ordinary objects, whose persistence conditions are grasped in terms of observational criteria, present us with a range of facts which point unavoidably to the conclusion that these ordinary objects are composed of, and are ultimately to be understood in terms of, persisting items of a quite different sort.

The range of facts to focus on contains as an instance just the sort of case discussed earlier, breaking a table to pieces. What we cannot avoid noticing in such a case is that the fragments which emerge from the table go together to add up to an object of at least roughly the size, and even form, of the table. And this is virtually a universal phenomenon: An object which contains no (observably) articulated parts is split up into a number of objects which add up to the original. How can one avoid trying to explain this by invoking the idea that the smaller objects which came out of the bigger one were in some sense *already in there* prior to their articulation? This conclusion seems so inevitable that one could scarcely take seriously my question about our basis for judging that (the wood in) the wooden fragment had always been lurking non-articulatedly in the table. And as far as the question *where* in the table it was, well, we adopt initially the simplest and most obvious hypothesis that it was always located right at the place in the table from whence it came. Such assumptions as this constitute a rudimentary commonsense theory of underlying matter, and all that is now required is for someone like Thales to enter the scene and the rest happens by itself.

But we can, I feel convinced, imagine what it would be like to live in a world whose articulated objects did not display those patterns of behavior which provide the primitive basis for our concept of persisting matter. In such a world the concept would have no use, at least not at a commonsense level. I will only sketch this peremptorily. But imagine that whenever you break a table to pieces the resulting fragments add up to five times the size of the table. Imagine that if ever you start out with a basin full of water and remove a glassful from it then when you pour the water back the basin overflows enormously. Imagine that whenever you dig a hole in the ground you wind up with a pile of dirt which looks thirty times higher than the hole next to it.

These imaginings would have to be generalized indefinitely before we reached the image of a world in which the concept of persisting matter had no immediate application. But I can see no reason to doubt that we can coherently broach this image. That it is extremely *difficult* for us to do so shows how deep in our experience the concept of matter penetrates; but that it is *possible* for us to do so shows that the concept is not, in the most ultimate sense, unavoidable. If we lived in that imagined world we would still have immediate use for the idea that "you can't get something out of nothing," since to get, for example, a new fragment of wood you would have to make one by separating it out of something else. The idea for which we would have no immediate use is that when you create a new articulated object by separating it out of another object there was all along something, the persisting matter, waiting there to be articulated. This idea (which is, I think, in some sense really a *strange* idea) would not impress itself upon us.

The essential simplification which our concept of matter contributes at a commonsense level might be thought of as follows. If we were to confine ourselves wholly to the observational level of the basic (or sortal) conception we would be able to formulate the following two kinds of laws. Type A laws would tell us what tends to happen in the special case in which one articulated object is created (or destroyed) by coming out of (or merging into) another. For example: When an articulated wooden object is broken to pieces the fragments which come out of it add up to the original in size and weight (and perhaps shape). Type B laws would tell us how articulated objects tend to behave in the more general case in which no articulated object is created (or destroyed) by coming out of (or merging into) another. An example might be: Under ordinary conditions an articulated wooden object tends to conserve its size, and weight, and shape. Now it is a contingent fact, which we can imagine otherwise, that these two types of observational laws are so related that they can be subsumed under, and hence explained in terms of, relatively simple type T laws which posit an underlying level of persisting matter. An example of a type T law is: Under ordinary conditions a portion of wood (whether articulated or not) tends to conserve its size, and weight, and shape. This type T law allows us to explain in a simple unified manner the two kinds of phenomena which we would have had to treat separately if we limited ourselves to the observational level.

The explanatory application of a type T law, which describes the behavior of underlying matter, presupposes the availability of some principles ("correspondence rules," "bridge principles") that connect observable facts about articulated objects with the posited facts about matter. We might perhaps represent the most rudimentary commonsense theory of matter as embodying such principles in the form of the three presumptive principles which have emerged in the course of this discussion, viz. (1) the presumption that the material composition of an articulated object remains pretty much constant, (2) the presumption that the location of a non-articulated bit of matter within an articulated object remains pretty much constant, and (3) the presumption that when a smaller articulated object comes out of (merges into) a larger one then the matter which makes up the smaller one is subtracted from (added to) the matter which makes up the larger one. In terms of these three principles we are able to construct a relatively coherent and satisfying picture of what happens to the wood in a table both before and after the table is broken to pieces. We can say that each fragment that comes out of the table is composed of wood which was originally in the table (presumption (3)), that this wood probably partially composed the table throughout its entire career (presumption (1)), and was always located roughly at the place in the table from which it eventually emerged (presumption (2)). And all of this happened in accordance with the type T law mentioned before (i.e., the law that a bit of wood tends to conserve its size, weight, and shape).

I have been at pains to establish that our concept of the persistence of matter is relatively theoretical as compared to our concept of the observable persistence of an ordinary articulated object, and that, as a consequence of this fact, we should be able to imagine what it would be like to live in a world in which we had a commonsense use for the latter concept but not the former. A somewhat different and perhaps easier point, which reinforces the previous one, is that we can imagine what it would be like for our concept of the persistence of ordinary objects to function normally while the concept of the persistence of matter is repudiated at the highest theoretical levels. (This is, I think, tantamount to imagining a world in which ordinary objects in fact persist without any matter in fact persisting.) It certainly seems that scientists might tell us that there is no such thing as an underlying level of persisting matter, but that some radically different conception affords the ultimate explanation of physical phenomena. (Indeed on some readings of contemporary physics it may possibly be that scientists *have* told us this.) But this would not (and should not) prevent us from continuing to judge in the normal way about the identity of ordinary observable objects.[8]

8. Compare with Sydney Shoemaker's criticism of Chisholm's position in "The Loose and Popular and the Strict and Philosophical Senses of Identity," in Norman S. Care and Robert H. Grimm, eds., *Perception and Personal Identity* (The Press of Western Reserve University, Cleveland, 1969), pp. 108–9.

It follows from the above account that I would regard our concept of the persistence of ordinary articulated objects as decisively more primary than our concept of persisting matter. This implies a repudiation of the common procedure (e.g., in Locke's discussions of identity) of stating identity criteria for ordinary objects in terms of a prior notion of persisting matter.[9] Often this procedure will take the form of substituting for the requirement of spatiotemporal and qualitative continuity the requirement that an object's material composition can alter only gradually. Now these requirements do in practice amount to virtually the same thing, but it is nevertheless a major error of principle to inject the concept of persisting matter into the very center of our ordinary identity criteria. The clear and observational concept of the persistence of an ordinary object deserves to be kept relatively disentangled from the more difficult and theoretical concept of persisting matter. We have, and have the right to have, a concept of persistence which operates essentially at the most straightforward observable level without much concern for what may be happening in the theoretical depths.

This is not necessarily to rule out the possibility that our relatively theoretical judgments about matter might marginally influence our judgments about ordinary objects. Such influence may be present in the following sort of case. Suppose that after breaking a table to pieces I manage to glue the fragments back together into a table. I should then probably want to say that it was the same table again, basing myself presumably on the judgment that "it's still the same matter." If this is correct then we have here a counterexample to the overall sortal analysis, insofar as we regard this analysis as implying that the identity of

9. Locke, *An Essay Concerning Human Understanding.* Chisholm's account of persistence seems to contain a variant of the same (I think objectionable) procedure. On his account our concept of the persistence of an ordinary object apparently depends upon our prior concept of the persistence of what he sometimes calls the "primary objects" which constitute ordinary objects, where these "primary objects" seem to be pretty much the same as what I am calling "portions of matter." Besides the previously cited works, see his *Person and Object* (Open Court, LaSalle, Ill., 1976), "Problems of Identity" in M. K. Munitz, ed., *Identity and Individuation* (New York University Press, N. Y., 1971), and "Identity Through Time" in H. E. Kiefer and M. K. Munitz, eds., *Language, Belief, and Metaphysics* (State University of New York, Albany, N. Y., 1970).

a standard object must be determined either by the observable sortal-covered continuity of the object, or by the observable sortal-covered continuity of the (major) parts that compose the object. In the present case the judgment about the identity of the table would be based neither on the sortal-covered continuity of the table, nor on compositional considerations about the observable sortal-covered continuity of parts of the table. It seems that we perhaps need to relax the compositional criterion by allowing into play theoretical compositional considerations *vis-à-vis* the identity of matter.

It should be remarked, however, that this possible counter-example to the sortal analysis of the identity of standard objects infects only the supplementary compositional criterion, but not the primary criterion of sortal-covered continuity expressed by the sortal rule. We have still found nothing to jeopardize the condition of sortal-covered continuity as logically sufficient for the identity of a standard object; and we can still uphold the general idea that a logically necessary and sufficient condition for the identity of a standard object is that it satisfy either the primary sortal rule or the supplementary compositional criterion, though the latter is perhaps seen now as infected by the identity of matter.[10] As regards the identity of matter, of course, my whole argument has been to show that the sortal analysis (at least at an observational level) is inadequate, and that theoretical considerations are required to define the identity of matter.

A question which might be addressed to my account is whether I would say that a continuous portion of matter can persist as that identical matter when it is fragmented. To this I would suggest that, as with all questions about the identity of matter, it must be settled on theoretical grounds, which means ultimately by the scientist. From the standpoint of elementary physics and chemistry it seems that various conservation laws imply that a portion of matter does not go out of existence even when it is fragmented. As to whether we should then say that a fragmented portion of matter, which was once continuous, is (still) in any sense an "object," this seems to be merely an inconsequential point of terminology which we can settle as we

10. This formulation of the general identity conditions for standard objects will be reconsidered in Chapter 7.

like. And, of course, elementary physics and chemistry may not give us the final answer.

Again, from my point of view it would be a question essentially to be settled by scientific theory whether or not matter can jump discontinuously through space (a possibility which some contemporary scientists may take seriously). I can see no decisive reason to rule this out a priori. This possibility, by the way, carries with it a correlative possibility with respect to standard objects, assuming that the compositional criterion is now properly regarded as embracing the identity of matter. Suppose that a table vanishes into thin air, and that immediately afterwards a table bearing all of the distinctive marks of the first appears in a different place. Insofar as our theoretical-explanatory needs might possibly induce us in such a case to hypothesize that the matter which constituted the first table jumped discontinuously through space and now constitutes the second table, we might also be entitled, via the compositional criterion, to judge that the first table is the same as the second.

I want to note that Russell sometimes explains the identity of matter in terms akin to the account that I have been presenting. After posing a problem about the identity of a drop of water in the sea in the passage last quoted he goes on to say: "The characteristic required in addition to continuity is conformity with the laws of dynamics."[11] If by "the laws of dynamics" Russell means the body of scientific laws that make reference to bits of matter then this seems fairly close to what I am saying.

Often, however, Russell seems also to be suggesting that the condition of conformity to laws has a special bearing not only on the identity of matter, but on the identity of standard objects as well.[12] But it seems to me excessively unclear what this could mean. Certainly even the most elementary laws of physics do not make reference to any standard objects, as ordinarily conceived. For example, the elementary law "For every bit of matter x, x's mass never changes" is not satisfied by a car as ordinarily thought of, since a car's mass changes whenever a tire is removed. All that this shows of course is that the physicist's

11. "The Relation of Sense-Data to Physics," p. 171.
12. Such a suggestion seems pretty clearly implicit in his discussion in *Human Knowledge, Its Scope and Limits* (Simon & Schuster, New York, 1948), pp. 458–60.

laws do not refer to (do not quantify over) standard objects as such, that a car is not (strictly identical with) a bit of matter. The physicist explains what happens to the car on the basis of what happens to the matter which makes it up. But then what precise bearing do the physicist's laws have on our concept of the identity of the car?

We can perhaps say (and this is what Russell seems sometimes to have in mind) that the career of a car exemplifies, if not the physicist's laws, at least some rough regularities in terms of which the successive stages of the car can be thought of as to some degree causally connected (in terms of which, as Russell sometimes puts it, the successive stages of the car can be thought of as forming a "causal line").[13] But whatever precisely this might mean it seems that we could certainly say the same thing about the career of a shrinking incar, viz. that it exemplifies some rough regularities in terms of which its successive stages can be thought of as to some degree causally connected. This very weak condition of causal connectedness does not, therefore, even rule out drastic part-whole tracing confusions. As such it seems to have no clear role to play in an analysis of identity.[14]

I am tentatively inclined to think that with respect to what is most plausibly regarded as a commonsense level of thought (as opposed to an expert or technical level) we should mention the condition of conformity to law only in the context of a discussion of the identity of matter. And here the idea is that the identity of matter is determined by theoretical considerations, and is ultimately clarified by the laws of science. As regards standard objects the essential condition to mention is sortal-covered, or change-minimizing, continuity.

Laws of physics (and chemistry), which describe the behavior of matter, are of course not the only laws of science there are, though it is often held that all laws are ultimately reducible

13. Ibid.
14. The relationship between causality and identity is examined further in Chapter 7. But let me here stress one point: If it is held that causal connectedness is an essential aspect of the continuity of a body's history, then the causal condition can be added to the other continuity conditions in the Simple Continuity Analysis of Chapter 1, the Sortal Rule of Chapter 2, and the Basic Rule of Chapter 3; the overall structure of my argument (including the contrast between matter and standard objects) remains essentially intact.

to these. We can perhaps think of the identity conditions associated with such essentially technical concepts as "bacterium"
and "cell" as determined by the theoretical needs of biology in
rather the way that the identity of matter is determined by the
theoretical needs of physics. But I think that we should resist
the possible suggestion that even such nontechnical notions
as "same tree" and "same cat" ought to be seen as ultimately
determined by how these notions can be made to figure in the
best laws of biology.[15] This suggestion can plausibly be resisted
at least to the extent of maintaining that there is a nontechnical
sense (level, part) of the concept "same tree," or "same cat,"
which operates quite independently of biological theory, and
which is determined essentially by relatively straightforward
considerations of observable sortal-covered, or change-minimizing,
continuity. If it is agreed that our ordinary concept of the persistence of a car is essentially unaffected by physical theory (e.g.,
by the principle of mass constancy), then what reason would
there be to suppose that our ordinary concept of the persistence
of a tree is somehow contingent upon biological theory? It seems
more plausible to characterize all of our ordinary concepts of
the persistence of standard objects, whether these objects be
man-made or natural, as operating in essential independence of
scientific-theoretic considerations, and as being essentially definable in the relatively simple terms of sortal-covered, or change-
minimizing, continuity. For the case of the identity of matter,
on the other hand, we apparently cannot coherently distinguish
any sense of the concept which is not already implicated in
essentially theoretical considerations, considerations which are
then eventually elaborated by science.

In summary, I have discussed altogether three commonsense
ideas of physical persistence: the basic conception, the sortal
conception, and now the theoretical-explanatory conception of

15. Such a suggestion might be implicit in the approach to "natural kinds"
that one finds in Hilary Putnam, "Is Semantics Possible?" in H. E. Kiefer
and M. K. Munitz, eds., Language, Belief, and Metaphysics, reprinted in
Mind, Language and Reality (Cambridge University Press, Cambridge, London, 1975); and in Saul Kripke, "Naming and Necessity," in D. Davidson and
G. Harman, eds., Semantics of Natural Language (D. Reidel, Dordrecht,
1972), republished as Naming and Necessity (Harvard University Press, Cambridge, Mass., 1980).

persisting matter. The connection between the first two of these was that the sortal conception serves primarily to clarify the basic one. Can we see any other connections here? I think we easily can. Perhaps any observational concept is amenable to theoretical extension. But there seems to be a sense in which our basic concept of persistence stands especially ready for this. The core of the basic conception was the rule that an object's career should be traced so as to minimize changes. But there seems to be a very natural movement of thought from saying "*Minimize* changes" to saying "*Simplify* changes." We can think of this movement as passing through the intermediary step "Do not countenance a change in an object unless it is necessary." This can be interpreted to mean "unless it is necessary for tracing the object in a continuous path," which gives us the basic rule, and its eventual sortal clarification. Or it can mean "unless it is necessary for providing the simplest explanation of the phenomena," which gives us the general procedure for judging of the persistence of matter.

As I see it, then, at the root of our concept of physical persistence is the vague rule of minimizing changes. From this rule there emanate two rather contrasting conceptions, on the one hand the relatively concrete and definite conception of the persistence of different sorts of articulated objects, and on the other the relatively abstract and indefinite conception of persisting matter.

5

The Metaphysics of Persistence

I. Do We Need Persisting Objects?

ONE KIND of question that may motivate a philosophical examination of the concept of physical persistence is whether this concept is indispensable to our thought about the world, or whether we could, on the contrary, conceive of the world in some radically different way. Let me first consider this question with regard to the observable persistence of standard objects, like cars, and tables, and trees; in later sections I will extend the discussion to include the persistence of matter. (But it should be understood that special problems revolving around the persistence of persons are not to be treated until a later chapter, except perhaps in an occasional parenthetical aside.)

It seems to follow immediately from the preceding account that the persistence of a car, or a table, or a tree boils down essentially to there being a continuously related succession of car-stages, or table-stages, or tree-stages. This point would admittedly need to be complicated to accommodate the compositional criterion. But there would seem to be nothing in this complication to discourage the general conclusion that, for any standard sortal F, our ordinary descriptions of the persistence of an F-thing could be dispensed with in favor of descriptions of F-stages and their interrelations.

There are in principle an indefinite number of possible constructions in terms of which ordinary talk about the persistence of, say, a car could be replaced by talk about the interrelations of car-stages. We could construct a language which allowed us to refer only to car-stages that last for one year or less, or to car-stages that last for as long as they maintain a constant color, or to car-stages that satisfy any number of other possible specifications. Each such construction would apparently allow us to redescribe what we ordinarily express about persisting cars in terms of descriptions of how car-stages (of this or that specification) are related to each other.

The most obvious, and also most radical, construction along these general lines is one in which we are allowed to refer only to *momentary* car-stages. This construction strikes us as particularly challenging insofar as it seems to depart as far as possible from the ordinary idea of an enduring object. I do not, however, want to get bogged down now over puzzles about whether momentary car-stages are to be conceived of as literally instantaneous or, if not, how long they last. Some of these puzzles would be merely reformulations of perennial puzzles in the philosophy of time, while others are perhaps specific to the present case.[1] I will assume that a "momentary" car-stage is of relatively short duration as compared to the normal duration of a car as ordinarily conceived of, but I will leave it open just how short this is.

We can imagine, then, a language, let us call it the M-language, within which only momentary object-stages (and their sets, successions, etc.) are referred to and described. In this language we could say "A car-stage is (spatially) in contact with a tree-stage," or "There occurs a continuous succession of tree-stages," or "There occurs a discontinuous succession containing tree-stages followed by car-stages." But we would not talk in ordinary ways about the persistence of a car or a tree.

To suggest that we could in principle dispense with our ordinary concept of the persistence of a standard object in favor of the M-language means essentially this. For any ordinary statement O which describes in ordinary terms the career of a standard object, there is some statement M within the M-language such that O and M are equivalent. But the kind of "equivalence" that is to obtain between O and M must not be construed too

1. Cf. my earlier questions about the duration of an "intrinsic car-stage"; Chapter 3, pp. 102–4.

stringently. Certainly we cannot expect that M should constitute a straightforward *translation* of the ordinary statement O, in the sense in which a French statement might constitute a translation of an English statement. Nor, even, do we want to require that O and M should be analytically equivalent (i.e., that they should analytically entail each other) in the strict sense in which, for example, "*x* is a triangle" is analytically equivalent to "*x* is a three-sided polygon." For one thing, an ordinary statement O will suffer from some margin of vagueness, in virtue of which certain states of affairs would render its truth-value indeterminate. And we have no reason to require that M should so perfectly match up with O as to mirror exactly this margin of vagueness. It would in fact be sufficient for our purposes if the force of M approximates even roughly to that of O. The question which concerns us is whether the M-language has as much fact-stating power as our ordinary language, whether the M-language would allow us to describe the world as we experience it without, so to speak, missing out on anything. Certainly the previous account of the nature of physical persistence would suggest an affirmative answer to this question (at least insofar as we continue to limit our attention to the observable persistence of standard objects). That account would seem to imply that, in terms of the idea of sortal-covered (or change-minimizing) continuity, we could in principle frame descriptions within the M-language that are loosely, even if not strictly, equivalent to our ordinary descriptions of persisting objects.

It might be suggested that the M-language does not really dispense with the concept of a persisting object since even in that language we can refer to successions of momentary stages, and these successions, insofar as they contain elements that exist at different times, are themselves in a sense persisting objects. Now it is a relatively unimportant point of terminology whether we apply the expression "persisting object," and kindred expressions, to an M-level succession. The more important point is that an M-level succession is not governed by any rules of identity through time of the sort that govern our ordinary thought. (I want to ignore any questions about *identity through space* in the present discussion.) At the M-level any succession of momentary stages, however the succession might be formed (i.e., even if it combines what would ordinarily be thought of as the stages of different objects), counts equally with any other. This is the essential contrast with our ordinary conception, which accords the special status of persistence, of unity through time, to just those select successions of object-stages that are related in some special way (e.g., by sortal-covered continuity).

The idea of the M-language is essentially the idea of a *language without rules of identity through time*, a language in which any succession of momentary object-stages is logically on a par with any other. Such a language is, in one very important sense, a language without the concept of persistence. And it appears now that we could describe the world in terms of such a language.

A question might be raised about the intelligibility of the idea of an "object-stage" within the M-language. Object-stages, it might be objected, are abstract items (perhaps ordered pairs of objects and times), which go together to make up another kind of abstract item, the career or history of an object. But our idea of these abstract items presupposes the idea of a concrete persisting object. If we, therefore, try to do without our ordinary concept of a persisting object we can no longer understand what an object-stage is.

Now this objection is well taken insofar as it emphasizes the kind of conceptual departure from ordinary thought which the M-language would have to embody. From the point of view of the M-language a "momentary object-stage" must be conceived of as a concrete entity, which has the various properties (of shape, color, etc.) which we ordinarily attribute to an object at a given moment. We would therefore do better, perhaps, to represent the M-language as containing such expressions as "succession of (momentary) trees," rather than "succession of (momentary) tree-stages." It may be admitted that ordinary language does not permit us to think of a persisting object as temporally divisible into concrete momentary parts. But there seems to be nothing incoherent about a conceptual revision which would permit this.

The legitimacy of thinking about an object as divisible into temporal parts has been amply defended in recent literature. Quine, for example, expresses this idea as follows: "A physical thing—whether a river or a human body or a stone—is at any one moment a sum of simultaneous momentary states of spatially scattered atoms or other small physical constituents. Now just as the thing at a moment is a sum of these spatially small parts, so we may think of the thing over a period as a sum of the temporally small parts which are its successive momentary states. Combining these conceptions, we see the thing as extended in time and in space alike."[2]

For my present purposes there is no important distinction to be drawn between the M-language and Quine's "space-time" conception. The essential characterization of both conceptions is that they contain no rules of identity through time, and are therefore in an important sense free of the concept of persistence. Quine's space-time idiom suggests the point that the momentary items that figure in the persistence-free conception are to be conceived of as concrete entities, on a parallel with the concreteness of the spatially small parts of objects. Moreover Quine's space-time idiom contains the intrinsically interesting (though, for my present purposes, not especially relevant) twist of regarding the successions ("sums," as Quine called them) that are formed from the momentary items as themselves concrete entities that are extended in space and time. From Quine's space-time vantage point reality is seen as comprised of concrete space-time portions, whether continuous or discontinuous, that can be characterized in many of the ways that we characterize ordinary objects. The all-important point that I want to keep in central focus is that the space-time portions of reality figuring in Quine's scheme crisscross and overlap in every conceivable way, and are not conceptually structured by the kinds of identity rules that govern our ordinary concept of persistence.

There is evidently no prima facie connection between the idea of a language that lacks rules of identity through time, a language in which any succession of momentary items is logically on a par with any other, and the idea of a language that lacks the distinction between subjective experience and objective physical reality. It is true that many philosophers of the past who have tried to conceive of the physical world as ultimately composed of momentary things were phenomenalists. Their momentary things were sense data and the like, items that were supposed to be mental (or private). But the kind of persistence-

2. W. V. Quine, *Methods of Logic*, 3rd ed. (Holt, Rinehart and Winston, Inc., N.Y., 1972), p. 222. For further discussion of "object-stages" and "temporal parts," see Chapter 6, below.

free conception that I have been talking about is not intended to be in the least bit tainted by phenomenalism. Certainly the momentary things that figure in Quine's space-time conception are supposed to be fully objective; and the conception as a whole is to be an analytic restructuring of our ordinary thought about the physical world, with no loss of any sense of objectivity.

Now there may possibly be some deep arguments to establish that our distinction between subjective experience and objective physical reality is inextricably linked to our conceptually structuring physical reality in terms of rules of identity through time. But such a linkage would certainly need to be established, and not merely taken for granted. I do not in fact know of any relatively clear argument which might establish this linkage. And my impression is that many recent discussions of the subjective-objective distinction simply take the linkage for granted without seeing the need to establish it.

Such seems to be the case in Strawson's discussion of the conditions of objectivity in his chapter "Sounds" in *Individuals*. Strawson is there concerned with two questions. The first is whether the conditions of a "non-solipsistic consciousness" can be fulfilled within a purely auditory experience, that is, roughly, whether a being whose experience was purely auditory could make sense out of a distinction between subjective experience and objective reality. The second question is whether there could be enduring (persisting) and reidentifiable sound-particulars in the purely auditory world. Strawson argues that an affirmative answer to the first question would necessarily carry with it an affirmative answer to the second:

For to have a conceptual scheme in which a distinction is made between oneself and one's states and auditory items which are not states of oneself, is to have a conceptual scheme in which the existence of auditory items is *logically* independent of the existence of one's states or of oneself. Thus it is to have a conceptual scheme in which it is logically possible that such items should exist whether or not they were being observed, and hence should continue to exist through an interval during which they were not being observed. So it seems that it must be the case that there could be reidentifiable particulars in a purely auditory world if the conditions of a non-solipsistic consciousness could be fulfilled for such a world.[3]

3. Strawson, *Individuals*, p. 72.

I want to focus on the second sentence in the above argument. The sentence begins with the correct observation that a non-solipsistic consciousness would necessarily require a conceptual scheme in which certain items are thought of as existing while unobserved. But then Strawson simply jumps at the end of the sentence to the unargued conclusion that, since these items are being thought of as *existing* while unobserved, they must be thought of as *continuing* to exist while unobserved, i.e., they must be thought of as enduring particulars. But why could not the auditory scheme fulfill the conditions of a non-solipsistic consciousness by including the idea of objective *momentary* sounds, and successions of momentary sounds, which exist while unobserved? How has Strawson established the necessity of *enduring* sounds?

Of course, if by a "reidentifiable sound," a "sound that continues to exist," Strawson merely meant *any* succession of sounds, then his conclusion would follow trivially. But it is evident that this is not Strawson's intention. He is clearly trying to establish the necessity of enduring sound-particulars in the sense of particulars that are governed by rules of identity through time, rules which are satisfied only by certain successions of sounds, and which accord only to these successions the special status of enduring particulars. But Strawson has failed to show (at least in the quoted passage) that a scheme of objective particulars must necessarily include any such rules of identity through time.

II. A Question about Spatiotemporal Continuity

Our ability to redescribe the world of standard objects in the persistence-free terms of the M-language (the space-time language) would depend upon our being able to express within that language the idea that a succession of momentary things is spatiotemporally and qualitatively continuous. The notion of qualitative continuity seems to present no special difficulty since the application of this notion requires nothing more than our ability to make qualitative comparisons between the momentary things which comprise a succession. But the notion of spatio-temporal continuity does present a special difficulty.

In Chapter 1, I defined several senses of spatiotemporal continuity, all of which revolved around the idea of two places over-lapping each other. Roughly, a succession S was said to be spatiotemporally continuous if the places which coincide with temporally neighboring stages in S overlap, where the extent of overlap that was required varied with each definition. Now to say that two places overlap each other is obviously to say that they overlap each other at a given time. That is, the places must exist simultaneously. Of course when we say that two places overlap each other we need not relativize this remark to some *specific* time, since if two places ever overlap they always overlap. The overlap relations, as well as the distance relations, between places cannot possibly change. But the fact that we need not specify a time must not obscure the point that for places to over-lap they must exist together, i.e., at the same time.

For S to be spatiotemporally continuous the place p_1, which is occupied by the momentary thing in S at t_1, must overlap the place p_2, which is occupied by the momentary thing in S at t_2, where t_1 and t_2 are neighboring times. This means that p_1 and p_2 must exist together at some time, that we cannot think of p_1 as existing only at t_1 and p_2 existing only at t_2. We cannot, that is, think of p_1 and p_2 as "momentary places," the counterparts of momentary things. It is necessary that we should think of p_1 and p_2 as ordinary persisting places, which exist not only at t_1, or at t_2, but throughout an extended period, during which they continually overlap. The upshot of this is that if the notion of spatiotemporal continuity is to be explained along the general lines discussed in Chapter 1, then this notion involves essentially the idea of a persisting place.

The difficulty now is that the idea of a persisting place seems to presuppose the idea of a persisting object. Indeed the iden-tity through time of a place must apparently be thought of as relative to some *specific* object or system of objects. A succession of lightning flashes that occur at the same place relative to the earth occur at different places relative to the sun. This suggests that our ordinary notion of "same place again" is in effect short for "same place relative to such-and-such objects," where the specified objects supply a coordinate system in terms of which any place can be assigned a unique, and permanent, set of co-ordinates. (Roughly, we are at the same place relative to such-and-such objects if we are at the same distance and direction from the objects.) Consequently the M-language (the space-time language), which excludes the ordinary idea of a persisting object, cannot be coherently thought of as containing the idea of a persisting place. How, then, can it contain the required notion of spatiotemporal continuity?

I think that there are essentially two ways in which we might respond to this question. The more moderate way would be to concede the force of the question, and accordingly to limit the scope of the persistence-free language; the more radical way would be to concede nothing to the question. Let me first explain the moderate approach.

Suppose that we concede the point that the notion of spatiotemporal continuity cannot be understood independently of our concepts of persisting objects and persisting places. This would imply that the world as we know it could not be adequately described at the persistence-free level, that a thoroughgoing reduction of our identity concepts in terms of the persistence-free level is not possible. However, we could still consider the following more limited possibility. We might designate some specific group of objects as providing our spatial framework. The identity concepts associated with these objects are not to be dispensed with in the persistence-free language but are to be taken for granted. Then, presupposing the spatial framework provided by these concepts, we could render all *other* identity concepts in persistence-free terms.

We might, for example, designate buildings and their parts as the objects that provide the framework. Presumably the class of buildings and their parts will contain a sufficient number and variety of rigid edges, movable rigid bodies, and whatever else may be required to coordinate in the ordinary manner a system of persisting places. Given a system of persisting places we can define spatiotemporal continuity as in Chapter 1. And now the persistence of every standard object other than buildings and their parts can be rendered in persistence-free terms.

According to the moderate account it is incorrect to say, "We could redescribe the world of standard objects in such a way that, for every sortal F, our language would not employ the concept of the persistence of an F-thing." But it remains correct to say, "For every sortal F, we could redescribe the world of standard objects in such a way that our language would not employ the concept of the persistence of an F-thing." We are not, that is, permitted to think of all our ordinary descriptions of persisting objects as eliminable *in toto* by the persistence-free language. We can, however, think of any specific range of such descriptions as eliminable without loss. Given a background of persisting buildings, and the spatial framework thereby provided, we can dispense with persisting trees; and perhaps vice versa. But some objects must remain to provide the framework. The general category of a persisting physical object would thus be seen as an irreducible and indispensable component of our thought about the world, but the specific embodiments of this category in our various concepts of specific kinds of objects may be severely limited without detriment to the facts.

This moderate account strikes me as adopting an uncomfortable half-way position. If we can, so to speak, get rid of any kind of persisting object that we choose then it seems unsatisfactory to insist that we somehow cannot get rid of all of them together.

I think that there is in fact no compelling reason to limit the scope of the persistence-free language in the way that the moderate approach suggests. The kind of explanation of spatiotemporal continuity that I gave earlier, in terms of a presupposed framework of persisting places, is one natural-seeming explanation of that notion within our ordinary conceptual scheme. This need not prevent us, however, from regarding the notion in a different light as it figures in the persistence-free scheme. In the latter scheme spatiotemporal continuity might be treated as a primitive idea which is explained ostensively, i.e., by exhibiting examples of spatiotemporally continuous successions. There seems in general to be no uniquely correct way to order our ideas; and in the present case, at any rate, the alternative of treating spatiotemporal continuity as primitive, rather than as defined in terms of other concepts, seems quite plausible. Certainly we may be inclined to think of the spatial continuity of an object at a given moment as directly observable and conceptually simple. Why then should we not treat the spatiotemporal continuity of a temporally extended portion of reality in the same light?[4]

4. Compare with Whitehead's treatment of the continuity of an "event," in *The Concept of Nature*, pp. 74–78. I defend the primitiveness of spatiotemporal continuity further in Chapter 6, Sections V and VII.

The analogy to spatial continuity may suggest a slightly different approach, much to the same effect. Spatial continuity might be treated as a primitive concept, but it may also be defined in several ways, one of which is this: "x is spatially continuous at time t" can be defined as meaning that, for any y and z, if y and z exhaustively comprise x at t (i.e., y and z are parts of x such that any part of x overlaps either y or z), and y and z do not overlap at t, then y and z touch each other at t. (I am allowing for the possibility that overlapping objects perhaps cannot be said to touch each other.) Here we define spatial continuity in terms of touching, though the reverse procedure seems equally plausible.

The term "spatiotemporal *contiguity*" is sometimes used to signify the spatiotemporal analogue of touching, to signify, that is, the relationship which stands to spatiotemporal continuity in the way that touching stands to spatial continuity. Hence "The succession S is spatiotemporally continuous" is equivalent to "For any S_1 and S_2, if S_1 and S_2 are temporal segments of S which exhaustively comprise S, and S_1 and S_2 do not overlap, then S_1 and S_2 are spatiotemporally contiguous to each other." If we can assume the notion of spatiotemporal contiguity in the persistence-free language then we can easily define spatiotemporal continuity in terms of it.

Now the ordinary notion of one thing turning into (being replaced by) another thing, in those cases in which the second thing might be said to come into existence when the first thing goes out of existence, is closely related to the idea of spatiotemporal contiguity. The proposition "x went out of existence and turned into y, which came into existence" (e.g., "The car went out of existence and turned into the block of scrap metal, which came into existence") can be roughly associated with the proposition "A terminal segment of x's career is spatiotemporally contiguous with an initial segment of y's career." To ascertain just how close this association is would require a more detailed examination of the ordinary notion of "turning into" than I now want to undertake. But even a rather loose association encourages the judgment that, if the ordinary notion of "turning into" can be treated as a primitive observational concept, and this seems quite plausible, then it should also be possible to treat spatiotemporal contiguity in the same spirit. And given spatiotemporal contiguity we can, as indicated before, immediately define spatiotemporal continuity. (Hence the idea of a spatiotemporally continuous succession can be loosely associated with the idea of a succession which is such that any early segment "turns into" a later segment.)

I conclude that the required notion of spatiotemporal continuity can be made available in the persistence-free language without relying on a presupposed framework of persisting places. Though it seems reasonable from the ordinary point of view to connect the notion of spatiotemporal continuity to our ordinary idea of a system of persisting places, severing this connection appears to impose no overwhelming strain on our understanding. It seems therefore that we can adequately redescribe the world of standard objects in wholly persistence-free terms.

III. Identity Schemes

The persistence of any standard physical object can be regarded as consisting simply in the occurrence of a succession of momentary things, which is spatiotemporally and qualitatively continuous, and sortal-covered or change-minimizing. This is obviously so if we accept the radical account, according to which the notion of spatiotemporal continuity can be made intelligible within a wholly persistence-free language. But even if we limit ourselves to the more moderate account, and think of the persistence-free language as presupposing a background of persisting objects, in terms of which the required notion of spatiotemporal continuity is explained, the conclusion still holds that, given some relatively limited background of persisting objects, the persistence of all other objects could be rendered in persistence-free terms. At the very least, then, we can regard the persistence of any specific object, or even any specific range of objects, as consisting simply in the successive existence of suitably related momentary things.

This conclusion may make us feel somewhat uneasy. We may be inclined to say that if the persistence of a given object boils down to nothing more than there being a certain kind of sequence of momentary things, then the object does not really persist at all, and our ordinary way of thinking about the matter is simply wrong. But the inclination to say this, however natural it may be, must, I think, be resisted. The inclination stems basically from the difficulty that we have in acknowledging that the world can be described, with equal completeness and correctness, in more ways than one. "If you could correctly describe the world, or some part of it, without mentioning any persisting objects," we are inclined to argue, "then there must not really *be* any persisting objects there to be mentioned." This argument, however, must be rebuffed by insisting on the point that the correctness of one mode of description does not necessarily preclude the correctness of some radically different mode of description. If the preceding account is accepted it would not follow that the world really consists of only criss-crossing sums of momentary things, but no genuinely persisting objects. The proper way to understand this, rather, is that what we ordinarily describe correctly in terms of the idea of a persisting object could also be described correctly in terms of the idea of a sum of momentary things. The compatibility of these two modes of description can be brought out by saying that what would be thought of in the persistence-free language as a certain kind of sum of momentary things is precisely *what we call* "a persisting thing."

The adequacy of the persistence-free language (whether this is understood in the radical sense or the moderate sense) is not, then, to be construed as in any manner denigrating the correctness of ordinary language. The persistence-free language is not an "ideal language" that gives us a glimpse into the world-as-it-really-is which is somehow hidden by ordinary forms of expression. The primary interest of the persistence-free language is that it affords a vantage point which is outside our ordinary identity scheme, and from which, therefore, we can gain a deeper insight into the character of that scheme. Such a vantage point may also have a certain intrinsic philosophical appeal, in that it provides a view of reality which is less structured, and hence in a sense less artificial, than our ordinary one. The relative non-structuredness of the persistence-free language, as compared to ordinary language, derives from the fact that in the former language any succession of momentary things is logically on a par with any other, whereas in ordinary language certain successions, but not others, are accorded the special status of constituting a unitary object. But there is no question of our having to decide which language gives us the uniquely correct view of reality.

If we define an "identity scheme" as a system of rules which determines which space-time portions do, and which do not, qualify as unitary objects, then we can perhaps say that the persistence-free language (which we can henceforth imagine on the model of Quine's space-time language) contains a maximally permissive identity scheme. In a sense it contains no identity scheme at all. From the space-time vantage point, "[a]ny arbitrary congeries of particle-stages, however spatiotemporally gerry-mandered or disperse, can count as a physical object."[5] "Each [object] comprises simply the content, however heterogeneous, of some portion of space-time, however disconnected and gerry-mandered."[6] Because of its extreme permissiveness the space-time language provides a kind of neutral ground to which a philosopher may naturally retreat when reflecting about identity schemes.

Adopting an identity scheme may be compared with attaching a particular sense to the expression "(same) object" and logically equivalent expressions. In the maximally permissive persistence-free scheme any sum of momentary stages can correctly be brought under the heading "one and the same object." The definitive feature of this scheme is that a statement of the form "Some object was A at t_1 and some object was B at a later time t_2" (where A and B are terms that attribute qualities or spatial relations) entails both "Some object (i.e., the sum of the A-stage at t_1 and the B-stage at t_2) was A at t_1 and B at t_2" and "Some object (i.e., the A-stage at t_1) was A at t_1 and non-existent at t_2." These entailments obviously do not hold given the ordinary sense of "(same) object."

The fact that the space-time language contains no rules of identity through time, so that in that language any space-time portion counts equally with any other, is what leads me to describe that language as being free of the concept of persistence. As intimated earlier, however, I could not strenuously object to someone's favoring a different terminology, according to which that language is said to contain, rather than no concept of persistence, a concept of persistence different from ours. At the other

5. Quine, *The Roots of Reference*, p. 54.
6. W. V. Quine, *Word and Object* (The M.I.T. Press, Cambridge, Mass., 1960), p. 171.

extreme, I could not object to someone's describing that language as being devoid not merely of the concept of persistence, but also of the very concept of an object (or body or entity). Often philosophers have characterized the space-time language (or kindred languages) as breaking reality down, not into *objects*, but into *processes* or *events* (or, in Strawson's suggestive expression, *process-things*).[7] These terminological nuances are less important than grasping the various logico-grammatical analogies and disanalogies between the space-time language (what I choose to call the "persistence-free language") and ours. Though I have not attempted to spell out these analogies and disanalogies in any detail, evidently the essential analogy is that the referential apparatus of the space-time language, as well as ours, centers upon items that are thought of as standing in spatial and temporal relation to each other, and as bearing ordinary sensible qualities like size, shape, color, and texture. And the essential disanalogy is that the space-time scheme contains no rules of identity through time.

The space-time language provides a maximally permissive identity scheme containing no rules of identity through time. We can also conceive of identity schemes different from our ordinary one which do contain rules of identity through time, rules different from the ordinary ones. This point can be illustrated by considering a somewhat generalized version of the previously discussed incar-outcar language. Let us now try to imagine a generalized in-out language which contains a great many strange-seeming descriptions on an analogy with the incar-outcar one. We can build up to the idea of this language by associating various kinds of objects with surroundings that are especially significant with respect to these objects, in rather the way that a garage is especially significant with respect to a car. Thus the language might allow one to refer to (and reidentify accordingly) *inpigs* and *outpigs*, depending on whether the object is inside or outside a pen, *onbooks* and *offbooks*, depending on whether the object is on or off a bookshelf, *onapples* and *offapples,* depending on whether the object is on or off a tree, and so on. The details of the language do not matter, so long as we have the general idea of a language containing many terms

7. Strawson, *Individuals*, p. 56. Cf. Quine, *Word and Object*, p. 171.

which stand to our ordinary terms in rather the way that "incar" and "outcar" stand to "car." Such a language could be said to contain a different identity scheme from ours.

Now it is surely an incontrovertible fact, which reflects a feature of our ordinary use of language, that when a car leaves a garage no object gets smaller in the process. Yet in the in-out language speakers describe the situation of a car leaving a garage by saying "An object, namely the incar, got smaller." This shows that they must be using the sentence "An object got smaller" differently from the way we do. It would perhaps not be incorrect to say that they use every word in that sentence (and perhaps indeed every nonlogical word in their language) differently from us. But it seems more natural to pin the difference on their use of "(same) object," and to say that they use this expression differently from us, that they operate with a different concept of (the identity of) an object.

Whereas I am inclined to characterize the space-time language as containing no concept of persistence, it seems natural, surely, to characterize the in-out language as containing a concept of persistence, but a different one from ours. This is because that language is analogous to ours in containing rules of identity through time, though these rules are, at least to a significant extent, different from ours. So the space-time language, as I want to look at this, gives us a persistence-free scheme, while the in-out language gives us an example of an identity scheme containing a different concept of persistence from our ordinary one.

Could there possibly be people who speak either of these strange languages, the persistence-free language or the in-out language, as their natural language, who learn one of these as their first language and who think in terms of it? My conjecture would be that this is probably an empirical impossibility, since, as the discussion of Chapter 3 suggested, these languages would contravene our basic concept of persistence, which I am inclined to regard as in some sense instinctive. But I hold that there is no logical inconsistency or incoherence in the idea of people speaking such languages, in people operating with those different concepts of the identity of an object. Nor, I believe, is there any sense in which these languages, if they were spoken, would give a less correct description of the world than our ordinary language.

This point may be especially hard to accept with respect to the in-out language. Insofar as this language does contain (what would naturally be regarded as) judgments of persistence, these judgments may appear to be simply logically incompatible with our ordinary judgments. If, as we ordinarily judge, nothing gets smaller when a car leaves a garage, how can they be correct in judging "An incar got smaller"? The futility of this sort of objection, however, can be brought out by turning it on its head. Since the incar-outcar description is (was introduced as being) merely an unfamiliar sentence used to describe the familiar facts, given that those facts obtain how could the sentence possibly fail to assert a truth? Again, what I think needs to be overcome here is the idea that there must be some uniquely correct way of describing reality.

There is at some level the inclination to say this. "Yes, there could conceivably be people whose conventions of language enjoined them to utter the words 'An incar got smaller' in a situation in which a car leaves a garage. But then what they would have to mean by uttering these words is simply that a car left a garage."

This seems to suggest that they somehow could not mean what they say but must instead mean what *we* say, as if they merely uttered the words of their strange language while secretly thinking in English. But if it is conceivable that they should speak that language then it surely must also be conceivable that they should internalize it, i.e., think in terms of it. Since, by hypothesis, our statement "A car left a garage" is roughly equivalent to their statement "An incar moved toward the exit of a garage and then diminished in size until it vanished, while simultaneously an outcar appeared at the outside of the exit and gradually grew to the size and form of the original incar," we can indeed say that their statement merely expresses the fact that a car left a garage. But by the same token we can also say (shifting now to their language) that the English statement merely expresses the fact that an incar moved toward the exit of a garage and then diminished in size, etc. There is no lack of symmetry here between the descriptions in the two languages.

It is easy to make the mistake of supposing that the incar-outcar description is incorrect because it would play havoc with science. How, it might be asked, could a physicist explain the strange loss of mass of a shrinking incar?

But the truth is that the physicist could easily explain this in precisely the way he explains the loss of mass of an ordinary car which has a part subtracted from it. The physicist could say that the mass of an incar decreases because the matter which makes it up at one moment is identical with only part of the matter which makes it up at a later moment (the rest of the matter going into the outcar). As noted once before even the most elementary laws of physics (e.g., the principle of mass constancy) do not refer (as such) to ordinary objects like cars, but refer instead to the matter which makes up these objects. There is therefore no reason to require that these laws refer (as such) to incars and outcars, nor less that these laws be rendered in some such terms as "inmatter" and "outmatter." It may indeed be conceivable that the hypothetical physicists of that language could develop some suitable in-out substitute for our ordinary concept of persisting matter. This possibility, or a variant of it, will be discussed in the next section. My present point is the much simpler one that our ordinary physics, in terms of our ordinary concept of persisting matter, can explain, without the slightest difficulty, all of the strange-sounding expansions and contractions of incars and outcars.

In short, if our ordinary statements about cars gaining and losing parts can be accepted as correct and essentially theoretically innocent descriptions of the observable phenomena, then the incar-outcar statements can be accepted in precisely the same spirit. Our ordinary identity scheme and the in-out scheme would be merely two conceptual devices for framing different but equivalently correct descriptions of what is in some sense the same observable phenomenon.

The metaphysical attitude which I have been expressing is familiar from much recent literature. It is an attitude that one associates with the later Wittgenstein, and with one sense of the word "relativism." A capsule summary of this attitude is aptly expressed by Urmson toward the end of his book *Philosophical Analysis*: "If two sentences are equivalent to each other, then while the use of one rather than the other may be useful for some philosophical purposes, it is not the case that one will be nearer to reality than the other. . . . We can say a thing this way and we can say it that way, sometimes; if we can it may be helpful to notice it. But it is no use asking which is the logically or metaphysically right way of saying it."[8]

I judge Urmson's dictum to be difficult, perplexing, and essentially correct. As it pertains to the present topic of persistence the dictum implies that an object's persistence is no less "real" or "genuine" just because statements which describe the object as persisting could in principle be replaced by equivalent statements in which the object's persistence does not figure.

IV. "Real" and "Fictitious" Persistence

I argued in the last chapter that the persistence of a portion of matter, in contrast to the persistence of a standard object, is in a sense ultimate and unanalyzable. Now it may seem to follow from that account that what I have been saying in the present chapter about the persistence of standard objects ought not to be said about the persistence of matter, that our concept of the persistence of matter, at least, could not be eliminated, or altered, without our thereby losing the ability to describe the world correctly. Perhaps this conclusion does follow; I confess to feeling considerably less than confident about this point. But I am inclined to think that it does not follow, and I now want to state why.

It may be that there are strictly two somewhat different questions to be considered. One is whether our ordinary concept of persisting matter could be eliminated in favor of a persistence-free conception. The second question is whether that ordinary concept could be eliminated in favor of some alternative conception of persistence, something, say, on the order of an "inmatter"-"outmatter" conception. I will focus on the first question, which seems a bit more tractable, though what I say would, I think, carry over rather directly to the second question as well.

The persistence of matter was argued to be "ultimate" in the sense that we cannot state observational identity criteria for matter. But I now want to suggest that there is nothing in this to

8. J. O. Urmson, *Philosophical Analysis* (Oxford University Press, London, 1956), p. 186.

prevent us from coherently regarding a persisting portion of matter as made up of temporal parts, and regarding its persistence as consisting in nothing more than its momentary parts standing in some unobservable relationship. We might give this relationship the name "genidentity," along the lines of one of the approaches that I sketched in the preceding chapter. (A completely parallel point could be made, perhaps with even greater plausibility, if we adopt the alternative a priori atomistic approach to matter.) We can then redescribe the persistence of a bit of matter in terms of the equivalent idea of the occurrence of a succession of momentary things that are genidentical with each other.

In general, I would suggest that we need to distinguish between these two questions: (a) "Can we coherently regard the persistence of x as consisting in the occurrence of a succession of momentary things that stand in some distinctive unity-making relationship?" and (b) "Can we give an account in relatively observational terms of what that unity-making relationship is?" My overall position commits me to holding that where x is a standard object the answers to both (a) and (b) are affirmative, whereas where x is a portion of matter the answer to (b) is negative. But I am now maintaining that a negative answer to (b) does not imply a negative answer to (a).

I think, in fact, that it is a general a priori truth that the answer to (a) must *always* be affirmative, no matter what kind of entity x is. This seems to follow from the bare idea of persistence through time. If x is an entity that persists through time then, no matter what sort of entity x is, we can make intelligible to ourselves a conceptual revision which allows us to redescribe x as made up of temporal parts. That we can "make it intelligible" is perhaps only another way of saying that we can draw many clear and persuasive analogies to the revisionary idea of the entity's having temporal parts from our ordinary idea of an object's spatial parts, and also from our ordinary idea of the temporal parts of a process, such as a game or a battle. In the face of these analogies I can see no point in someone's insisting that the contemplated redescription (and this is all that it would be, a *redescription* of the accepted facts) is somehow illegitimate or incomprehensible. But, now, if we have gotten ourselves to think about x as made up of temporal parts then we can, indeed must, think of those parts as standing in some relationship which constitutes x's unity through time. This conclusion remains valid even in a case in which the unity-making relationship for x must be regarded as nonobservational.

Our concept of the persistence of matter is, on my view, something on the order of a theoretical extension of our concept of the observable persistence of standard objects. What we mean even at a commonsense level by "the persistence of matter" is something to the effect of "that underlying mode of physical persistence which can ultimately provide the simplest and most coherent explanation of the observable phenomena." It is therefore scientific theory which eventually fills in the detailed facts about the behavior of matter. But once the scientist presents us with those facts there cannot, I think, be any factual or metaphysical error in redescribing them in persistence-free terms, in terms of the idea of a genidentical succession of momentary things. There is, at least on my intuition, no way to attach any sense to the question "How is it really in the world? Does matter persist or are there merely momentary things related to each other by genidentity?" These are two ways of saying the same thing. If we describe the world in terms of persistence we can say that the underlying persistence of matter is what ultimately explains the observable persistence of standard objects. And if we describe the world in persistence-free terms we can make the correlative and equally correct remark that the underlying relationship of genidentity is what ultimately explains the observable relationships of sortal-covered or change-minimizing continuity. There is no question of fact at stake here.

It will be objected perhaps that what is wrong with the persistence-free rendition of the facts about matter is that this rendition would be less simple and less coherent than the ordinary formulation. This assessment may indeed seem to follow directly from my view that our concept of persisting matter is essentially the concept of a mode of persistence in terms of which it would be possible to formulate theoretically best explanations.

But there are difficulties here. What needs to be borne in mind is that our ordinary concept of persisting matter presupposes our general commitment to the concept of persistence, our general commitment, that is, to describing the world in terms of a category of temporally extended units that do not merely correspond to arbitrary successions. Given this general constraint our concept of persisting matter implies that these units are to be selected in such a way as to maximize simplicity and coherence. What is at issue at present, however, is precisely the possibility of removing this general constraint by repudiating the concept of persistence altogether. It is not clear that an overall description of reality in persistence-free terms would have to be less simple than an overall description in terms of persistence. (Contemporary science, on some readings, may in fact favor a kind of persistence-free description.)

More specifically, it would seem that our ordinary concept of persisting matter presupposes, and is indeed an outgrowth of, a background of ordinary descriptions of standard objects. It is against this background that an identity judgment about matter is assessed. Now let S and T be sets which contain all of the true statements that could be formulated in ordinary terms about, respectively, standard objects and persisting matter; and let S' and T' be the persistence-free reformulations of these statements. It may seem clear that the composite view S-plus-T is simpler and more coherent than S-plus-T'. It is less clear that S-plus-T is simpler and more coherent than S'-plus-T'. It is not clear, in other words, that a thoroughgoing and consistent repudiation of persistence would constitute a theoretical loss.

Let us, however, suppose for the sake of argument that a persistence-free description of reality would be less simple and less coherent than a description in terms of persistence. It would seem to follow that there is a theoretical gain in describing reality in terms of persistence. But this would have to be regarded as a mere gain of elegance, rather than a gain of truth. Of two logically incompatible hypotheses it seems correct to say that, other things being equal, the one that is simpler and more coherent is more likely to be true. But where two propositions are logically equivalent, so that the truth of either entails the truth of the other, it could make no sense to say that one is more likely to be true than the other. Since, as I am assuming, statements about successions of genidentically related momentary things are logically equivalent to (are merely reformulations of) statements about persisting matter, it could make no sense to say that the latter are more likely because they are simpler.[9]

A lot more needs to be said about these points, much of which baffles me. The conclusion which this discussion suggests, however, is that the persistence of matter, despite its "ultimacy," can be legitimately redescribed in persistence-free terms.

(Let me state briefly, without argument, how I would want to connect these ideas to the persistence of persons. Here too I would urge that we distinguish between the question (a) "Can we coherently regard the persistence of a person as consisting in the occurrence of a succession of momentary person-stages that stand in some distinctive unity-making relationship?" and the question (b) "Can we give an account in relatively observational terms of what that unity-making relationship is?" I am inclined to think that we *can* give such an account, so that both (a) and (b) should be answered affirmatively.[10] But even if it is the case, as many philosophers have held, that our concept of the persistence of a person cannot be analyzed in terms of identity criteria, so that (b) must be answered negatively, I would still say that (a) should be answered affirmatively. For it would still be legitimate for us to regard a person as made up of person-stages that stand in some distinctive relationship. We can, if we want, give this relationship a name, say "person kinship."[11] This way of thinking about the identity of a person remains legitimate even if we have to construe the unity-making relationship of person kinship as in some sense simple and unobservable.)

The "relativistic" attitude toward persistence which I have been expounding in these sections runs counter to an important

9. Compare with Reichenbach's distinction between "simplicity as a criterion of truth" and mere "descriptive simplicity," in *The Philosophy of Space and Time*, pp. 34–35. A similar idea is expressed in Rudolf Carnap, *Philosophical Foundation of Physics* (Basic Books, Inc., N.Y., 1966), pp. 83–85.

10. The kind of account that I have in mind is suggested in Derek Parfit, "Personal Identity," *Philosophical Review*, 80 (1971), 3–27. For a discussion of the issue of personal identity, see below, Chapter 10. (The argument in this paragraph is elaborated in Chapter 10, Section II.)

11. Compare with Quine's use of "river kinship" and "water kinship" in *From a Logical Point of View* (Harvard University Press, Cambridge, Mass., 1961), p. 66. My view would be that river kinship is observable in a way that water kinship is not.

tradition. Many philosophers, notably Butler, Reid, and more recently Chisholm, have held the view that the persistence of ordinary objects like tables and trees is in some sense "fictitious" (or "imperfect" or "loose"), as compared to the "real" (or "perfect" or "strict") persistence of other entities, such as, perhaps, persons or bits of matter.[12] Shoemaker has illuminated this view in his book *Self-Knowledge and Self-Identity*. A passage in which he summarizes his explanation of what underlies the view is worth quoting at length:

There is a common inclination to say that if the persistence of a [particular kind of object] through time can be regarded as consisting simply in the occurrence of a temporal succession of momentary states or events that are empirically related to one another in certain ways (by resemblance, spatiotemporal contiguity, and so on), or in the successive existence of momentary things . . . , then what is called the persistence of [that kind of object] is not really the persistence of anything. Where persistence can be so regarded, one is inclined to say, the unity attributed to those sequences that are regarded as histories of persisting things does not derive from anything intrinsic to the sequences themselves, but is somehow imposed on them by conventions of language. In such cases it seems to be only our need to have economical ways of talking about the world that leads us to describe any sequences at all as histories of persisting things, and only our practical or theoretical interest in certain kinds of sequences that leads us to single out these, and not sequences of other kinds, to be described in this way. Now if someone thinks that the persistence of some things is of this sort, and that the persistence of other things is not, then it will be natural for him to mark this distinction by saying that only the latter is *real* persistence involving *real* identity.[13]

Up to a point I am quite sympathetic to the Butler-Reid-Chisholm doctrine, as Shoemaker here explains it, since I would also want to emphasize a distinction, of roughly the sort suggested by that doctrine, between two kinds of persistence, between the criterially determined persistence of standard objects and the "ultimate" persistence of matter. As I see this distinc-

12. Joseph Butler, "Of Personal Identity," in *The Whole Works of Joseph Butler, LL.D.* (Thomas Tegg, London, 1836), pp. 263–70; Thomas Reid, "Of the Nature and Origin of Our Notion of Personal Identity," in *Essays on the Intellectual Powers of Man*, essay III, ch. III, sec. II; and Chisholm in all the previously cited works.
13. Shoemaker, *Self-Knowledge and Self-Identity*, pp. 37–38.

tion, however, it is a potentially serious distortion to express it by saying that the persistence of a standard object, as compared to that of a portion of matter, is somehow less than "real" (or that a standard object persists in only a "loose" sense, whereas a portion of matter persists in a "strict" sense).

This seems to me a distortion, summarily, for two reasons, the second of which is somewhat clearer than the first. The first reason is that even where the persistence of an entity, such as a bit of matter (or, on some views, a person), is not governed by observational identity criteria, we can still, or so I am inclined to think, legitimately regard that persistence as consisting in the occurrence of a succession of momentary things that are related in some unobservable way. As I see it, there is not, and cannot conceivably be, any "intrinsic" unity through time, in the sense of a unity that cannot be adequately redescribed in different terms. Nor can there be any relationships that are "intrinsically" unity-making, in the sense of a relationship that cannot be coherently separated from its unity-making role in our identity scheme. Hence the persistence of any conceivable entity can be construed as a "mere succession," if we want to look at it that way.

But, second, even if it were correct to say that the persistence of a standard object can be redescribed in terms of the idea of a succession, in a way that the persistence of a bit of matter (or a person) cannot be so redescribed, it would still be unreasonable to conclude that the former kind of persistence is "unreal" (or "loose"). That the persistence of an object can be redescribed in different terms does not discredit the descriptions that we actually employ. There seems no question that our ordinary descriptions of standard objects provide one essential paradigm of our use of the ordinary concept of persistence. The persistence of a standard object is therefore properly regarded as an especially clear and obvious kind of persistence; here we have as "real" a kind of persistence as we know of.

V. Can We Justify Our Identity Scheme?

Though I have professed myself to be a "relativist" about persistence I am not, in at least one important sense of the word, a "conventionalist." As a relativist I hold that our identity scheme is not the only one that could in principle be employed in making true statements about the world. But, as I stated earlier, I am inclined toward the empirical speculation that our ordinary identity scheme, or at least the basic core of that scheme, is instinctive to human beings. My conjecture would be that, as a matter of contingent fact, each of us enters the world innately disposed in some manner to interpret experience in terms of our basic idea of persistence, in terms, that is, of the idea of persisting objects whose careers unfold along continuous change-minimizing paths. So I would not suppose that our identity scheme is a "mere convention," in the sense of something that we could easily decide to alter. In fact I doubt whether we could in any way get ourselves, or our descendants, to perceive the world in terms of an identity scheme radically different from the one presently employed by a speaker of English.

I shall not at present attempt to develop these rather vague speculations about our "instincts" and "innate dispositions."[14] Instead I want to raise certain questions about a common assumption among philosophers which may seem to render such speculations philosophically superfluous. I think that it is often taken for granted that, at least from a philosopher's point of view, the interesting explanation of why we operate with our identity scheme, rather than with another one, is that it is *reasonable* for us to operate with the scheme that we have. Sometimes this position will take the bald form of the claim that no other identity scheme could allow us to make true statements about the world. Against this I have already argued. But I think that even many philosophers who would allow that reality could in principle be described in terms of some other identity scheme, often take it for granted that the philosophically relevant explanation of why we operate with this particular identity scheme is that, given our human needs and purposes, this scheme is the reasonable one for us to have.

I want to question whether anything of this sort is correct. I will suggest that there is reason to doubt that there is any important sense in which our identity scheme can be said to be especially right, or reasonable, or practical, or convenient, or anything of that sort. This is not to suggest that our identity

14. This issue will be addressed in Chapter 8.

scheme may be especially wrong, or unreasonable, or impractical, or inconvenient. Rather I doubt that any such assessments really make much sense, or that they have any fundamental bearing on explaining why we think about persistence the way that we do.

The kind of assumption that I want to call into question seemed implicit in one of the remarks quoted previously from Shoemaker. Our reason for treating certain successions as persisting objects, Shoemaker suggests, is "our need to have economical ways of talking about the world," and "our practical and theoretical interest" in certain kinds of successions rather than others.[15]

Let us consider the principle

(1) We tend to treat a kind of succession as corresponding to the career of a persisting object when that kind of succession is especially important or interesting to us.

It is not immediately clear what it means to say that a kind of succession is important to us. This may mean that it is often important to us whether that kind of succession occurs. Or perhaps it means that, given the occurrence of that kind of succession, it would often be important to us what the properties and interrelations are of the items that comprise the succession. But in whatever way we make this out I think that if we consider the principle carefully we can see that it really has no plausibility at all. More often than not we are especially interested in facts about the successive stages of *different* objects that may be related in various ways. More often than not, therefore, we are especially interested in successions that do not correspond to unitary careers.

Consider, for example, all of the following sorts of successions: (a) a succession which consists in the stages of every car that I have every owned during the periods when I owned them; (b) a succession which consists in a stage of the car x when x leaves a particular parking space, followed by a stage of the car y when y enters that space immediately afterwards; (c) a succession which consists in a stage of an object x immediately prior to x's impact with the object y, followed by a stage of y immediately after the impact; (d) a succession which consists in the stage of a tree while

15. Shoemaker, *Self-Knowledge and Self-Identity*, pp. 37–38.

it is blooming, followed by the stage of an apple that grows and falls from the tree.

I think it is unnecessary to multiply these examples, or to make them out in any detail, in order to see that there is really no evident connection between the idea of a succession that is important to us and the idea of a succession that corresponds to a persisting object. There is no apparent truth to the principle that we generally treat important kinds of space-time portions of reality as unitary objects.

I think this principle may have a specious plausibility because we can easily confuse it with a different and much more limited one. Suppose we take the basic rule of identity as given, and suppose we take it for granted, furthermore, that this rule is to be refined in terms of the introduction of a list of sortal concepts under which the careers of objects are traced. The question then arises why we introduce just the sortal concepts that we have. Part of the answer to this question, I have already suggested, lies in the idea that the sortal refinement must not issue in an overly drastic departure from the basic conception. Hence our sortals must be nondispersive, they must allow us to trace paths that minimize nonlocational change, and they must not force us to terminate careers in ways that conflict too often with the basic rule. But even granted these constraints imposed upon our sortal introductions by the basic rule there would still be in principle a great deal of leeway, and the question persists why we have just the sortals that we have. Now to *this* question it may be quite plausible to suggest

(2) We tend to treat a property as a sortal when (besides satisfying the constraints imposed by the basic rule) that property is especially interesting or important to us.

In other words we tend to resolve change-minimizing conflict by tracing paths in such a way as to stabilize important properties. I am prepared to believe that some such principle as this is acceptable, though I find myself unable to make even this much out with any clarity. But this limited principle, which already takes for granted the general structure of our identity scheme, is not at issue. A philosopher who holds that our identity scheme is to be justified by reference to our human needs and interests must be able to show that the general structure of that scheme, the fact that it includes the basic rule and the sortal rule, can be explained in these terms. This he cannot show by appealing to any such limited principle as (2). Nor can he show it by appealing to the false principle (1) that we generally treat important successions as persisting objects.

Now actually it is not clear that this discredited principle (1) is the one that is crucial to the case which this philosopher would want to make. We need to distinguish between saying

(1) We tend to treat a kind of succession as corresponding to the career of a persisting object when that kind of succession is especially important or interesting to us

and saying

(3) We tend to treat a kind of succession as corresponding to the career of a persisting object when it is especially important (or convenient or useful) for us to treat the succession in that way.

Though it seems tempting to equate (1) with (3) there is really no obvious connection between these principles. There is no obvious reason to suppose that it would be especially important for us to treat a succession as a persisting object when (or only when) the succession is especially important to us. Though (1) seems quite definitely unacceptable it might still be maintained that (3) is correct. And it is surely (3) that is most directly relevant to the claim that, given our needs and interests, our identity scheme is the reasonable one for us to have.

Is it, then, important (or convenient or useful) for us to think about persistence in the way we do, to treat as persisting objects just those successions that we do so treat? Here we should perhaps distinguish between *theoretical* importance and *practical* importance.

The discussion in the last section suggested that there are difficulties in maintaining even that our concept of persisting matter affords a gain to theory. What can be said with reasonable confidence is that given our general commitment to describing the world in terms of persistence, our concept of persisting matter attempts to realize that commitment in the theoretically optimal fashion. It seemed unclear, however, whether we could say unqualifiedly, and without already presupposing our commitment to persistence (and, specifically, our commitment to the ordinary persistence of standard objects), that our concept of persisting matter is theoretically advantageous.

Be this as it may, it seems quite definitely impossible to maintain that our ordinary concept of the persistence of standard objects is especially advantageous to theory. There seems to be no special theoretical point in our reidentifying cars, and tables, and trees in the way that we do rather than any number of other possible ways. We say that the same car persists with different parts when parts are added and subtracted, though the physicist's description of the world may mention no entities that persist with new parts. Here, with respect to the identity of a standard object, scientific-theoretic considerations are apparently not relevant as arbiters of the truth. Our ordinary description of the persistence of a car is, on my view, a literally (and "strictly") true description of the observable facts. But there appears to be no special theoretical gain in our describing the facts the way that we do rather than in some other way (e.g., by requiring of an object's identity that no parts are added or subtracted). Indeed from the standpoint of scientific theory the most that could safely be said about our ordinary identity scheme is that it might possibly have been worse.

This does not, as far as I am concerned, show that there is anything especially bad about our identity scheme, but only that there is nothing especially good about it from the point of view of our scientific-theoretic needs. Those needs are apparently not to be regarded as the primary determinants of our thought about persistence. We might perhaps try to imagine a purely intellectual creature, given our sensory intake, who confronts his experience in terms of the exclusive disposition to seek unity-making principles which would yield the simplest laws of nature. Such a propensity seems quite alien to our own overall perspective. It is unclear whether the exclusively theorizing creature could have any basis for adopting even a concept of persisting matter. It seems certain that he could have no basis for adopting our scheme of standard objects.

So at least the major brunt of our ordinary identity scheme, the part of it that deals with standard objects, cannot apparently be justified in terms of theoretical purposes. Can we perhaps say, however, that there is some decisive *practical* gain in the way that we think about the persistence of a standard object? A point which is often made, and which may be suggested by Shoemaker's remarks about "our need to have economical ways of talking about the world," is that if we tried to describe the world in terms of a different identity scheme, we would have to use many more words than we now do to convey the kinds of information that we typically need to convey.

Now there really seems to be no very close connection between the number of words that we need to describe a given situation and the kind of identity scheme that is being employed in the description. Suppose that the in-out language contained the relational term "ancestor" which functioned in such a way that the statement "x is an ancestor of y" is true if and only if either x is identical with y, or some finite sequence of in-out transformations leads from x to y. Hence, the statement "The incar x is an ancestor of the outcar y," a case in which x and y are assumed to be nonidentical, would in effect assert that either the outcar y came out of the incar x, or y came out of an incar which came out of an outcar which came out of x, or . . . , etc. Would this construction not perhaps allow speakers of the in-out language to say many of the things that we typically say about cars in a reasonably limited number of words? Where we say of a car, for example, "It broke down five times last year," they could perhaps say, "Its ancestors broke down five times last year" (where, as follows from the previous definition, any incar or outcar is degenerately an ancestor of itself). Even here the in-out sentence is longer by one word than its English counterpart, and certainly more difficult cases would have to be considered. But there is always the possibility of introducing additional abbreviations into the in-out language which would not apparently affect the essential character of their identity scheme. (For example, they might have one word for "broke down.") Given the fairly unlimited prospects for such abbreviations it seems entirely unclear that there could not be an in-out scheme which might allow for roughly as "economical" a way of talking as our ordinary way.

Again, suppose that Quine's space-time language contained such expressions as "longest car-continuum" to denote a continuous succession of momentary car-stages that is not a segment of any longer continuous succession of momentary car-stages (to denote, that is, roughly what in the ordinary scheme is the whole career of a persisting car). Given such constructions, in conjunction with other well-placed abbreviations, it seems that we might be able to express with a comparable number of words many of the things that we ordinarily express. It would in fact be quite difficult to understand how the space-time language could necessitate our using more words than we now use. That language, with its wholly permissive identity scheme, would allow us to single out any space-time portion of reality as a unit, including of course the select few space-time portions which our ordinary identity scheme accords the special status of unity. The space-time language might in principle contain any number of abbreviated, or even syntactically simple, expressions which denote various space-time portions, including, among others, the ones that we ordinarily talk about. The permissibility of singling out units in addition to the ones that we ordinarily single out, would seem to promise, if anything, the prospect for a possible gain of brevity, not a loss.

In short, I am unable to see any relatively clear connection between our identity scheme and our supposed need for brevity.

But actually there is, to begin with, something faintly embarrassing in philosophers' continually seeming to tell us that the underlying rationale of our language is to enable us to talk less. The fact is of course that people like to talk, apparently as much as possible, and a breath saved here and there is simply not credited by us as enhancing the felicity of our condition. There may be, I suppose, an outer limit to human garrulity. If it required three hours of steadfast oration to convey that a car broke down this would probably not be good. But there seems no reason to suppose, or to hope, that our language is, or ever will be, even close to the realization of some philosophical ideal of maximally condensed talk. From the standpoint of taciturnity the most that could safely be said about our ordinary identity scheme is that it might possibly have been worse.

Word-count aside, can we conceive of any other practical gain that we might derive from talking about persistence in the way we do rather than some other way? Suppose that there were people who talked about (and thought about and experienced) the world in terms of some generalized in-out language, a language in which many (though perhaps not all) objects stood to our ordinary objects in rather the way that incars and out-cars stand to cars. Would it follow from the fact that they talked this way that their lives would be essentially different from ours? Would it follow that their actions and attitudes would be different from ours?

In one sense this would have to be so. In a sense, someone who spoke that language could not intend (or wish or fear) that a car would leave a garage, and perhaps could not therefore be said (intentionally) to bring it about that a car would leave a garage. But of course he might have the equivalent intention (or wish or fear) that an incar would go out of existence and be replaced by an outcar. The relevant question is whether this difference in the way that he thinks about things would have any practical implications. Would his actions and attitudes be different from ours in the sense that when they are, so to speak, translated into English they fail to match our own actions and attitudes?

I suggest that there is no a priori answer to this question. It is a priori possible that the lives of the in-out speakers would be in the relevant sense exactly like ours. This would mean roughly that if there is a situation S such that a typical speaker of our language who found himself in S would entertain an intention (wish, fear) which he could express, for example, in the words "I intend (wish, fear) that the car will leave the garage," then a typical speaker of the in-out language who found himself in S would entertain an intention (wish, fear) which he could express in the words "I intend (wish, fear) that the incar will go out of existence and be replaced by an outcar." It would mean that when the rules which define their practices and institutions are translated into English what comes out are the rules which define our practices and institutions. (So it would perhaps be a law of their land that if you own an incar or outcar then, unless you sell it, you automatically own its immediate "descendant.")

It is a priori possible that their lives would be just like ours. But it is also possible that their lives would be very different from ours. Perhaps the rapid fluctuations of the identities of objects, as they experience this, would express itself in some distinctive way in their attitudes and behavior. (Maybe they would be saintly nomads who flit from place to place without possessions or property rights, or maybe crazed hoarders compulsively staked out against the ins and outs of their fate.) Perhaps all of their practices and institutions would seem radically alien to us. There is no (a priori) way of saying. Nor less is there any way of saying that, if there were such alien practices and institutions, they would be less practical, convenient, or useful than ours.

(It is possible, though problematical, that these remarks would remain valid even if the discussion could be extended to include personal identity. Perhaps we can imagine an in-out language which affects the concept of a person and correlative personal pronouns. Someone might be called an *inperson* or an *outperson*, and be reidentified accordingly, depending upon whether he or she is, let us say, inside or outside the village. It may still be conceivable that their actions and attitudes would be in the relevant sense just like ours. This would mean that in a situation where one of us would announce with equanimity "I am about to be taken out of the village," one of them would announce with equanimity "I am about to cease to exist and be replaced by an outperson."[16]

But it may also be conceivable that their actions and attitudes would be in the relevant sense very different from ours, in that they might be, in terms of their concept of personal identity, as predominantly self-regarding as we are in terms of our concept. This would mean that one of them who is about to be carried out of the village would judge with horror "I am about to cease to exist (and be replaced by an outperson)," and attach to those words all of the dismay, and resistant behavior, that we ordinarily attach to the prospect of personal extinction.[17]

It may well be that these fantasies about inpersons and out-

16. That is, ". . . and be replaced by an outperson who will remember everything about me." For the kinds of revisions in the concepts of memory, intention, and related notions that would be required in the inperson-outperson language, see Parfit, "Personal Identity," and Sydney Shoemaker, "Persons and Their Pasts," *American Philosophical Quarterly*, 7 (1970), 269–85.

17. The connection between our concept of personal identity and our sense of self-interest is explored in Chapter 10. This issue is discussed in Parfit, "Personal Identity"; in Bernard Williams, "The Self and the Future," *Philosophical Review*, 79 (1970), 161–80, reprinted in Bernard Williams, *Problems of the Self* (Cambridge University Press, London, 1973), pp. 46–63; and in Shoemaker's comments in "The Loose and Popular and the Strict and Philosophical Senses of Identity." (See also Shoemaker's remarks there about the connection between our concept of physical identity and our interests in objects.)

persons are in some fundamental way incomprehensible. Insofar as the fantasies are entertainable, however, and entertainable in the two forms mentioned, they suggest that it may not even be possible to draw any evident connections between our concept of personal identity and our actions and attitudes. But this point is much clearer with respect to standard objects, other than persons, which are the only cases that I am seriously treating.)

My conclusion is that there is no evident sense in which it is especially practical (or useful or convenient) for us to think about the persistence of standard objects in the way we do rather than some other way. There is no evident benefit or gain which our identity scheme seems peculiarly adept at securing for us. Insofar as our concepts may be said to enter into our intentions and attitudes there is a trivial sense in which we could not do or feel any of the things that we ordinarily do or feel except by having our ordinary concepts. In a trivial sense, therefore, we need our ordinary concepts to do and feel all of the ordinary things that we like to do and feel. So we can say that thinking (and acting and feeling) in the ordinary way serves our need to think (and act and feel) in the ordinary way. This near-tautology obviously does not explain, or justify, why we (need to) think in the ordinary way.

Looked at in one way, then, the attempt to justify our identity scheme by reference to our practical needs is futile because those needs, as conceptualized by us, already presuppose the identity scheme. (For example, in order for someone to think "I need to move the car out of the garage," he must be operating with the ordinary concept of the persistence of a car.) On the other hand, to the extent that it makes sense to distinguish between our needs as such and our ways of conceptualizing them, it is no longer clear how our identity scheme is especially adept at serving these needs.

The impulse to assume that ours is (for us) the best of all possible identity schemes sometimes takes an evolutionary turn. Quine, who holds (as I do) that our identity scheme is "rooted in instinct,"[18] drops the casual remark that "man and other animals are body-minded by natural selection; for body-minded-

18. Quine, *The Roots of Reference*, p. 55.

ness has evident survival value in town and jungle."[19] This is precisely what is not evident to me. To be "body-minded," in Quine's sense, is to experience objects in terms of our ordinary unity-making principles. A creature who experienced the world in terms of the in-out language (or in terms of Quine's space-time language) would not be body-minded. I would want to see how Quine could make out that such a creature would be less fit to survive than we. I doubt that this can be made out. We can say that in the struggle to survive we discover ourselves to be two-eyed body-minded survivors, and that being two-eyed and body-minded is, other things remaining equal, evidently better for survival than various other possibilities (for example, being totally blind or totally unconscious). As to whether we (or creatures otherwise like us) would have necessarily been in any sense worse off with some different number of eyes, or some different identity scheme, I think no one can say.

My aim in this section has been to stress, perhaps at some risk of exaggeration, the seemingly implacable primitiveness (non-derivativeness) of our ordinary commitment to our identity scheme. At the level of common experience we think about persistence in the only way that we know how, in the only way that makes sense to us, perhaps in the only way that is psychologically possible for us. This, I think, is essentially the only "justification" that we can give for thinking the way that we do.

19. Ibid., p. 54.

PART TWO

MINDS AND BODIES

Introduction to Part Two

THIS PART attempts, first, to clarify and defend some of the views already presented, and, second, to open up some additional questions about the nature of identity. Each chapter is designed to be an essentially self-complete essay, though there is inevitably a considerable amount of cross-reference.

The first two chapters deal directly with several objections to the previous views. Chapter 6 addresses in detail the crucial objection that an analysis of our concept of bodily identity is necessarily circular because the concept is more fundamental, both metaphysically and epistemologically, than any concepts in terms of which the analysis might be couched. In Chapter 7 I take up Shoemaker's suggestion that causal connectedness is necessary for identity, and the radical suggestion that there are *no* logically sufficient criteria of identity. Here I also show how Putnam's notion of a stereotype might be applied to an analysis of identity.

Several times in Part One, I expressed the conjecture that our concept of bodily identity is innately determined. This is elaborated and defended in Chapter 8. The question of innateness leads to a consideration of the essential connection between the issue of "unity" and the issue of "similarity," a connection which is pursued in Chapter 9. The notion of a natural kind is prominent in recent literature, and in the latter chapter I explore various points of connection between that notion and what I call a "natural unit."

The topic of personal identity, which I studiously avoided in Part One, is now addressed in Chapter 10. This chapter extends various issues of relativism, conventionalism, and innatism into the realm of personal identity. In this discussion I adopt the rather extreme device of assessing at length an utterly alien conception of personal identity; the device will not, I hope, overly tax the reader's indulgence for the philosophy of the weird.

Running through a number of these discussions is my preoccupation with the issue already broached in Chapter 5 of what the status is of our ordinary identity concept. There I considered the claim that:

There are compelling *reasons* for us to describe the world in terms of ordinary objects.

And now in Chapter 6 I go on to consider the claim that:

Ordinary objects are *basic*,

and in Chapter 9 the claim that:

Ordinary objects are *natural units*.

These are three ways of conferring upon ordinary objects a special and exalted status.

The three status claims are evidently not unrelated, but they do carry rather different philosophical associations. The first claim suggests that we could cite some *ordinary reasons* in support of our identity concept, theoretical or practical reasons akin to those—e.g., of probability or efficiency—which we ordinarily give in support of a belief or practice. I have already criticized this position, and will argue against it again in somewhat different contexts in Chapters 8 and 10.

The claim that ordinary objects are "basic" can be taken in two senses. From a metaphysical standpoint the claim suggests that the ordinary concept of an object cannot be analyzed or defined in terms which do not already presuppose the concept. From an epistemological standpoint the claim suggests that our knowledge of the world depends on our knowledge of ordinary objects. The metaphysical claim does not seem to me convincing; some of the central issues here have partially emerged in Chapter 5, and will be clarified and developed in Chapter 6. As regards the epistemological claim it is necessary to distinguish between two questions. We can compare the status of an ordinary object to the status of the momentary stages of an object; or we can compare the status of an ordinary object to the status of other successions of stages, successions, that is, which do not correspond to what we ordinarily conceive of as persisting objects. Whereas I will suggest in Chapter 6 that the stages may be epistemologically more basic than the objects, I would certainly hold that the objects are epistemologically more basic than other successions; obviously this is so if, as I think, our minds are innately determined to synthesize the stages into ordinary objects. Note that from the metaphysical standpoint this distinction between the two comparisons seems inconsequential: ordinary objects, it seems, are more basic metaphysically than the other successions if and only if they are more basic metaphysically than the stages.

What is suggested by the claim that ordinary objects are "natural units"? When philosophers talk about "natural *kinds*" they seem to imply that there is an objective distinction, apart from our human attitudes and practices, between kinds and artificial constructions. The analogous claim with respect to objects is that there is an objective distinction between ordinary persisting objects and other successions of stages, a distinction that can be drawn without reference to our attitudes or practices. But that claim seems almost trivially correct; and certainly it does not confer any *special status* on the objects. That ordinary objects are objectively distinguishable from the other successions surely does not exalt the objects above the other successions. The objects are, I think, exalted and "natural" only in the psychological sense that it is *natural for us* to conceive of the world in terms of such objects. If it is held that there is an objective distinction between natural kinds and artificial classes— a position which (as I explain in Chapter 9) is denied by certain nominalists—then it may perhaps also seem plausible to regard the natural kinds as metaphysically basic, as presupposed in any adequate conception of the world. But this connection between "naturalness" and "metaphysical basicness" is, I shall maintain, *not* plausible for "natural units." Though there is an objective enough distinction between the natural units—i.e., the ordinary objects—and other successions, the special status of the ordinary objects seems to be essentially *subjective,* essentially a function of how we think.

And it is not just physical things that seem to lack an objectively or metaphysically exalted status but persons too; or so I argue in Chapter 10. But here especially the psychological centrality of our concept of identity seems strikingly evident. One aspect of my view, then, is that our concept of identity, in its application both to bodies and to persons, suffers from a certain kind of metaphysical arbitrariness. That theme has already been sounded at the end of Part One, and will be amplified in this part. But in the ensuing chapters I want also to lay stress on the correlative point that our concept of identity is psychologically not arbitrary at all; there are probably deep psychological constraints which determine that just this concept should structure our understanding and knowledge. If our identity concept disappoints us as metaphysicians, it may yet fulfill our expectations as philosophical psychologists and epistemologists.

6

Foundations of Identity

IN THE recent literature a number of philosophers, including myself, have attempted to analyze our concept of bodily identity in terms of the interrelations between the successive momentary stages of a body. This kind of analysis implies that there is a conceptual connection between bodily identity and various conditions which might be satisfied by a succession of body-stages. These conditions have often been called our "criteria" of bodily identity.

These criteria of identity have typically been regarded as essentially comprising two kinds of elements: an element of continuity, and an element of sortal-coverage. The idea is that there is a special class of "sortal" terms, which can perhaps be specified by a list, such that if F belongs to this class, then the identity through time of an F-thing can be (more or less) equated with the continuity of a succession of F-stages. The kinds of continuities that have generally been most stressed are spatio-temporal and qualitative, though other continuities have sometimes been mentioned, typically in a derivative role. As regards the condition of sortal-coverage, in my own work this has been seen as based upon a more rudimentary condition of "minimizing change."[1] I shall ignore these various complications in the present chapter; but everything I say here about "sortal-covered continuity" could be said just as well about "change-minimizing continuity," and might apply regardless of what precise form the continuities take.

1. See above, Chapter 3.

There are two general kinds of questions that might be raised about this analysis of bodily identity. It might be questioned, obviously, whether there is the required conceptual (or semantic or a priori) connection between bodily identity and sortal-covered continuity. But even if this connection is granted it might still be questioned whether we have what can properly be called an *analysis* or *criteria* of bodily identity. For it might be insisted that the analysis or criteria of a concept must be more *basic* than the concept itself. And what can be more basic than our concept of bodily identity? Bodies, it might be said, are more basic than body-stages, and bodily identity is more basic than any relationship between body-stages. Hence the purported analysis moves in the wrong direction: It moves from the more basic to the less basic.

This latter question about analytical priorities is the only issue I want to discuss in the present chapter. For the purposes of this discussion I will therefore simply take it for granted that there is in fact the required conceptual connection between bodily identity and sortal-covered continuity. Since I suspect that doubts about this connection often conceal concerns about the priorities, a discussion of the latter issue may interest even those who entertain such doubts.

I. Metaphysical Priorities and Epistemological Priorities

I want, first of all, to draw a tentative distinction between two kinds of philosophical issues concerning "basicness": There are issues of *epistemological basicness* and issues of *metaphysical basicness*. A kind of thing is epistemologically basic if our knowledge of it belongs to the "foundations of knowledge"; or, more generally, one kind of thing is epistemologically more basic than a second if our knowledge about the second kind of thing derives from our knowledge about the first kind of thing. What is epistemologically basic depends on our sense organs and other aspects of our human situation. But the issue of metaphysical basicness is supposed to depend not at all on our human situation. Something is metaphysically basic if it "ultimately exists," if it belongs to the "ultimate structure of the world," if it figures in the "ideal description of reality." I think it is immediately apparent that the metaphysical notion is more proble-matical than the epistemological one; and it is equally clear that the metaphysical notion looms very large in the history of philosophy.

That there is at least a prima facie distinction between these two notions can be brought out by considering our attitude toward the particles of physics. Certainly these particles are epistemologically nonbasic, for whatever we know about them we derive from our knowledge of ordinary bodies. Yet we may be strongly inclined to regard these particles as metaphysically basic, as belonging to the most ultimate level of reality.

It may not be easy to give an equally convincing example of the reverse situation, something which strikes us as epistemologi-cally basic but metaphysically nonbasic. The sort of example to look for is one in which a complex "gestalt" seems to present itself directly to our experience, though we are still inclined to regard it as metaphysically derivative of its constituents. Of course ordinary bodies are arguably just such examples, but this is precisely the controversial issue we are about to consider. A possibly less controversial example would be a song, which we may want to regard metaphysically as merely a construction of certain kinds of notes in certain kinds of relations, though our recognition of the song seems quite direct.

There are of course many examples which may strike us as both metaphysically and epistemologically nonbasic. Many typi-cal processes, such as an economic depression, are likely to strike us in this way.

As regards our analysis of bodily identity I think it is im-portant to consider the issues of both metaphysical and episte-mological basicness. Perhaps the first issue relates more to the word "analysis," and the second to the word "criteria." Certainly the word "analysis," in the traditional use of a philosopher like Russell, suggested a movement toward metaphysical ultimates. The word "criteria" perhaps carries no such suggestion. In its or-dinary nonphilosophical use there is not even the suggestion that criteria must be conceptually connected to that of which they are criteria. In current philosophical usage, however, "criteria" (as opposed to "evidence" or "symptoms") conveys the idea of conceptual connectedness, while retaining the ordinary associa-tion with the epistemic basis for a judgment. Criteria of bodily identity would, then, have to be conditions which are conceptually related to identity, and upon which we can base our judgments of identity.

It might therefore be said, perhaps, that a question about the *metaphysical* basicness of bodily identity challenges the possibility of *analyzing* bodily identity, whereas a question about the *epistemological* basicness of bodily identity challenges the possibility of stating *criteria* for bodily identity. I will first discuss the metaphysical question, and then later turn to the epistemological question.

II. Body-Stages

The proposed analysis of bodily identity in terms of the sortal-covered continuity of body-stages may give rise to several issues about metaphysical priorities. I shall address only two of these, which are perhaps the most prominent: an issue about the status of *body-stages* and an issue about the status of *spatio-temporal continuity*.[2] I think it has seemed to some philosophers that the analysis must be misguided in principle, since body-stages are derivative of bodies and spatiotemporal continuity is derivative of bodily identity. These philosophers might agree that there are conceptual connections between bodily identity and the spatiotemporal continuity of body-stages (that perhaps bodily identity is essentially equivalent to the sortal-covered spatiotemporal and qualitative continuity of body-stages), but they would say that this is because both the notion of a body-stage and the notion of spatiotemporal continuity are derivative of the notion of bodily identity, not the other way around.

Let us first consider the question about body-stages. There may be a metaphysically innocuous construal of the notion of a body-stage for which an issue of metaphysical priorities need not even arise. By a body-stage we might simply mean *how a body is at a given time*. The analysis, on this construal, shows us how to translate ordinary statements about bodily identity in terms of the relations between the descriptions-at-a-moment of a body. Where F is a sortal, and t and t' are neighboring times such that

2. Both of these issues were discussed briefly, and from a less general standpoint, in Chapter 5.

the body x exists at t and the body y exists at t', the analysis tells us that $x = y$ if x is F at t, y is F at t', and the continuity conditions prevail. On this construal the analysis refers only to ordinary persisting bodies; no metaphysically dubious "momentary things" are brought into play. It is not that descriptions of bodies are analyzed in terms of descriptions of certain other items, but rather that one kind of description of bodies, that pertaining to persistence through time, is analyzed in terms of another kind of description of bodies, that pertaining to continuity and sortal-coverage.

It may seem unclear how the continuity conditions can be understood in the context of this construal. These conditions require that a succession of body-stages should be related in certain ways. Does this not imply that body-stages are treated as special kinds of things to be related in these ways? But no, it may be the bodies themselves which are related in these ways. We might take "$Qxtyt'$" as signifying a four-termed relationship, where x and y are bodies which may or may not be identical, and t and t' are neighboring times. We can read "$Qxtyt'$" as "x at t is qualitatively continuous with y at t'." (Compare with "x at t is bigger than y at t'," where it may be that $x = y$.) Similarly we can take "$Sxtyt'$" for "x at t is spatiotemporally continuous with y at t'." Now the analysis tells us that, where F is a sortal, $x = y$ if Fxt, Fyt', $Qxtyt'$, and $Sxtyt'$. There is still no reference here to anything but ordinary bodies (and times). Of course there may be a major problem in understanding what these continuity relations amount to, especially the relation of spatiotemporal continuity, but that is another problem, to which I will return.

If body-stages in the analysis are supposed to be literally instantaneous, then the innocuous construal might seem to require the idealization of "neighboring instants." At least this is suggested by my formulation of the analysis in the previous paragraph. I doubt, however, that this is a decisive problem; the idealization could probably be dispensed with at the cost of some complications.

Be this as it may, the fact is that most proponents of the sort of analysis being considered have *not* adopted the innocuous construal. Body-stages are typically construed as momentary things, distinct from persisting bodies. The analysis is interpreted as showing how the persistence of a body boils down to the inter-relations between these other kinds of items.

What are these other kinds of items? If we try to stay fairly close to common sense we might answer that body-stages are parts of a body's *history*. Each body has a history, which can be thought of as comprised of momentary segments or parts; ac-cording to the present suggestion these are what we are calling "body-stages."

Given *this* interpretation of what a body-stage is, it is not difficult to appreciate the critic's complaint that the analysis moves in the wrong direction. For it may seem obvious that bodies are more basic than their histories or the parts of these histories.

Are there any arguments, any general considerations, which we can adduce in favor of this judgment? If we ask why the existence of an economic depression strikes us as less basic than the existence of a person, the first answer that might come to mind is that it is logically possible for there to exist persons without there existing any depressions, but there could not possibly exist depressions without there existing any persons. This kind of answer can apparently not help us to establish that bodies are more basic than their histories. For just as it is logically impossible for there to be body-histories without bodies, it is equally impossible for there to be bodies without histories.

The answer may anyway be of dubious value. Our judgment about the relative basicness of depressions and persons cannot depend simply on the fact that "There are depressions" entails "There are persons," but not vice versa. "There are things which are red" entails "There are things which are red or yellow," but not vice versa. This does not lead us to say that being red is less basic than being red or yellow.

Perhaps what we really wanted to say about the case of eco-nomic depressions is this. It seems logically impossible that some-one should have the concept of an economic depression without having the concept of a person, whereas it is possible that some-one should have the latter concept without having the former. This is perhaps why the existence of an economic depression is less basic than the existence of a person. This approach may also give us the intuitively right line on the case of "red" and "red or yellow." It seems on the face of it impossible that some-one should have the concept "red or yellow" without having the concept "red," but not vice versa. And our intuitive judgment indeed is that being red or yellow is less basic than being red.

How will this approach apply to bodies and body-histories? It seems evidently impossible for someone to have the concept of the history of a body without having the concept of a body. A problem arises, however, in that it may seem equally im-possible that someone should have the concept of a body without having the concept of a body-history. Can one conceive of a body without conceiving of something which has different properties at different times, something, that is, which has a history? But perhaps it can be answered that while it is necessary to conceive of a body as changing in various ways, it is not necessary to *reify* this; it is not necessary to conceive of a distinguishable item called the body's *history*, which itself has various parts or stages.[3]

I am not sure how convincing this answer is. Let us note, how-ever, that for the purposes at hand it may be quite unnecessary to press this point. The critic of our analysis need not show that body-histories are *less* basic than bodies; it is enough for him to show that body-histories are *not more* basic than bodies. A legitimate piece of analysis, at least by the critic's standards, must move from the less basic to the more basic. This the analysis fails to do, if body-stages are not more basic than bodies. And that they are not is perhaps shown by the fact that to have the concept of a body-history, or the concept of a stage of such a history, necessarily depends upon having the concept of a body.

The test for metaphysical priorities which I have been dis-cussing might be called the *concept-dependence test*. It amounts to this:

(1) If it is logically impossible for someone to have the con-cept of F without having the concept of G, then the concept of F is not more basic than the concept of G;

(2) If in addition to the condition stated in (1) it is logically possible for someone to have the concept of G without hav-

3. Compare with P. F. Strawson's suggestion that our concept of an animal may depend on our concept of being born, but not on our concept of partic-ular *births*, in *Individuals*, p. 42.

ing the concept of F, then the concept of F is less basic than the concept of G.

I think it is clear that the concept-dependence test captures the essential point that the critic is trying to make. He thinks that there is a uniquely correct way to order our concepts, an ordering that corresponds to the true logical or metaphysical structure of the facts. The concept-dependence test merely expresses the idea that it cannot be correct to order our concepts with F preceding G if it is not even logically possible that someone should have the concept of F without having the concept of G. Hence it cannot be correct to treat the (concept of the) histories of bodies, or the (concept of the) stages of these histories, as more basic than the (concept of the) bodies themselves.

(Throughout this discussion I allow myself to be rather careless about a distinction that in other contexts might be crucial, viz. the distinction between saying that (a) the concept of F is more basic than the concept of G, and saying that (b) particular instances of F are more basic than particular instances of G. It is the (a)-claim that figures most directly in the present argument.)

III. Temporal Parts

If body-stages are construed innocuously then the analysis does not even purport to explain the persistence of bodies in terms of the interrelations between momentary things. And if body-stages are merely segments of the histories of bodies then the analysis does not appear to move in the right direction. This does not, however, exhaust the main possibilities. In fact many philosophers regard body-stages in neither of the two ways just mentioned.

Many philosophers regard body-stages as the "temporal parts" of bodies. We are invited to conceive of these temporal parts on the analogy of a body's ordinary spatial parts. The temporal parts are said to bear the qualities and relations that we would ordinarily ascribe to a body at a given moment. On this account the momentary things which figure in the analysis have colors, shapes, textures, and stand to each other in various spatial relations.

In some literature we are presented with the issue whether there are such things. The question is sometimes put: Do bodies have temporal parts? But it seems to me that the question, so put, is *verbal*: the philosopher who says that there are temporal parts is using language differently from the philosopher who denies that there are such things. I am not here endorsing any kind of positivist view to the general effect that issues of ontology are always verbal. Each issue has to be taken separately, on its own merits. Indeed I will in the next section want to turn to an issue about temporal parts which I am not inclined to regard as merely verbal, viz. an issue about the *metaphysical basicness* of temporal parts. All I am now suggesting is that the stark question "Are there such things as temporal parts?" is verbal.

Let me underscore this point, so that my position is not misunderstood. I have been assuming throughout this discussion that we are often prepared to talk about the existence of certain kinds of things (e.g., economic depressions) which we might then want to regard as metaphysically nonbasic. Consequently when a philosopher talks about the existence of temporal parts I assume that he has not (as yet) committed himself to anything about metaphysical priorities. (He may indeed not even acknowledge any such notion as "metaphysical prorities.") And it is only this "pure" existence question about temporal parts that I regard as verbal.[4]

Certainly the question is a priori. We could not begin to understand a philosopher who said the following: "It seems probable that in the actual world bodies have temporal parts. For example, when a tree grows the chances are that it has early parts and later parts, and the early parts are smaller than the later parts. But we can imagine a different situation. We can imagine a situation in which a tree grows without its having any temporal

4. I do not of course regard as verbal all "pure" existence questions (i.e., questions about existence which do not broach on issues of basicness), but only those which succumb to the kind of argument I am about to give. (Very roughly these would be questions about the existence of F's where both parties to the dispute agree on certain facts which only one party regards as logically equivalent to the existence of F's.) For a similar approach see G. A. Paul's classic paper "Is there a Problem about Sense-data?" *Supplementary Proceedings of the Aristotelian Society* (1936), reprinted in A. Flew, ed., *Logic and Language,* 1st ser. (Basil Blackwell, Oxford), 1951.

parts." That remark would be utterly incomprehensible. It is clear that the philosopher who says "The early parts of a tree are smaller than its later parts" regards this statement as *logically equivalent* to "The tree was first small and then large." And the philosopher who denies the statement about the tree's temporal parts refuses to treat these statements as equivalent. My suggestion is that the source of this disagreement, whether the philosophers acknowledge it or not, is that they have adopted different ways of talking. (As in all verbal disagreements the disputants may not simply have adopted different uses of language, but they may also be tacitly disagreeing about which is the *ordinary* use of language; this is still not a "substantive disagreement" in the relevant sense.)

Now I am not suggesting that any issue about logical equivalence must be verbal. People often make substantive mistakes about what is equivalent to what. If someone says that "There are twenty-seven times eighteen objects" is equivalent to "There are five hundred eighty-six objects" we would not assume that his mistake is merely verbal; we would not assume, that is, that he is merely making a strange use of language, and that in his idiolect the statements really are equivalent. We would expect rather that his general methods of arithmetical calculation would reveal that these statements are not equivalent in his idiolect.

Again, we would suspect someone of a substantive mistake if he says that "*a* knows that *p*" is equivalent to "*a* believes *p* with good reason and *p* is true." Presumably this person's response to Gettier examples would belie this equivalence, and would show that, even within his own idiolect, his remark was mistaken.

Let us consider, however, what we would say if this person responded to Gettier examples by insisting that these *are* cases of knowledge. Perhaps we would want to present him with more examples, and develop these examples from various different angles; and perhaps also give him some time to think about it. But suppose that after all of this he persists in his evaluation of the examples. Eventually I think we would have to judge that in *his* idiolect "knowledge" *is* equivalent to "true, rational belief." In this case his mistake was verbal, merely revealing that his use of language is strange.

A reasonable rule of thumb seems to be this: If someone claims that two statements are equivalent in his idiolect, and this is borne out by his formal calculations and/or his responses to particular examples, then there is a strong presumption that the statements are indeed equivalent in his idiolect.

Let us now return to the philosopher who claims that "The tree grew larger" is equivalent to "An earlier part of the tree is smaller than a later part." All of this philosopher's responses to particular examples, as well as his formal calculations, indicate that in his (philosophical) idiolect the statements *are* equivalent. It seems indeed clear that this philosopher has adopted a way of talking in which any statement of the form "The body x is A at t and B at t'" is equivalent to the statement "The body x contains the temporal parts y and z such that y exists only at t and z exists only at t', and y is A and z is B."

We can approach this point from a slightly different direction. Suppose that we explicitly introduce a new way of talking, which we might call "the language of temporal parts." We can introduce this language informally by saying that we are going to treat time on the analogy of space, and then giving a few examples to show how this works. This might suffice to teach the language to anyone who cares to learn it. In principle we should be able to introduce the language more formally, by stipulating a range of transformation rules which equate various English statements with their counterparts in the language of temporal parts. One such rule might indeed be that any English statement of the form "x is A at t and B at t'" can be transformed into "x contains the temporal parts y and z such that y exists only at t and z exists only at t', and y is A and z is B." I do not want to minimize the formal difficulties that might arise in a rigorous presentation of the new language. But I doubt that anyone could deny that this language is in principle intelligible and consistent (if English is).

Once this point is granted I think it is quite impossible to fail to see that the philosophical exponent of temporal parts has in effect adopted this new language of temporal parts; and that the philosophical antagonist of temporal parts refuses to speak the new language, but carries on in ordinary English. So this is an exemplary case of a verbal dispute. (It follows from my account that the exponent of temporal parts may be trivially mistaken, if, that is, he is tacitly claiming that his is the ordinary use of language; but he may be entering no such claim.)

The dispute is verbal, but not therefore entirely trivial. Here we should recall the lesson continually emphasized by John Wisdom, that a metaphysician's use of language, and especially his *mis*use of language, is often designed to reveal unnoticed aspects of reality, unnoticed analogies and disanalogies.[5] Certainly we can say that the language of temporal parts discloses a startlingly new perspective on the world.

Philosophers sometimes express their antagonism toward temporal parts by insisting that the expression "the temporal part of x at t" merely refers to the ordered pair (x, t). But this seems wrong, in just the way that it would be wrong to maintain that "the depression of 1929" refers to a set of people (i.e., the people involved in the depression). We say that the depression began in 1929, but we do not say "A set of people began in 1929." By the same token, if we speak the language of temporal parts we will say "The part of the tree at t was short, and straight, and smooth," whereas we would not ascribe such properties to an ordered pair. How precisely to characterize the relationship between an object and the various sets which might be said to "correspond" to it, is one of the great mysteries of metaphysics; and I am not suggesting anything to dispell this mystery. But this problem is not peculiar to temporal parts; and it remains sufficiently clear that a temporal part cannot be straightforwardly identified with any set-theoretical item.

IV. A Question of Priorities

If there is a legitimate issue to raise here it must be this: Assuming the notion of a temporal part, which is metaphysically more basic, a body or its temporal parts? Is a body merely a "logical construction" out of its temporal parts, or is it rather the temporal parts which are merely "logical constructions"? We may

5. See the essays in John Wisdom, *Philosophy and Psychoanalysis* (University of California Press, Berkeley and Los Angeles), 1969, especially "Metaphysics and Verification."

well begin to wonder whether our notion of metaphysical basicness is sufficiently clear to make good sense out of these questions.
Whereas the stark question about the existence of temporal parts
is merely verbal, the deeper issue about basicness may be too
obscure.

(In the metaphysical tradition a number of closely related
questions about the basicness of temporal parts might be formulated, for example: Do statements about temporal parts have
the logical form which their superficial grammatical form suggests? Or is the language of temporal parts merely a "code"
which allows us to express in distorted form what is better expressed in ordinary terms? On the other hand is it perhaps our
ordinary statements about persisting things which distort the
true logical structure of the facts, and which cannot be taken at
face value? All of these questions are, I take it, essentially varia-
tions on the issue of metaphysical priorities, an issue which in
the present context is coming to look exceedingly problematic.)

The proposed analysis of bodily identity is, on the present
construal, couched in terms of the language of temporal parts.
The critic cannot simply insist that the analysis must not be
couched in such terms. His objection must rather be that, even
given the language of temporal parts, the momentary things
which the analysis talks about do not have the required metaphysical priority over persisting bodies.

How can he show this? In terms of the concept-dependence
test considered earlier, the key question here would seem to be
whether it is logically possible that someone should have the
concept of a momentary thing without having the concept of a
persisting body. Why should this not be possible? Momentary
things, as now construed, have various sensible qualities and
stand to each other in various spatial relations; and persisting
bodies are constituted by distinctive kinds of successions of these
things. Why should it be logically impossible for someone to
have the concept of the momentary things without having the
concept of these distinctive kinds of successions?

Our question might be seen as arising from two steps. First
we introduce the language of temporal parts, a language in terms
of which we can render all of our ordinary English statements.
Then we ask whether we can imagine someone who speaks only

a *segment* of this language, i.e., the segment which refers only to momentary things.

Here perhaps we have nothing to appeal to but our intuitions about the possibilities of conceptualization. And these intuitions seem to be especially flimsy in the present case. It may seem immediately obvious than no one could possibly have the concept of the history of a body without having the concept of a body; or even that no one could possibly have the concept of an economic depression without having the concept of a person. I do not doubt that serious questions could be raised even about these examples. But it does not seem even prima facie obvious that no one could possibly have the concept of a momentary thing without having the concept of a persisting body.

Suppose it is granted that the critic cannot show that bodies are more basic than momentary things. The fact is, however, that the proponent of the analysis, if he is to meet the critic's standards of analysis, must maintain the opposite, that momentary things are more basic than bodies. And how can he show this? Perhaps we have reached a standoff.

It may seem, however, that we should be able to develop an argument in behalf of the priorities set by the analysis. For there is surely a pervasive tendency in metaphysics to regard a thing's parts as more basic than the thing. A general argument in behalf of the primacy of parts over wholes can perhaps be formulated in terms of the concept-dependence test. Suppose that we divide bodies up into two great classes, those which are of size N or greater, and those which are less than N. Then it may seem that our concept of the larger objects necessarily depends upon our concept of the smaller objects, but not vice versa. If this is so then it follows that the existence of the smaller objects is more basic than the existence of the larger ones. Assuming that this holds for any size N, we seem to have the general result that the smaller the object the more metaphysically basic it is.

Whatever may be the merits of this argument with respect to spatial parts, it runs into obvious problems when applied to temporal parts. The argument requires two assumptions: first, that the concept of a momentary thing does not necessarily depend upon the concept of a persisting body; and, second, that the concept of a persisting body *does* necessarily depend upon the concept of a momentary thing. Even if the first point is conceded, the second looks hopelessly wrong. For unless we adopt the language of temporal parts, which is a philosophical creation, we apparently do perfectly well without the concept of a momentary thing.

Something of the argument may yet be salvageable. For we need not limit ourselves to comparing the category of persisting bodies to the category of momentary things. We may instead compare the more general category of persisting items of all sorts to the more general category of momentary items of all sorts. Of course the analysis I have been discussing pertains to ordinary bodies, and does not apply directly to various other kinds of persisting items, such as persons, or places, or the theoretical particles of physics. But it might be maintained with some plausibility that our concept of a persisting body is the most central application of our general category of persistence through time. So if it has been conceded that the concept of a momentary thing is in principle independent of the concept of a persisting body, then it might not be difficult to maintain that the general category of momentary items is in principle independent of the general category of persistence. On the other hand it may be argued that the general category of persistence is not in turn independent of the general category of momentary items. For though the thought of persistence through time obviously does not require the concept of the concrete momentary things which figure in the analysis it may seem to require at least the concept of a *moment of time* or a *momentary event*, or some other kind of item which will represent the category of the momentary. Along these lines it might perhaps be argued that the general category of momentary items is more basic than the general category of persisting items, so that at least in this sense the analysis moves in the proper direction.

Though this argument does seem to me to have some weight, it is obviously less than decisive. And I think it is rather doubtful that some other argument will strike us as settling this issue. (We might perhaps attempt an argument from Occam's razor. But first of all it seems thoroughly unclear whether simplicity considerations should favor persisting things or momentary things; and moreover it is not even clear how such considerations can provide us with the required insight into why one kind of thing—or one way of talking—is more basic than another.)[6] Indeed the slippery twists and turns of this whole debate may encourage the response that we should simply admit that our intuitions about metaphysical basicness are quite tenuous and inconclusive, and that perhaps the very notion of metaphysical basicness is not to be taken very seriously. I will return to this negative note after first addressing the question of spatiotemporal continuity.

V. Spatiotemporal Continuity

The standard treatment of spatiotemporal continuity consists in defining this notion on the basis of bodily identity. This obviously presents a problem for the proposed analysis of bodily identity on the basis of spatiotemporal continuity.

The standard treatment actually contains two separable parts. In the first part, place-identity is defined in terms of bodily identity. The definition, roughly put, states that a place at one time is identical with a place at a second time if the first place and the second place stand in the same relations of distance and direction to a framework-defining system of persisting bodies. Place-identity is thus relativized to the choice of a framework, and presupposes the notion of a persisting body.

In the second part, spatiotemporal continuity is defined in terms of place-identity, roughly as follows. A body is said to move in a spatiotemporally continuous manner if it occupies closely neighboring places at closely neighboring times. Given the previous definition of place-identity, what this amounts to is that at closely neighboring times the body stands in very similar spatial relations to the framework-defining system of persisting bodies. Or to recast this idea in terms of momentary things, a succession of momentary things is spatiotemporally continuous if temporally neighboring elements of the succession stand in very similar spatial relations to the framework-defining system of persisting bodies. On this account the proper ordering of our

6. It is on the face of it quite absurd to be told that a mere change of language, which allows us to make statements logically equivalent to those made in the first language, could have the effect of generating an ontological problem of "overpopulation." Is this "problem" supposed to explain why the second way of talking is necessarily parasitic on the first? Or why the second way of talking misrepresents "true logical form"?

concepts evidently must take bodily identity prior to spatio-temporal continuity.

Both parts of the standard treatment can be challenged. Obviously the relativization of place-identity to a choice of framework presupposes the rejection of the doctrine of absolute motion. That doctrine would have to treat place-identity as basic, for the whole point of the doctrine is that place-identity does not depend upon the comings and goings of bodies. If place-identity is treated as basic, then our analysis of bodily identity may proceed smoothly. The ordering of concepts might be: place-identity, then spatiotemporal continuity, then bodily identity.

Though we seem to have some rather strong and, I think, not easily expungible intuitions in favor of absolute space, science has presumably taught us that there is no such thing. And this scientific lesson has obviously not gotten us to repudiate our concept of bodily identity; indeed the lesson does not even appear to impose any great strain on our concept of bodily identity. So it could not be right for the analysis to base our concept of bodily identity on absolute place-identity.

Let us assume, therefore, that the standard treatment of relativized place-identity is accepted. We are still left with two alternatives: We can define spatiotemporal continuity on the basis of bodily identity, as in the standard treatment; or we can define bodily identity on the basis of spatiotemporal continuity, as suggested in the analysis. On the first approach we arrive at the ordering: bodily identity, then place-identity, then spatiotemporal continuity. On the second approach we have the ordering: spatiotemporal continuity, then bodily identity, then place-identity.

I think it is not easy to decide which is the correct ordering. And we may indeed wonder, as we did with respect to the issue of body-stages, whether it even makes good sense to suppose that there is "*the* correct ordering." If there is a metaphysical issue here, to be distinguished from various epistemological and psychological issues, it cannot be settled on the basis of any contingent facts about human concept formation. The crucial question would seem to be whether it is at least logically possible that someone should have the concept of spatiotemporal continuity without having the concept of bodily identity. My own intuitions certainly do not decisively indicate a negative answer to this question.[7] And if there is no compelling reason to regard spatiotemporal continuity as *less* basic than bodily identity, the justification for regarding it as *more* basic might simply be a corollary of the earlier argument for regarding the momentary things, and hence their interrelations, as basic.

It must be understood that the question here is not whether every case of spatiotemporal continuity must be a case of bodily identity. No one is claiming this. There are many kinds of cases of spatiotemporal continuity which are certainly not cases of bodily identity. The most obvious case is where a spatiotemporally continuous succession combines the early stages of an object with the later stages of its parts. Another kind of case is where we judge an object to go out of existence and be replaced by another object, e.g., where a gold coin is melted down and replaced by a lump of gold. But according to the standard definition all of these cases of spatiotemporal continuity can only be understood against some background of persisting bodies which define a spatial framework.

The case of something being replaced by something else does, however, suggest a problem for the standard treatment. If we can conceive of a body going out of existence and being replaced by another body, can we conceive of this happening simultaneously to every body in the universe? This seems to be logically possible, and may even be empirically possible. But the standard treatment would rule this possibility out. To say that one body *replaces* the other must surely imply a spatiotemporally continuous connection between the initial stage of one body and the terminal stage of the other. But if this happens at a certain time to every body in the universe then at that time there would be no framework of persisting bodies, and hence, according to the standard treatment, there could be no spatiotemporal continuity, and consequently no replacement of bodies by bodies, contrary to the hypothesis. This is, I think, a fairly serious problem, which argues again for the basicness of spatiotemporal continuity.

We should briefly consider another alternative to those so far

7. An affirmative answer might be suggested by the tempting comparison between spatiotemporal continuity and *spatial* continuity; cf. above, pp. 147–49.

mentioned. It is tempting to suggest that both spatiotemporal continuity and bodily identity derive from something more basic than either, viz. the successive spatial relations between the momentary things. Any momentary thing x has what we might call a *global context*. The description of x's global context would include such statements as this: "x is 30 thousand miles from a green spherical thing," "x is touching a hard blue thing," etc. The description of x's global context would be a description of the whole momentary universe from, so to speak, x's standpoint. If x is a momentary thing that exists at t, and y is a momentary thing that exists at t', it is intuitively obvious what could be meant by saying that x's global context is *very similar* to y's. This would imply that if x is 30 thousand miles from a green spherical thing, then y is approximately 30 thousand miles from something which is approximately green and approximately spherical.

It might now be suggested that we can define spatiotemporal continuity in terms of the continuity of global contexts. A succession of momentary things is spatiotemporally continuous, according to this definition, if temporally neighboring elements of the succession have very similar global contexts.

This definition will immediately raise an epistemological problem, insofar as it apparently implies that spatiotemporal continuity is not observable (since one cannot presumably be said to observe something's whole global context). Apart from this, the definition has some rather counterintuitive metaphysical implications. Perhaps the most glaring of these pertains to imaginary cases in which there is radical duplication of objects.

Max Black has imagined a universe which consists exclusively of two spheres that are descriptively indiscernible, i.e., that are alike with respect to all general qualitative and relational characteristics.[8] It seems that we can also imagine these spheres as descriptively indiscernible relative to one time, but discernible relative to earlier and later times. For example, they might first differ in color, then become indiscernible, then differ in color again. In order for us to make sense out of this possibility we must be able to distinguish between the following two cases.

---

8. Max Black, "The Identity of Indiscernibles," in *Problems of Analysis* (Cornell University Press, Ithaca, N.Y., 1954), pp. 80–92.

D_1: The universe contains nothing but two spheres, and these spheres never differ in any respect except color. One of the spheres is initially red while the other is initially yellow. The sphere which is initially red undergoes a continuous change of color, in which it passes from red to orange to yellow. While this is taking place the other sphere also undergoes a continuous change of color, in which it passes from yellow to orange to red. There is a time t during this period when both spheres share the exact same shade of orange, so that at t the spheres are descriptively indiscernible.

D_2: The universe contains nothing but two spheres, and these spheres never differ in any respect except color. One of the spheres is initially red while the other is initially yellow. The sphere which is initially red undergoes a continuous change of color, in which it passes from red to orange and back to red again. While this is taking place the other sphere also undergoes a continuous change of color, in which it passes from yellow to orange and back to yellow again. There is a time t during this period when both spheres share the exact same shade of orange, so that at t the spheres are descriptively indiscernible.

D_1 says that the sphere which was initially red winds up yellow, and the sphere which was initially yellow winds up red, whereas D_2 says that the sphere which was initially red winds up red, and the sphere which was initially yellow winds up yellow. Intuitively it seems clear that we can distinguish between these two cases. But given the previous definition of spatiotemporal continuity in terms of contextual continuity, it would seem to follow that we cannot make the distinction, at least not on the basis of spatiotemporal continuity. For suppose that D_1 is true. Then we can derive D_2 by combining the pre-t stages of one sphere with the post-t stages of the other. And there would be no considerations of spatiotemporal continuity to block this, assuming the previous definition. For the succession which combines the pre-t stages of one sphere with the post-t stages of the other would be spatiotemporally continuous, given that definition, since there is evidently no lack of continuity of global context. Intuitively we want to say that this succession will lack spatiotemporal continuity, which is why the truth of D_1 precludes the truth of D_2.

I am therefore disinclined to accept the definition of spatiotemporal continuity in terms of contextual continuity. Of course this definition would have been congenial to our analysis of bodily identity in terms of spatiotemporal continuity, since it would ground spatiotemporal continuity in something other than bodily identity. But, as I have already indicated, I can see no decisive reason why spatiotemporal continuity needs to be grounded in anything.

VI. Analyzing Bodily Identity

All in all, I would conclude that a modestly plausible case can be made out for the metaphysical priorities set by the analysis. At least these priorities seem no less plausible than those advanced by the critic.

We might be tempted to draw a more general and negative conclusion from this whole discussion. Perhaps the discussion suggests that the notion of "metaphysical basicness" makes no real sense and has no real use. If this is so we must jettison the notion of "analysis" in its traditional sense, and with it the traditional sense of such kindred notions as "logical construction," "logical simplicity," and "logical form." Perhaps none of these notions can really be separated from various contingent facts about human concept formation and human knowledge.

Though I have some considerable sympathy for this negative attitude, I think we might reasonably adopt it with respect to some issues without necessarily adopting it across the board. Our intuitions about metaphysical basicness may be dim but they are not necessarily benighted. And where we have a clear and decisive intuition (as *perhaps* with the case of economic depressions) then I can see no reason to reject it. But with respect to the sorts of issues I have been raising about bodily identity it is doubtful that we do have any such clear intuition.[9]

9. Here as elsewhere in this book I challenge, though only selectively and partially, various traditional doctrines of "metaphysical basicness" and "analysis"; but I draw short of waging a full-scale or head-on assault on these doctrines. For a general critique of such doctrines, and a historical perspective, see Urmson, *Philosophical Analysis*.

Some of our strongest intuitions about metaphysical basicness, I think, relate to the relative priority of "natural kinds" over "artificial classes." See Chapter 9, especially Section V, and ftn. 24. In the present discussion I am in effect maintaining that we have no comparably strong intuitions about the meta-

So I would say this: If to give an "analysis" of bodily identity means to explain this notion in terms which seem to be decisively more basic in some noncontingent metaphysical respect, then I think it is doubtful that we can ever give an analysis of bodily identity.

But we might of course give an "analysis" in various less stringent senses. We can try to depict the logical interconnections between (the "logical geography" of) the concept of bodily identity and various other concepts, such as sortal-coverage and continuity. We can try to determine whether bodily identity is equivalent to some combination of these other concepts. And we can try, as I have been trying, to decide whether these other concepts are, if not decisively more basic, at least not decisively less basic than bodily identity. And of course we might also examine the epistemological relations between these concepts, which is indeed the topic I next want to consider.

VII. Epistemological Priorities

I continue to assume in this discussion that bodily identity is essentially equivalent to the condition of sortal-coverage in conjunction with the continuity conditions. It is important to be quite clear that this assumption does not by itself commit us to holding that a person's judgments about bodily identity must be derived from some prior judgments about sortal-covered continuity. In general, if a proposition is logically equivalent to a conjunction of certain other propositions, it does not follow that a judgment about the first proposition must be derived from judgments about the other propositions.

This point was already implicit in an illustration mentioned earlier. It may seem plausible to say that the playing of a particular song is equivalent to the playing of certain kinds of notes in a certain kind of relationship. The proposition "That was the Star Spangled Banner," for example, might be regarded as essentially equivalent to a complicated conjunction of proposi-

---

physical priority of "natural units" (i.e., bodies). I would maintain this negative attitude even with respect to the special case of persons; see Chapter 10, especially Section II. (See also the last two paragraphs of the Introduction to Part Two.)

tions about individual notes (together perhaps with certain facts about the social status of the song). But this does not imply that the ordinary person's judgment "That was the Star Spangled Banner" derives from judgments about the notes. Most people cannot even recognize notes.

So even on the assumption that bodily identity is equivalent to sortal-covered continuity, it must remain an open possibility that judgments about bodily identity are not based on judgments about continuity or sortal coverage. And from a phenomenological standpoint this possibility seems immediately appealing. At least a superficial exercise of phenomenological inspection does not seem to reveal that our judgments of bodily identity derive from any other kinds of judgments. As I look around me the perceptual judgments that seem to form directly in my mind are such as "The pen is moving on the paper," "The cigarette is burning down," "The cup remains stationary." These are evidently judgments about how bodies persist and change. It is not clear that I make any judgments at all about continuity or sortal coverage, let alone that I derive from these my judgments about the vicissitudes of bodies.

Yet it is a rather common philosophical assumption that our judgments of bodily identity must derive from such "criteria" as sortal-covered continuity. Indeed, as I noted earlier, a standard use of the philosophical expression "criteria of bodily identity" seems to imply not only that judgments about bodily identity are logically equivalent to judgments about the presence of the criteria, but also that the former judgments are inferentially derived from the latter. The first point I take for granted here; but I am questioning the second assumption.

I think that this second assumption frequently derives from a certain fallacious argument, which I will call *the argument from immediacy*. It might be put as follows: "Obviously we cannot see into the future, or into the past. This means that a perceptual judgment, properly speaking, can only describe what is happening at a particular moment. So a perceptual judgment cannot possibly be about identity through time. Rather our judgments about identity through time must be inferred from various observed facts about particular moments, which facts constitute our criteria for these judgments."[10]

10. Cf. Quinton, *The Nature of Things*, pp. 58–59.

Let me temporarily grant the argument's premise, viz. that a perceptual judgment can only describe what is happening at a particular moment. The main point I want to make is that this premise cannot sustain the argument's conclusion. If a perceptual judgment can only describe what is happening at a particular moment then it would indeed follow that a perceptual judgment cannot possibly be about identity through time. But it would *also* follow that a perceptual judgment cannot be about *spatiotemporal continuity*, which is a relationship between bodies (or body-stages) at different times. So it would follow from the argument's premise that spatiotemporal continuity, which is supposed to be a criterion of identity, is itself unobservable. This contradicts the argument's conclusion that we infer bodily identity from observable criteria.

The argument wants to have it both ways. It wants to say both that (1) perceptual judgments cannot be about identity through time, and (2) perceptual judgments can be about conditions which logically entail identity through time. But the same considerations which might induce us to accept (1) will induce us to deny (2). I single out spatiotemporal continuity for special attention because, first, this condition is most widely accepted as a criterion of identity, and also because with respect to this condition the conflict between (1) and (2) is most glaring.

If the premise of the argument were correct then there could be no observable facts which logically entail bodily identity. Even the mere temporal ordering of events would be problematical, though perhaps it could be said that we order event A as temporally prior to event B if the observation of B is accompanied by the memory of A. But a mere sequence of temporally ordered momentary observation-reports could not possibly entail any facts about identity through time, for it could not even entail that a succession of body-stages is spatiotemporally continuous.

Given the premise of the argument the most basic level of objective knowledge would consist of temporally ordered facts about the qualities and spatial relations of momentary body-stages. From this we could perhaps deduce certain facts about qualitative continuity and continuity of local (as opposed to global) context. At this point some kind of mysterious leap would have to take place, perhaps inspired by instinct, to the level which includes both judgments about bodily identity and judgments about spatiotemporal continuity. There is no argument here at all for regarding the former judgments as criterially based upon the latter.

So even if we accept the premise of the argument from immediacy, the conclusion does not follow. And I do not in fact think that we should accept the premise. The truism that "we cannot see into the future or past" does not compel us to deny that we can, in the most literal and proper sense, observe facts which relate different moments of time, facts which can perhaps be characterized, in one traditional jargon, as belonging to a single "specious present." So we need not rule out a priori the possibility that we simply observe how bodies persist and change.

Let us consider an example in which it seems straightforwardly correct to say that a judgment is based on criteria (in the philosophical sense of "criteria" under discussion). I might judge that a figure is an octagon on the basis of (a) observing that it is a polygon, and (b) counting eight sides. Its being an octagon is equivalent to its satisfying the two conditions. And my judgment that it is an octagon consciously derives from my prior judgment that each condition is satisfied.

I think it is clear that our perceptual judgments of bodily identity are not typically based on criteria in this way. When we observe a body, our judgments about its persistence and change are not consciously derived from any prior judgments about the satisfaction of some identity conditions. In this sense, our judgments about bodily identity, at least in optimal conditions of observation, are not based on any criteria whatever.

But we also need to consider a weaker and more nebulous sense of "basing a judgment on criteria." Some of the murkiness of this issue can be brought out immediately by comparing the case of judging that something is an octagon with the case of judging that something is a triangle. It seems correct to say that I can simply *see* that something is a triangle, and that I need not consciously derive this judgment from any prior judgments that the figure is a polygon and that it is three-sided. On the other hand it may also seem correct to say that I see that it is a triangle *insofar as* I judge it to have three sides and to be a polygon. Perhaps we want to say that the perceptual judgment that it is a triangle is based on an unconscious, or implicit, in-

ference from the judgments that it is three-sided and that it is
a polygon.

Now an interesting possibility, I think, is that our perceptual
judgments of bodily identity also involve an unconscious or
implicit inference from criteria. Though I cannot venture any
general explanation of the nature of "unconscious" or "implicit"
inference from criteria, I suggest that the primary kind of
situation in which it may seem correct to apply this notion might
be roughly characterized as follows. A person S judges that a
proposition p is true, where there exists a certain set C of conditions such that: (1) p is logically entailed by the proposition that
the conditions in C are satisfied; and (2) S does not consciously
or explicitly judge that he perceives the conditions in C to be
satisfied; but (3) if S's attention were redirected, perhaps by his
being asked certain questions, then S *would* explicitly judge
that he perceives the conditions in C to be satisfied.

To the extent that these three clauses apply it may seem correct
to say that in a sense S's judgment that p is true is based on the
criteria C; that S's judgment that p is true is based on the unconscious or implicit inference from the judgment that each
condition in C is satisfied.

Clause (3) requires that the criterial conditions should be
accessible to S, in the sense that S's perceptual and conceptual
abilities would enable him on that occasion to form the conscious perceptual judgment that the conditions obtain. Though
this requirement is rather vague, and may admit of degrees, it
seems obviously to be met in the case of recognizing a triangle.
If the case is typical we can easily induce the explicit judgments
that the thing is a polygon (or a closed figure) and that it has
three sides. This is why we may be inclined to say that recognizing a triangle is implicitly based on these judgments.

I think it can now be argued that judgments of bodily identity ought to be compared to the case of recognizing a triangle.
One source of resistance to this proposal may be that the conditions of identity seem rather technical, and therefore inaccessible
to the typical observer. But this is, I think, a rather superficial
point. First of all, for our present epistemological purposes a
body-stage can be understood in terms of the essentially common-
sensical notion of the stage of a thing's history. Of course the
typical observer will not be readily induced to judge "There goes

another sortal-covered continuous succession of body-stages." But he can be readily induced to make judgments which, in a rudimentary fashion, amount to much the same thing. Suppose he is observing a pen. Then we can easily get him to attend to the fact that at any time during this stretch of observation the body he observes is a pen; that the qualities of the body he observes at any time are very similar to what the qualities were of the body he observed at the just previous time; and that the location of the body he observes at any time is very close to what the location was of the body he observed at the just previous time. These facts amount in our philosophical terminology to his having observed a succession of body-stages which all come under the sortal "pen," such that the succession is both qualitatively and spatiotemporally continuous. So I think it is fair to say that the conditions of bodily identity are in the relevant sense accessible to the typical observer. And this argues for the conclusion that typical judgments of bodily identity are implicitly or unconsciously based on the conditions as criteria.

If we accept this conclusion we need not deny that people can, in the most strict and proper sense, perceive how objects persist and change. Just as we might want to say that someone can perceive that a figure is a triangle *insofar as* he implicitly infers this from the conditions of triangularity, so we can say that someone perceives the persistence and change of a body insofar as he implicitly infers this from the criterial conditions of bodily identity.

There is, to be sure, an important difference between perceiving a triangle and perceiving bodily identity. Almost anyone can state what the conditions of triangularity are, whereas no one except perhaps a few philosophers (who even disagree among themselves) can state what the conditions of bodily identity are. But it seems clear that there are many cases in which we recognize a complex kind of object or phenomenon on the basis of perceiving certain features, without our being able to state authoritatively what the features are that define that kind of object or phenomenon.

An interesting example of this sort, which may indeed be very similar to the case of bodily identity, concerns our judgments about how things form into groups. When we look at the following figure we are likely to see pairs of dots and triplets of crosses,

· · ✕ ✕ ✕ · · ✕ ✕ ✕ · · ✕ ✕ ✕ · ·

rather than various other possible combinations of these elements. Gestalt psychologists have attempted to formulate the principles of grouping which in effect define what we mean in this kind of context by a "group," or "cluster," or "arrangement." These principles are complicated and controversial. It may seem evident that in the exhibited case the conditions of proximity and similarity play some role in determining our perception of the group-units; but it is by no means obvious how to combine or weight these conditions, nor what other conditions might be relevant. But though we may be unable to state precisely what the conditions of group-unity are, I think that few would doubt that our perception of the groups is in some manner derived from the implicit recognition of these conditions. I am suggesting that the conditions of bodily identity may play very much the same kind of role in determining our perception of how bodies persist and change.

I believe that the only serious objection to this position stems from the widely accepted view that judgments of spatiotemporal continuity must derive from judgments of bodily identity. This view seems to follow directly from the standard treatment of spatiotemporal continuity, according to which spatiotemporal continuity must be relativized to a framework-defining system of persisting bodies.

Now there are some philosophers who appear to think that our judgments of spatiotemporal continuity must always depend on judgments of bodily identity, and *also* that our judgments of bodily identity must always depend on judgments of spatiotemporal continuity.[11] Such a view seems quite baffling. How could these two kinds of judgments feed off each other in that way? If the standard treatment of spatiotemporal continuity is accepted then at least our judgments about the identities of the framework-defining bodies cannot possibly derive from judgments of spatiotemporal continuity. And if this is so the obvious conclusion to draw is that our judgments of bodily identity need *never* derive from judgments of spatiotemporal continuity. As I have repeatedly emphasized such a view of the epistemological priorities may be fully compatible with the

11. See especially Strawson, *Individuals*, p. 26.

conceptual point that bodily identity is essentially equivalent to sortal-covered continuity.

But I am inclined to think that this is the wrong view of the epistemological priorities. I have already suggested that there are some metaphysical problems with the standard treatment of spatiotemporal continuity. From an epistemological standpoint this approach is even more obviously vulnerable. Certainly it seems plausible to say that we can observe spatiotemporal continuity, that we can observe that a body moves continuously through space. And surely our ability to observe a case of spatio-temporal continuity does not depend on their being any framework-defining bodies within the scope of our observation. We can imagine someone who observes a single body in total isolation from all other bodies. (We can even imagine that the observer suffers from some abnormality which prevents him from perceiving his own body.) Surely the isolated body could be observed to move continuously, to move without any discontinuous jumps. How can we make sense out of this if, as in the standard treatment, spatiotemporal continuity must be relativized to some framework-defining bodies?

Perhaps there is some way to get around this question. But I think the most obvious and plausible response is to reject the standard treatment. Spatiotemporal continuity can be regarded as an observable phenomenon that is as primitive, as indefinable, as color, or shape, or contact.

This does not necessarily imply that our perception of spatio-temporal continuity is in no sense based on something. Perhaps all of our perceptions are based on the having, or even on the implicit recognition, of our subjective sense data, as so many philosophers have thought. And perhaps, as noted earlier, there is even an *objective* level of perception, more basic than either spatiotemporal continuity or bodily identity, which embraces only momentary facts. These issues need not be settled here. I am only arguing for the position that our perception of spatio-temporal continuity need not derive from any judgments about bodily identity.

If this position is accepted then nothing stands in the way of saying that our perception of bodily identity *does* derive from judgments of spatiotemporal continuity, as one criterion of bodily identity. And if nothing stands in the way of saying this then the analogy to other cases (such as that of group-unity) seems to indicate that we should say this.

I conclude this discussion of the epistemological aspect of bodily identity on much the same tentative note that concluded my previous discussion of the metaphysical aspect. Certainly I have presented no very conclusive argument for the epistemological priorities I recommend. But I think a fairly good case has been made for the position that our perception of bodily identity derives from the implicit recognition of the conditions of bodily identity, so that these conditions can rightly be called *criteria* of identity.

7

Matter, Causality, and Stereotypes of Identity

I. Optimal Cases

I AM inclined to maintain—with various reservations to be discussed—that the following is a conceptual truth: If a succession of car-stages is spatiotemporally and qualitatively continuous, then it constitutes some portion (perhaps the whole) of the history of a persisting car. This principle, to put it somewhat less technically, states that if there exists a car at one moment, and there exists a car at the next moment, and there exists a car at the moment after this, and so on, and the car that exists at any moment is located very close to where the car at the next moment is located, and also the car that exists at any moment has qualities that are very similar to the qualities of the car at the next moment, then this is one and the same car that exists at each of these moments.[1] I will call this principle SQ, after the conditions of spatiotemporal and qualitative continuity. Of course I would suggest the corresponding principle for various other sorts of things, such as trees, rocks, and tables. The principle, relativized to each sort of thing, would state that any spatiotemporally and qualitatively continuous succession of stages of that sort of thing constitutes some portion of the history of a thing of that sort.

To say that SQ is a conceptual truth means, trivially, that its truth follows from the nature of the concepts involved, or, if

1. Here as elsewhere I allow the loose but intuitive notion of a "next" or "neighboring" moment.

one prefers, from the meanings of the relevant words. Another way to put this is that we cannot so much as conceive of what it would be like for SQ to turn out to be false. I will have something more to say later about the notion of a conceptual truth, and its connection to the notion of metaphysical necessity.

I place one general limitation on my commitment to SQ as a conceptual truth. I do not necessarily deny that there could be a case which seems to satisfy the SQ conditions but which is nevertheless a *borderline case* of the identity of a car. In such a case a decision might be made as to what to say, and some might decide against the identity claim. But according to my suggestion SQ is a conceptual truth *up to* borderline cases: There is no case, actual or possible, which both clearly satisfies the SQ conditions and also clearly is not a case of identity.

Before proceeding let me mention a weaker version of the SQ principle, which may strike some readers as immediately more attractive. The weaker version would say that it is a conceptual truth that the presence of the SQ conditions constitutes *prima facie* evidence, though not *conclusive* evidence, for an identity claim.[2] Toward the end of this chapter I will broach an analysis which would sustain this weaker version. For now, however, I want to try to show that even the stronger version may be viable.

Assuming the general notion of a conceptual truth, there are two kinds of objections that might be raised against my claim that SQ is a conceptual truth. First, it might be maintained that, in addition to the two conditions mentioned in SQ, certain other conditions are necessary for the identity of a car. Two conditions which have often been mentioned in the literature are compositional continuity and causal continuity. The first condition would require that the matter which makes up the car at any moment be almost the same as the matter which makes it up at the next moment. And the second condition would require that the car's qualitative state at each moment be causally related to its qualitative state at the next moment.

2. It may be noted that even the weaker version of SQ could sustain, with suitable modifications, the general approach to identity presented in Part One. (For example, we could define F as a sortal if it is a conceptual truth that the presence of an F-succession satisfying the SQ conditions constitutes prima facie evidence for the identity of an F-thing.)

The first objection to SQ is an objection of detail; it does not question the possibility of stating some nontrivial combination of conditions which suffices to guarantee conceptually the identity of a car. A philosopher might, however, deny even this general possibility. Such a philosopher might insist that the identity of a car is "primitive" and "indefinable," and therefore cannot be entailed by any combination of spatiotemporal, or qualitative, or compositional, or causal conditions. (Of course even this philosopher would admit that we could trivially define some new expression, e.g., "car kinship," in such a manner as to make it tautologous to say that a succession of kindred car-stages constitutes a persisting car.)

Let me first address this extreme form of objection. I will try to describe a case, which I will call the *optimal* case, in which every possible source of doubt about a car's identity has been removed. Doubts might arise about the degree of spatiotemporal continuity that is typically required for a car's identity. So let us assume that in the optimal case we have a very high degree of spatiotemporal continuity. Similar doubts might arise about the degree of qualitative continuity required. But also doubts might conceivably arise about how *much* a car can change, even continuously, and still be the same car. So let us assume that in the optimal case we have not merely a high degree of qualitative continuity, but a high degree of qualitative *stability*, i.e., any two car-stages in the succession are qualitatively very similar to each other. For the same reason let us assume that in the optimal case we have a high degree of compositional stability, i.e., any two car-stages in the succession are composed of almost the same matter. And we will assume that in the optimal case there is a high degree of causal connectedness between the car-stages in the succession.

In sum, in the optimal case we have a succession of car-stages which is to a high degree spatiotemporally continuous, which is highly stable both qualitatively and compositionally, and which has a high degree of casual interconnectedness. Could anyone seriously deny that it is a conceptual truth that the optimal case is a case of identity? Such a denial would seem on the face of it extremely paradoxical. If we have a succession of car-stages which satisfies all of the conditions of the optimal case, then it seems that we cannot conceive of anything *more*

that might be required for this succession to qualify as a persisting car. Of course a philosopher might respond that something more *is* required, viz. that it be *the same car*. But this
response, barring some special explanation, seems simply
unintelligible.

So I think that reflection on the optimal case will convince
most people that it is indeed possible to specify some (nontrivial)
conditions which are logically sufficient for the identity of a car.
The only question then is what these conditions are. I suggest
that one set of logically sufficient conditions is the SQ conditions. Note that I do not suggest that these conditions are
necessary, but only that they are sufficient. The objection that
now concerns me implies that the SQ conditions are *not* sufficient
because certain other conditions *are* necessary, i.e., the conditions
of compositional and causal continuity. I suggest that these
latter conditions are not necessary. Note again that I do not
necessarily deny that these conditions may be sufficient in their
own right.

Before pursuing this issue let me introduce another kind of
case which I will call the *nearly optimal* case. In the optimal
case we had qualitative and compositional stability; in the nearly
optimal case we merely have qualitative and compositional
continuity. This means that in the latter case two car-stages in
the succession may be qualitatively very *dissimilar* or composed
of entirely *different* matter, so long as temporally neighboring
car-stages are qualitatively similar and composed of almost the
same matter.

There may be, at least prereflectively, the impulse to maintain
that continuity of qualitative or compositional change is not
enough, but that there is an upper limit on the degree of change
in these respects that a car can suffer while retaining its identity. (There is, for some reason, not even the slightest impulse
to impose such a limit on how much a car can *move* and still
be the same car.) Of course if the car changes so much that it
ceases to be *a car* then it will indeed not qualify under any of
the conditions I have so far been discussing. All of these conditions are relativized to the sortal "car"; it is a succession of *car*-
stages that is always presupposed. But even given that we have
a succession of car-stages there may still be the impulse to hold
that, in order to have a case of identity, this succession must

be to some extent stable with respect to its qualities or material composition.

I think that this impulse is for most people rather decisively quelled by simply considering a few examples in which we obviously do not require stability. For example, the material composition of a living thing, such as a tree, may alter entirely over a period of time without that thing's going out of existence. And so long as a tree remains a tree, there is apparently no general limit on how much it can change with respect to its qualities of size, or shape, or color.

There is a more general consideration which seems to show that if stability suffices for identity so must continuity suffice. Let x be a car that is picked out at t_1, y a car that is picked out at t_2, and z a car that is picked out at t_3, where t_1, t_2, and t_3 are neighboring times. Suppose that x is the same car as y because (in addition to the other conditions being satisfied) x at t_1 is almost like y at t_2 with respect to qualities and composition, and that y is the same car as z because y at t_2 is almost like z at t_3 with respect to qualities and composition. Then, by the transitivity of identity, x must be the same car as z even if x at t_1 is *not* almost like z at t_3 with respect to qualities and composition. In other words, if a car can retain its identity through a small qualitative or compositional change, it seems that it must be able to retain its identity through any sequence of such small changes, even if they add up to a large change. But a sequence of small changes is precisely what we mean by a continuous change.

It might be suggested that this is just another case of the familiar sorites argument. It is like arguing that, since a poor person who is given a penny remains poor, therefore no sequence of such gifts could ever make the person rich. But there is an important difference between these cases. In the typical sorites argument we can at least in principle stipulate a *cut-off point*, e.g., the point at which getting one more penny will change the person to being not poor. The fact that there is in practice no such definite cut-off point might then be regarded as merely reflecting the vagueness of our concept of poverty. But in the identity argument it seems that there cannot be even in principle a cut-off point, for the transitivity of identity precludes our saying that $x = y$ and $y = z$ but $x \neq z$.

Perhaps there are some subtle maneuvers to escape this argument.[3] But I think it is more plausible to assume that if stability suffices then so does continuity. And from this it follows that, since the optimal case is a case of identity, so is the nearly optimal case. In the nearly optimal case we have the four kinds of continuities, each to a sufficiently high degree. I will not attempt to specify what constitutes a "sufficiently high degree"; perhaps it is not possible to specify this in any useful way.

Now my argument will proceed as follows. The conjunction of the four continuity conditions suffices for identity; this is the nearly optimal case. It seems plausible to assume that any condition which is either necessary or sufficient for identity is some combination of the four continuities. Suppose that it can now be shown that neither compositional continuity nor causal continuity (nor their disjunction) is necessary for identity. It then would follow that the other two conditions, i.e., the SQ conditions, suffice.

II. Compositional and Causal Continuity

It is quite easy to think of examples which at least strongly suggest that compositional continuity is not necessary for the identity of a car. Suppose that in the next issue of *Scientific American* we read that whenever a car backfires the majority of its subatomic particles simultaneously go out of existence and are replaced by other particles. This would amount to a massive *discontinuity* of material composition. Would this announcement induce us to say that, as it has turned out, cars go out of existence when they backfire? I think not. We would say rather that it has turned out that cars wind up with new subatomic particles when they backfire.

3. One interesting possibility, noted by Alan Brody, is that the identity of a car depends on its qualitative and compositional similarity to how it was *when it was first created*. This suggestion would allow us to stipulate a cut-off point, and hence even cast a kind of doubt on the optimal case (for even a minute change might be too much relative to the cut-off point). Certainly this suggestion could not apply to many things, such as trees; and I doubt that it really has much plausibility even for cars.

I think we can imagine a more extreme possibility.

Could we not reject the concept of matter and build a pure field physics? What impresses our senses as matter is really a great concentration of energy into a comparatively small space. . . . A thrown stone is, from this point of view, a changing field. . . . There would be no place, in our new physics, for both field and matter, field being the only reality.[4]

Einstein and Infeld, from whom this passage is quoted, put this forward only as a possibility. But suppose that such a possibility were generally accepted by scientists. If the concept of matter is rejected then apparently the condition of continuity of material composition can never be satisfied. But surely we would still continue to assert that a stone can be thrown (cf. the quoted passage), or that a car can move down First Avenue. Evidently the identities of such bodies do not in general depend upon any facts about the existence or persistence of underlying matter.

It might be questioned whether Einstein and Infeld should have expressed their speculation in the words "The concept of matter is rejected (i.e., there is no such thing as matter)," rather than in the words "Matter has turned out to be very different from what people thought." But I think this is like asking whether it is correct to say "There is no such thing as phlogiston," rather than "Phlogiston has turned out to be very different from what people thought." Our concept of matter is defined by its role in our most general theory of the underlying structure of physical reality. If this theory changes in ways which seem very drastic or essential than it may be natural and correct to conclude "There is no matter."[5] But even if we draw this conclusion we will surely continue to assert that cars move down First Avenue.

4. Albert Einstein and Leopold Infeld, *The Evolution of Physics* (Simon and Schuster, New York, 1961), pp. 242–43.
5. If "There is matter" simply means "There are material bodies" then the existence of stones and cars would trivially entail the existence of matter. That, however, is not the sense of "matter" at issue. The question is whether such observable bodies as cars and stones are made up of some underlying material substance which can be said to persist and change independently of these observable bodies.

Our judgments about the identity of a car do not in general depend on our theories about the underlying structure of reality.

There may still be a question to raise about compositional continuity as a necessary condition of identity. Suppose it is granted that a body's ultimate composition (e.g., at the atomic or subatomic level) can alter discontinuously without the body's going out of existence. It might still be suggested that a body's *observable* composition cannot change discontinuously. This would imply that most of a body's observable parts at any moment must continue to be parts of the body at the next moment.

This suggestion is difficult to assess, for it is not clear how a body's observable parts could alter discontinuously without there also being a lapse of spatiotemporal and qualitative continuity. So it is difficult to see how this suggestion could threaten the claim that the SQ conditions suffice. I am able to think of one possible kind of example. Suppose that we have a wicker chair composed of observable strands of wicker. Because of moisture in the air the strands gradually meld together. Perhaps it would eventually be correct to say that the wicker strands have been destroyed. This might happen (i.e., the process of destruction might be completed) at the same moment to all the strands. So here we would have a massive discontinuity in the chair's observable composition without there being any lapse at all in spatiotemporal or qualitative continuity. Presumably in this case we have little inclination to deny that it is still the same chair. So at least in this kind of example the proposed compositional condition seems not to be necessary.

I turn now to the condition of causal continuity. There are several considerations which seem to suggest that this is not a necessary condition of identity. Perhaps most obviously, if this were a necessary condition of identity then it would seem to be logically impossible for there to be such a thing as *miraculous survival*. Suppose that because of some internal force a car is about to explode, dispersing its particles to the four corners of the Earth, but that God intervenes with a miracle and keeps the car intact. Surely this does not strike us as a logical contradiction. But a miracle is by definition a suspension of causal laws, so that presumably the car's post-miracle stages are not causally determined by its pre-miracle stages. The causal requirement would seem to render God impotent in effecting miraculous survivals, which is perhaps one of His major traditional functions.

Miracles aside, there actually exists in the world a kind of physical thing (I do not say physical *body*) which moves and changes without satisfying the causal requirement. I have in mind *shadows*. It is certainly correct to say that we can observe a shadow moving across the floor or changing its shape. But the stages of a shadow are causally independent of each other, each shadow-stage being the effect of the body which has the shadow.

It will be said perhaps that shadows are not to be compared to bodies with respect to their identity conditions. (It might also be questioned whether the SQ conditions suffice even for shadows in all circumstances, for example, where shadows temporarily merge.) I agree that this comparison should not be pushed too far. Still I think that reflecting on the phenomena of shadows can help to raise a question in our minds as to whether our thought (and experience) of identity through time depends essentially on a causal condition.

Sydney Shoemaker has presented an example which he thinks demonstrates that causal continuity is a necessary condition of bodily identity.

Suppose, contrary to fact, that the following remarkable machines are possible. The first is a table canceller; if you have set its controls to pick out a certain location, then pushing a button on the machine will cause any table at that location to vanish into thin air. The second is a table producer; if you have set its controls so as to pick out a certain location, then pushing a button on the machine will cause a table to materialize out of thin air at that location, and the properties of that table will depend on the setting of the machine and on nothing else. . . . [N]ow we set the controls of the machines so that the location picked out on both is that of my dining room table, and we push both buttons simultaneously. Assuming that the controls of the table producer are set to produce tables of the shape, size, and color of my present dining room table, it will look as if nothing has happened. There will be a spatiotemporally continuous series of table-stages, and it will appear to the casual observer as if the same table has persisted throughout. But knowing the powers of the machines, we know that this is not so. If t is the time at which the buttons were pushed, then the nature of the table-stages that occurred after t is due to the pushing of the button on the table producer at t, and not at all due to the properties of the table that was there before t; given that the button was pushed, we would have had such a table there after *t* even if there had been no table, or a very different table, there before. It seems plain that in this case one table has been replaced by another.[6]

I think Shoemaker has drawn a too hasty conclusion. Suppose that the way the machines work is as follows. The table canceller disperses the subatomic particles of the table at any target location. On the other hand the table producer operates on the particles at a target location (or if there are insufficient particles in that location, draws from particles at the closest available location) and rearranges them into the specified form of a table. What happens now if both machines are simultaneously activated upon a certain target location which contains a table of the specified form? Presumably the table producer in effect prevents the table canceller from dispersing the particles. So we are left after *t* with a table containing exactly the same particles arranged in (more or less) the same way. When the story is filled out in this way is it not plain that the table after *t* *is* the same table as the one before *t*? I think that no one would doubt this, even though the causal requirement seems not to be satisfied. (The causal requirement seems not to be satisfied because "the nature of the table-stages that occurred after *t* is due to the pushing of the button on the table producer at *t*, and not at all due to the properties of the table that was there before *t*"—Shoemaker's characterization of the absence of causal continuity. If we are asked to explain why there is a table with certain properties at the target location after *t* then it will apparently be *no part* of

6. Sydney Shoemaker, "Identity, Properties, and Causality," in P. A. French, T. E. Uehling, Jr., H. K. Wettstein, eds., *Midwest Studies in Philosophy*, vol. 4 (University of Minnesota Press, Minneapolis, 1979), p. 326.

There are a couple of minor problems in Shoemaker's exposition. Why does he require *both* machines to be activated? Even if just the table producer is activated it would still follow that "given that the button was pushed, we would have had such a table there after *t* even if there had been no table, or a very different table, there before." He must hold that if just the table producer is activated then the pre-*t* stages would be, though not a necessary cause, at least part of a sufficient cause for the post-*t* stages, and this would suffice to satisfy the causal requirement.

Why does he suppose that if both buttons are pushed simultaneously then the net result would be the existence of a table at the target location? He must be assuming that the producer machine is in some sense *stronger*. That should be made explicit.

this explanation to say that there was a table with certain properties there before t.)[7] If this is correct then Shoemaker's kind of example may serve very nicely to demonstrate that causal connectedness is *not* a necessary condition of identity.

Shoemaker is probably thinking of another version of the example. In the second version the table canceller annihilates not just tables but the matter which composes them, whereas the table producer creates tables *ex nihilo*. Would we say in this second version that the table after t is not identical with the table before t?

In the second version we may perhaps grant that the table after t is not composed of the same matter as the table before t. Even this conclusion is by no means straightforward, since there is no obvious reason to assume that the best scientific theory of matter would necessarily imply that, say, the history of an electron must be causally connected. But perhaps we can imagine that in the second version of Shoemaker's example our simplest theoretical explanation of what transpired at t would include the judgment that the matter which made up the table was replaced by different matter. (This judgment can be made to seem more plausible if we imagine that the original particles are replaced by particles with somewhat different properties at somewhat different locations.) But even if we do grant that the table after t is not composed of the same matter as the table before t, that could not be our reason for denying that this is one and the same table, for we have seen reason to think that continuity of material composition is not a necessary condition of identity.[8] Nor could our reason be the lack of causal continuity, if the first version of the

7. If it is held that the causal requirement is still satisfied because the composition of the table after t is caused by the composition of the table before t (I think a dubious formulation), then change the example as follows: The table producer draws particles *randomly* from neighboring areas (simultaneously dispersing the particles in the target location if they are not drawn), and it happened *by chance* that the particles were drawn from the original table, so that we wind up with a table composed of the same particles (arranged by chance in roughly the same way). There still seems to be no doubt that this is the same table, though the causal requirement seems quite definitely not to be satisfied.

8. As Shoemaker himself agrees: see his "The Loose and Popular and the Strict and Philosophical Senses of Identity," in Care and Grimm, *Perception and Personal Identity*, pp. 108–9.

example shows that this is not a necessary condition of identity. But perhaps our reason could be that the *disjunction* of these conditions is necessary for identity; perhaps there must be *either* compositional continuity *or* causal continuity.

Let me not exaggerate my opposition to this suggestion; it may be correct. But I am not convinced. Even in the second version of Shoemaker's example my intuition is that we perhaps *can* treat the tables as identical. The most that I could unreservedly concede is that this is a *borderline case*. Perhaps it would be appropriate in this case to say, "In a sense it's the same table and in a sense it isn't." It does not seem to me clearly *unacceptable* to say, "By an incredible fluke the table survived, because both buttons were pushed at the same time." If someone claims that his intuition says that this clearly *is* unacceptable I would have to wonder whether he has properly distinguished between the question "Is it the same table?" and the question "Is it the same matter?"[9]

I am aware that my intuition about this example may not be universally shared. And I will eventually offer a kind of compromise account which may accommodate differing intuitions about such a case. For the moment, however, I will simply conclude that the SQ conditions may suffice at least up to borderline cases.

Let us now inquire what other combinations of the continuities might suffice for identity. First of all we may wonder whether spatiotemporal continuity by itself (of course relativized to the sortal) might suffice even without qualitative continuity. If we have a spatiotemporally continuous succession of car-stages which suffers some massive qualitative discontinuity would we perhaps still judge it to be the same car? I will not attempt to settle this question.[10] The possibility remains open then that the SQ conditions can be simplified to the single condition of spatiotemporal continuity.

On the other hand it is clear that qualitative continuity by

9. I wonder if Shoemaker was really trying to show that the SQ conditions are not sufficient for the identity of matter. But that point can be conclusively established without appealing to any science fiction examples: see above, pp. 113–19.

10. For a discussion of this question see Quinton, *The Nature of Things*, pp. 67–69.

itself does not suffice for identity. We might have two cars C_1 and C_2 which are qualitatively indistinguishable. A succession of car-stages which combines stages of C_1 with stages of C_2 would be qualitatively continuous but would obviously not correspond to a single car.

It might be suggested that this is because the hybrid succession must compete with both of the successions corresponding to C_1 and C_2, and these win out in virtue of having other continuities in addition to the qualitative one. But suppose that C_1 was destroyed before C_2 was created (out of different material). Then we could prolong the C_1-succession in a qualitatively continuous manner by combining it with the C_2-succession. Obviously we do not do this; we do not identify the car that is destroyed with the car that is later created, even though there is no other identification competing with this one. So it is clear that qualitative continuity by itself amounts to nothing as a sufficient condition of identity.

It seems equally clear that causal continuity does not in general suffice for identity. We can imagine a machine which creates an exact copy of a given car out of new material, destroying the original car in the process. Here there may be the most intimate causal connection between the final stages of the original and the initial stages of the copy. Still there is no inclination to identify the two cars. In this example there was both causal and qualitative continuity; so we see that the conjunction of these two conditions does not suffice for identity.

What about compositional continuity? I think a case can be made for saying that this condition, or some close variant of it, *does* suffice for identity. A car can be taken apart and put back together again, retaining its identity through a lapse of spatio-temporal continuity. In this case we can appeal to continuity of *observable* composition. But it seems plausible that the more general condition is continuity of material composition, whether observable or not. In a famous science fiction example (from the TV show "Star Trek") bodies are "beamed" aboard a spaceship. The observable facts are that some apparatus on the spaceship is in some manner set to the location of the body, whereupon the body vanishes into thin air, and a short while later a similar body materializes on the spaceship. I think that our understanding of this example is probably premised on the assumption that compositional continuity is satisfied, though at a nonobservable level. We can conceive of the body that vanishes as being identical with the body that later materializes, because we assume that (most of) the particles of the first body somehow wind up on the spaceship, where they are again arranged into the form of that body.

In these examples it is perhaps also required that the matter which made up the original body is later arranged in the recomposed body in pretty much the same way as in the original. This might incidentally assure some fairly high degree of qualitative continuity. Furthermore in these examples, and other typical examples, compositional continuity is accompanied by at least some degree of causal continuity: typically there will be some causal connection between the properties of the body prior to decomposition and its properties after recomposition. So perhaps these additional factors should be understood as implicit in the condition of compositional continuity.[11]

The compositional condition complicates our concept of bodily identity in two very important ways. First of all, it relates the identities of such observable bodies as cars, and stones, and trees to theoretical speculations about the underlying reality. This is why our concept of the identity of a car can in principle accommodate such exotic possibilities as a car disappearing in one place and reappearing in another place (cf. the "Star Trek" example). There is an important sense in which our concept of the identity of matter is indefinable; it is doubtful that there are any definite a priori constraints on the identity of matter.[12] The compositional condition thus invests even the identity of a car with a derivative dimension of indefinability.

The second important complication is that the compositional condition can generate *conflict* cases, i.e., cases in which the condition directs us in contradictory ways. The most famous example of this sort is the case of the ship of Theseus.[13] In that case the compositional condition would permit us to make the judgment that the original ship suffered a continuous and total

11. The condition of compositional continuity might also have to be complicated by reference to the *importance* of the parts that are preserved in a compositional change. See above, p. 66.

12. Cf. above, Chapter 4.

13. See above, pp. 68–71.

replacement of its material, and also to make the contradictory judgment that the original ship was later reconstituted by its original material. Perhaps we might favor the first judgment on the grounds that this is bolstered by the SQ conditions as well. (Note how the compositional condition can conflict both with itself and with the SQ conditions.)[14] But I am inclined to doubt that there is a definitively "correct" answer to this question. We can say that the original ship is in a sense identical with one ship, and in a sense identical with the other ship. So in this kind of case we seem to have at worst only a borderline counter-example to the SQ principle.

But I cannot deny the possibility of constructing some exotic conflict examples in which the pull of the compositional condi-tion might strike many as decisively stronger than that of the SQ conditions. One such example might be developed along the following lines. Assuming that our theory of matter might co-herently allow for the discontinuous motion of matter (which I am inclined to think is possible), then we can imagine a situa-tion in which we are able to predict how matter will jump dis-continuously from one place to another. In this situation it might be commonplace to rely on the compositional condition to pre-dict how standard objects like cars jump discontinuously from place to place. Suppose now that in this situation there are two very similar cars, and we are able to predict that the matter which makes up one car will jump discontinuously to the place of the second, while at the same instant the matter which makes up the second car jumps discontinuously to the place of the first (both portions of matter maintaining their forms as cars during this process of displacement). Here the compositional condition dictates the judgment that these cars retain their material com-position while instantaneously exchanging places, whereas the SQ principle implies that the cars stay where they are while in-

14. It is sometimes supposed that even the SQ conditions can give rise to conflict cases if, e.g., a car splits into two like an amoeba. But that is an error. If a car splits into two there will be a moment during the process of splitting when we have a monster object, followed at a later moment by the two resultant cars. First of all it is not clear that the monster object qualifies as a "car," so there may not even be sortal coverage. And certainly the jump from the monster object to each resultant car will not be spatiotemporally or qualitatively continuous.

stantaneously exchanging their matter. In this kind of example I think that many people (if indeed they can accept the premise of the example) might feel that the compositional condition decisively predominates. If such an example can qualify as *clearcut* (i.e., nonborderline) then I shall have to relinquish my commitment to the SQ principle to that extent.

And there are other important complications that I pass over, such as the possibility of taking into account *degrees* of SQ or compositional or causal continuity in attempting to resolve a conflict case. In general I have no very firm position about these conflict cases, except to suggest that by and large they seem to me to be left indeterminate by our ordinary identity concept.

The discussion up to this point suggests the following analysis of the identity of a car:

> *Analysis A*. A succession of car-stages constitutes a persisting car if and only if *either* it satisfies the SQ conditions *or* it satisfies the condition of compositional continuity.

This analysis, as well as those which follow, should be understood as containing the implicit proviso that (with the reservations noted) a case is indeterminate if the specified conditions yield conflicting judgments.

(A possible emendation of Analysis A, which I have been only mildly resisting, is to add the condition of causal continuity to the first disjunct, so that the two sufficient conditions of identity will be (1) SQ continuity together with causal continuity, and (2) compositional continuity. I resist this to the extent of suggesting that the emended and unemended versions may differ only in borderline cases.)[15]

---

15. Analysis A corresponds substantially to the position adopted in Part One; on the possible emendation see Chapter 4, ftn. 14.

It should be noted that even given the emendation conflict cases of the sorts I have mentioned still arise. The example of the ship of Theseus remains unaffected. And in the more exotic example last considered we can easily imagine that the cars interact in such a manner that some properties of both of them after the "jump" causally depend on some previous properties of both of them. (Think of how the temperatures of two objects in contact causally depend on the prior temperatures of both of them.) Indeed we can even imagine that some relationship between the cars causes the instantaneous displacement of their matter. In this case the condition of causal continuity

III. Stereotypes of Identity

I now want to consider a somewhat different approach to these issues. In a number of publications Hilary Putnam has presented a distinctive pattern of analysis which seems to apply to a wide range of concepts.[16] It is worth considering how Putnam's kind of analysis might apply to the concept of identity through time.

Putnam's basic idea is that often the concept of F is associated with a *stereotype* of F, which fixes the reference to a *hidden structure*. The stereotype is defined by some superficially observable characteristics, and the concept refers to the hidden structure via the stereotype.

The term "lemon," for example, is associated with a stereotype consisting of a certain characteristic shape, color, texture, taste, and perhaps observable origin and growth. But the concept of a lemon is not to be equated with the stereotype of a lemon. The connection between the concept and the stereotype is rather to be understood along the following lines:

x is a lemon if and only if x has that (rigidly designated) underlying structure distinctive of most local cases satisfying the lemon-stereotype.

Suppose that S represents the relevant underlying structure common to most of the stereotypical lemons that human beings might have encountered. Then the above definition implies that something is a lemon if and only if it has that structure S.

This account has two kinds of interesting consequences, one about the actual world and another about possible worlds. As regards the actual world, there may be objects that are lemons even though they do not satisfy the stereotype, and objects which are not lemons even though they do satisfy the stereotype. It all depends on whether the object has the hidden structure S, i.e.,

---

would be satisfied by the judgment that accords with the SQ principle, viz. the judgment that the cars stood still and exchanged their matter. We would then have both SQ and causal continuity pitted against compositional (and causal) continuity; many will still feel that compositional continuity wins.

16. Hilary Putnam, "Is Semantics Possible?" "Explanation and Reference," and "The Meaning of 'Meaning,'" all reprinted in *Mind, Language and Reality*.

the structure which is common to most of the objects around here which satisfy the stereotype.

Because "that hidden structure" in the definition is taken rigidly, when we consider whether an object in some counterfactual situation is a lemon we have to ask whether that object has the structure S, i.e., the structure which in *the actual world* corresponds to the stereotype. If there would have been a situation in which all of the objects which satisfy the lemon-stereotype have the hidden structure S' rather than S, then *none* of those objects would have been *lemons* (though they would have had all of the superficial properties of lemons).

Thus according to this account the statement "Most of the objects around here which satisfy the lemon-stereotype are lemons" is a *conceptual truth,* i.e., it follows from the definition of "lemon."[17] But the statement is not *metaphysically necessary* since, as we just saw, there is a possible situation in which it is false. The statement is, in Kripke's terms, an a priori contingency.

On the other hand if S turns out to be the structure shared by most of the local stereotypical lemons, then the statement "Any lemon has S" is metaphysically necessary, for in any possible world whether something is a lemon depends on its having S. But the statement is not a conceptual truth: it does not follow from the concept of a lemon that S is the related structure. The statement, if true, is a posteriori necessary.

Let us now see what happens if we try to apply this pattern of analysis to our concept of the identity of a car. The first point I would suggest is that we take the SQ conditions (relativized to the sortal "car") as defining the stereotype of car-identity. The SQ conditions seem to provide us with our basic *picture* of the persistence of a car. The difficult question is how exactly to relate the stereotype, the picture, to the general concept. If we try to conform as closely as possible to the preceding analysis of "lemon" we wind up with this:

Analysis B: A succession of car-stages constitutes a persisting car if and only if it has that (rigidly designated) underlying

17. There are several complications here which I ignore. One rather obvious question is what we should say if it turns out that there is no underlying structure (nor even some few underlying structures) corresponding to the stereotype. Putnam suggests that in this case the concept is simply equivalent to the stereotype; see "The Meaning of 'Meaning,'" pp. 240–41.

structure distinctive of most local cases satisfying the stereotype of car-identity (where the stereotype is defined by the SQ conditions).

What should we say this underlying structure is? Assuming some standard notions of physics (and ignoring for the moment the kind of comment made by Einstein and Infeld), it seems plausible to identify this underlying structure with *continuity of material composition*. That is, in the stereotypical case of car-identity we have a succession of car-stages, each stage consisting at the underlying level of a swarm of particles of matter, where closely neighboring stages contain almost the same particles arranged in almost the same way. If we assume that compositional continuity is the relevant underlying structure of the stereotypical cases, then Analysis B implies that a given succession of car-stages constitutes a persisting car if and only if it satisfies the compositional condition.

How does this compare to Analysis A? In that analysis there were two independently sufficient conditions of identity, the SQ conditions and the compositional condition. On Analysis B the story is more complicated and in many ways more interesting (though not perhaps more accurate).

According to Analysis A it is a conceptual truth that any succession of car-stages which satisfies the SQ conditions constitutes a persisting car. This is *not* a conceptual truth according to Analysis B. What is a conceptual truth according to the latter analysis is that *most local* successions which satisfy the SQ conditions constitute persisting cars.[18] Analysis B allows for the exceptional case in which, though the stereotypical SQ conditions are satisfied, the relevant underlying structure is absent, and hence the case cannot qualify as one of identity.

According to Analysis A the statement "Any succession of car-stages which satisfies the SQ conditions constitutes a persisting car" is not only a conceptual truth but also metaphysically necessary: the statement holds in any counterfactual situation. This unqualified statement is not, as we just saw, a conceptual truth on Analysis B; nor obviously is it metaphysically necessary. But even

---

18. Here again we would require the stipulation mentioned in ftn. 17, viz. that if it should turn out that there is no relevant hidden structure the concept of persistence collapses into the stereotype.

the qualified statement "Most local successions of car-stages which satisfy the SQ conditions constitute persisting cars" is not necessary on Analysis B, though it is a conceptual truth; the analysis implies that this statement is a priori contingent. For imagine a counterfactual situation in which the cases which satisfy the SQ conditions do not satisfy the condition of compositional continuity. Assuming that compositional continuity is the underlying structure related to the stereotypical cases in the actual world, *none* of those counterfactual cases satisfying the SQ conditions would qualify as cases of identity.

So two ways in which Analysis B departs from Analysis A is that according to the former analysis only the qualified statement is a priori, and even this statement is not metaphysically necessary. And there is a third difference. According to Analysis A it is both a priori and necessary that a case of compositional continuity is a case of identity. According to Analysis B this is not a priori; for it is not a conceptual truth that compositional continuity is the hidden structure related to the stereotypical cases. It may yet turn out that some other structure (e.g., of the sort discussed by Einstein and Infeld) has that status. But if compositional continuity *is* in fact the relevant structure then it is metaphysically necessary that all (and only) cases of compositional continuity are cases of identity. According to Analysis B the connection between compositional continuity and identity is a posteriori necessary.

It should be clear that Analysis B does not have the implausible consequence that our ordinary judgments about bodily identity must in general depend upon some specific theory about the underlying reality. In general we can base ourselves on the conceptual truth that at least most of the stereotypical cases we encounter are cases of identity. The analysis only requires that our concept of identity should incorporate the vague idea of there being a distinctive kind of hidden structure related to the stereotype. Detailed theories about the nature of that structure (e.g., theories about the persistence of matter) only come later, after we have built up sufficient knowledge of the stereotypical cases.

It is evident that Analysis B cannot sustain all of the intuitions that I tried to promote earlier. The analysis will depart from these intuitions with respect to cases in which the SQ conditions are satisfied but the underlying structure is atypical. The second version of Shoemaker's example was such a case. Here the SQ conditions were satisfied but the underlying structure was assumed to involve a wholly atypical lapse of compositional (and causal) continuity. Analysis B would decisively disqualify a judgment of identity in this case, whereas my intuition is that such a judgment would at least be borderline correct.[19]

Let me therefore suggest an emendation of Analysis B, still somewhat in the spirit of Putnam's approach, but more in line with my intuitions:

> *Analysis C*: A succession of car-stages constitutes a persisting car if and only if *either* it satisfies the stereotype of car-identity *or* it has that (rigidly designated) underlying structure distinctive of most local cases satisfying the stereotype (where the stereotype is defined in terms of the SQ conditions).

Analysis C implies that it is both a priori and necessary that any case which satisfies the SQ conditions is a case of identity (with the exception of conflict cases which remain indeterminate). In this respect it is just like Analysis A. The difference between the two analyses concerns the second condition. In Analysis A this condition is specified as compositional continuity, whereas in Analysis C the condition is specified to be whatever is the hidden structure generally characteristic of the stereotypical cases. It cannot be determined a priori what the nature of that hidden structure is. If this structure *is* compositional continuity then it will follow from Analysis C that it is metaphysically necessary that any case of compositional continuity is a case of identity. But this is only an a posteriori truth.

The difference between Analysis A and Analysis C is perhaps not very great. But Analysis C, in contrast to Analysis A, invests our identity concept with a kind of open-endedness or indefiniteness which may seem intuitively appealing. Suppose it turns out that the theoretically correct description of the underlying struc-

19. Note that Analysis B would not even allow it to be a conceptual truth that the presence of the four continuities suffices for identity (since these continuities may not typify the stereotypical cases), a consequence which I think many (including Shoemaker) would find unacceptable.

ture of cars and other observable bodies is not in terms of persisting matter, but is rather in terms of some field structures (as
in the Einstein-Infeld remark), or perhaps in terms as yet not
conceived of by anyone. The second condition of Analysis C
would enable our identity concept to absorb these new theoretical structures, whatever they might turn out to be. Whether the
structure corresponding to the stereotype is continuity of material composition, or some facts about fields, or some facts as
yet undreamed of, that structure is according to Analysis C a
sufficient condition of bodily identity.

The element of indefiniteness in Analysis C can be brought
out by considering again the science fiction fantasy in which
bodies are "beamed" aboard spaceships. I suggested earlier that
we understand this fantasy by conceiving that the particles which
make up the beamed body travel (perhaps discontinuously) to the
spaceship. And I think it is indeed plausible to suppose that most
people would conceive of the case in that way. But what about
a small child, or even an extremely uneducated adult, who may
have no clear idea, or perhaps no idea at all, of there being any
such things as invisible particles which make up a body? Surely
it would seem that such a person could still understand the
fantasy. Analysis C can account for this fact. All that is required
for understanding the fantasy is that one should vaguely conceive
of there being some kind of underlying reality characteristic of
the stereotypical cases, which is in some manner present in the
beaming case. It is unnecessary that one should have any definite
ideas about what that underlying reality is like.

I think our ordinary concept of the identity of a car might
plausibly be placed somewhere between Analysis B and Analysis
C. The latter analysis is more elementary, less theoretical, than
the former; for in the latter analysis the superficially observable
SQ conditions, which define the stereotype, suffice for identity,
whereas in the former analysis only the associated hidden structure suffices. I think our ordinary concept of the identity of a car
may be said to vacillate vaguely between the relatively elementary sense defined by Analysis C and the relatively theoretical
sense defined by Analysis B. And this kind of vagueness may
characterize many of our concepts. For example, our concept of
a lemon may vacillate between a more elementary sense in which
the presence of the stereotypical properties suffices and the more

theoretical sense defined earlier, in which only the presence of the associated hidden structure suffices.[20]

If this is correct then it follows that the SQ conditions suffice at least for typical cases. Where the SQ conditions are satisfied but the relevant hidden structure is absent, then we have a case for which the two competing senses, the more elementary and the more theoretical, yield different judgments, and perhaps either judgment is acceptable.

We can say something, I think, about the kinds of conversational contexts which are likely to encourage someone to employ the more elementary sense, or the more theoretical sense. If a philosopher presents us with a complicated example, and asks us to consider what identity judgment is appropriate in that example, then since we know that philosophy is a serious business that aims at deep truths, in considering the example we are naturally going to be propelled in the direction of the more theoretical sense approximating to Analysis B. Indeed the solemnity of the philosopher's question "Is x *really* identical with y?" has often propelled a response at a level of theoreticalness much beyond that of analysis B. I have in mind those philosophers (such as Reid, and Butler, and Chisholm)[21] who have maintained that "strictly speaking" bodily identity requires identity of matter, so that, for example, a car cannot survive the loss of a hubcap. This response, I would say, simply *replaces* our ordinary concept of the identity of observable bodies, like cars and tables and trees, with the quite different concept of the identity of the matter which makes up these bodies. On the other hand if we respond to a philosopher's identity-question by employing the relatively theoretical sense of Analysis B, then I think we are still within the vague bounds of the ordinary concept. We are merely pushing the concept in a certain direction, in the theo-

20. It may be possible to combine Putnam's relatively theoretical definition of "lemon" with the elementary definition of "the persistence of a lemon." If S represents the hidden structure associated with the lemon-stereotype then Putnam's definition implies that a succession of lemon-stages must be a succession of stages of bodies with the structure S. We can still say, in accordance with Analysis C, that a sufficient condition for a succession of lemon-stages to constitute a persisting lemon is that it satisfy the SQ conditions. There are to be sure complications here, which could be worked out in different ways.

21. Cf. above, pp. 161–62.

retical direction induced by the solemnity of the question. That may be alright so long as we do not conclude that there is something *wrong* with employing our identity concept in the more elementary sense of Analysis C. Indeed in the most typical conversational contexts, which tend to be casual and theoretically carefree, the more elementary sense may well predominate.

If philosophizing has a tendency to propell us toward the more theoretical sense of bodily identity then obviously scientific theorizing will have the same effect. A biologist who theorizes about the persistence and change of a tree will perhaps be likely to employ a concept of the identity of a tree corresponding to Analysis B (with the sortal "tree" replacing the sortal "car"). Again I would maintain that there are more casual levels of discourse about trees for which the more elementary identity concept may legitimately predominate.

It would of course be possible to define an identity concept even more elementary than that corresponding to Analysis C. The most obvious possibility is a concept which is simply equivalent to the stereotype, a concept, that is, for which the SQ conditions are not only sufficient but also necessary. A somewhat more complicated possibility would add the sufficient condition of continuity of *observable* composition, but still with no regard at all for the underlying reality even as a sufficient condition. It may be that these concepts can be said to operate at some very primitive levels of thought; but it seems fairly clear that they are not dominant at any ordinary level (though for all practical purposes there is a quite negligible difference between either of these concepts, especially the latter, and the ordinary concept which acknowledges the underlying reality). A more important point is that the discussion of this whole chapter has assumed a concept of identity relativized to such sortals as "car," "table," and "tree." However, the basic core of our identity concept can be understood without appeal to such sortals; at the most basic level the condition of *minimizing change* takes the place of sortal coverage.[22] In terms of the notion of a stereotype we might say that our most basic stereotype of bodily identity is the picture of a succession of body-stages which satisfies the SQ conditions while minimizing change. At a level of knowledge which allows for the

22. See above, Chapter 3.

application of sortals, however, this most basic stereotype gives way to the more refined sortal-relativized stereotypes.

To summarize: I have considered in this chapter three closely related analyses of our concept of bodily identity. One may regard these as providing competing accounts, or, I think more plausibly (at least for the last two analyses), as characterizing different senses of identity, each with some legitimate claim to ordinary usage. In any case the point which emerges clearly, and which is common to all of these analyses, is that there is the most intimate connection between our concept of the identity of a specified sort of body and the idea of a spatiotemporally and qualitatively continuous succession of body-stages of that sort. It is implicit in the identity concept that the presence of a succession satisfying those conditions constitutes at least a prima facie basis, and perhaps even a conclusive basis, for making a judgment of identity.

8

A Sense of Unity

PHILOSOPHERS HAVE often raised questions about our concept of the unity of a thing. Most typically what is sought is an analysis of what our concept of unity consists in. The answer to this question commonly takes the form of citing various conditions that seem to provide a definition of our judgments of unity. These conditions may be said to constitute our criteria of unity, our criteria of identity.

The question I want to raise in the present chapter is somewhat different from this typical one. Suppose that we have already ascertained what our criteria of unity are. Then I want to ask why it is that we employ just those criteria rather than others. What determines us to base our judgments of unity on just those conditions?

I. Criteria of Unity

Let me present an example to illustrate the difference between these two kinds of questions: the one I am asking and the more typical one. Suppose that you have a tree in your backyard and that next to the tree there stands a table. Common sense would judge that the tree is a single object and the table is a single object. Each of these objects is of course *composite*; the tree, for example, is composed of a trunk, some branches, twigs, leaves, and so on. Now something that common sense would definitely not judge is that there is a single object that is composed of the tree together with the table. If I am, say, touching the tree and you are touching the table, common sense would not say that there is some single object that you and I are both touching. But why not? Why should we not say that the tree and the table add up to a unitary object?

At one level the answer to this question would consist in citing relevant criteria of unity through space, i.e., criteria that determine whether or not an aggregate of matter can properly be said to add up to a single thing. In the case under discussion two relevant criteria would seem to be *spatial connectedness* and *dynamic cohesiveness*. Generally an object must be spatially connected, in the sense that any of its parts can be connected by a continuous curve whose points all touch the object. And generally an object must be cohesive, in the sense that all its parts tend to remain together under various pressures. I do not mean to suggest that these two conditions (connectedness and cohesiveness) are strictly necessary for an object's unity in all imaginable circumstances; nor am I suggesting that they are sufficient for unity. But these conditions are pretty likely to figure in any general analysis of an object's unity through space, and with respect to our simple example they seem enough to rule out the tree-*cum*-table as a unitary object.[1]

At one level, then, we can explain by appealing to criteria why the tree and the table do not add up to one object. The question I want to raise, however, is why these criteria function the way they do. What is it that induces common sense to base a judgment of unity on the particular conditions of connectedness and cohesiveness? Why allow *those* conditions to dictate the matter? Why does common sense not choose some other criteria of unity, criteria that might allow for the judgment that the tree and the table compose a single object (where this object happens to be disconnected and noncohesive)?

Let me extend this example a bit, so as to bring identity through time into play. The tree is not just spatially composite; it is also, in a sense, temporally composite. Insofar as the tree persists through time, it (or its history) can be thought of as comprising a succession of temporary stages, where these stages can be delimited in any number of ways. (For example, we can

1. On our criteria of unity through space, see above, Chapter 3, Sections V and VI.

think of the tree as combining an early stage in which it is short followed by a later stage in which it is tall, or as combining stages in which it is in bloom with stages in which it is not in bloom.) And the same can be said for the table; this too is temporally composite. If, however, we were to combine in thought some early stage of the table with some later stage of the tree we would not, at least by the lights of common sense, arrive at a unitary persisting thing. In the case I am imagining, where a tree and a table are situated together in a normal way, common sense could not even take seriously the idea that some single persisting thing is first a table and then a tree. But why not? Why should we not judge in this case that there is a single persisting object that combines a table-stage and a tree-stage?

Again, the answer at one level consists in citing criteria, in this case criteria of unity through time. Two criteria that seem to suffice for the case (though they do not suffice for all cases) are *qualitative continuity* and *spatiotemporal continuity*.[2] If we tried to think of there being a single object that is first a table and then a tree we should have to say that this object changed discontinuously, as regards both its qualities and its location. Our criteria of unity through time do not (in general) allow us to say this.

And again, my question is: What induces common sense to credit those particular criteria of unity through time? Why not choose other criteria which might accommodate the judgment that a table changed discontinuously into a tree?

There are philosophers, notably W. V. Quine, who in fact recommend a revision in our commonsense notion of an object which would have precisely the effect of accommodating the judgments that I have just instanced as conflicting with our ordinary criteria of unity. In terms of Quine's revised concept of an object we would indeed say, in the imagined example, that there is at a given moment some object that is composed of the table and the tree, and that there is over a period of time an object that is first a table and then a tree. On Quine's proposal an object "comprises simply the content, however heterogeneous, of some portion of space-time, however disconnected and gerry-

2. Cf. above, Chapters 1–3, *passim,* and Chapter 7.

mandered."[3] Any space-time portion of reality qualifies as an object, in Quine's terms. But this technical notion of an object is crucially different from the ordinary notion, as Quine himself amply stresses. In terms of the ordinary notion only a select few space-time portions qualify as objects, namely, those which satisfy our criteria of unity. It is the ordinary notion that concerns me. Quine often marks off the ordinary notion from his technical one by using the word "body" for the ordinary notion. Hence he says: "Man is a body-minded animal."[4] In these terms what I am asking for is an explanation of why common sense is body-minded.

What is at stake in this question is not merely the use of two or three words (such as "body," "object," "thing"), but a whole way of thinking. Exactly how to characterize that way of thinking is itself an essential part of the philosophical difficulty. But one can say, to begin with, that the category of a body seems to constitute for common sense the primary way of breaking up the world into units. And this category is defined in terms of various specific and complicated criteria of unity, for example, spatial connectedness, dynamic cohesiveness, spatiotemporal and qualitative continuity. The question, then, is why common sense should divide reality up in just that particular way.

II. Unity and Similarity

A possible answer to this question, which I want to consider and defend, is that we think of the world in terms of our criteria of bodily unity because we are innately disposed to think in this way. According to this hypothesis, a sense of bodily unity is part of our inborn constitution, and this is what determines us to interpret our experience in the way we do.

This hypothesis has something in common with Kant's view about the a priori category of substance. I want to stress, however, two differences between the hypothesis under consideration and Kant's view. First of all, Kant had little, if anything, to say about specific criteria of bodily unity. In fact Kant's category

3. Quine, *Word and Object*, p. 171.
4. Quine, *The Roots of Reference*, p. 54.

of substance is not equivalent to the commonsense idea of a body. Ordinary bodies, like trees and tables, are created and destroyed, but Kant's idea of substance referred to the underlying matter that was supposed to persist forever. The second difference is that Kant maintained that his category of substance is a necessary ingredient of understanding. This necessity claim is no part of my hypothesis. My hypothesis claims only that, as a matter of contingent fact, human beings are innately disposed to interpret their experience in a certain way.

This hypothesis is more closely related to some of Chomsky's ideas about innate grammatical schemata. And it is even closer to the views expressed by gestalt psychologists like Wolfgang Köhler, who have maintained that, as a matter of empirical fact, our sensory fields are "naturally" and "spontaneously" organized in terms of distinctive kinds of units.[5]

I want to broach this idea by way of an analogy. I want to compare the idea of an *innate sense of unity* to the more familiar philosophical idea of an *innate sense of similarity*. It has been persuasively argued by Quine, and also by Anthony Quinton, that our grasp of general concepts must ultimately be rooted in an innate tendency to classify objects in certain definite ways.[6] In order for a child to acquire the use of a general term, he must be able to extrapolate from observed cases of the term's application to new cases. This extrapolation evidently requires that the child have some basis for deciding which new cases go together with the observed cases. At least with respect to the most elementary vocabulary, the basis for this decision would apparently have to be innate. The idea here is not that our fully developed scheme of classifications depends on nothing but our primitive classificatory impulses. Perhaps the scheme is eventually affected by various practical and theoretical needs. At bottom, however, there must be the innate tendency to classify things in certain ways rather than others.

Quine sometimes refers to this innate tendency as an innate "sense of similarity"; sometimes he refers to it as an innate

5. Köhler, *Gestalt Psychology*, chaps. 5 and 6.
6. See W. V. Quine, "Natural Kinds," in *Ontological Relativity and Other Essays* (Columbia University Press, N.Y., 1969), p. 116ff; *Word and Object*, p. 83ff.; *The Roots of Reference*, p. 19; and Quinton, *The Nature of Things*, pp. 261–65.

"quality space." It should be borne in mind that the first expression ("sense of similarity") is not meant to imply any special views about the possibility of reducing properties to similarity relations; and the expression "quality space" applies not just to qualities properly speaking, since all properties, including relational properties, would have to be treated in the same manner. The general point is simply that we are innately disposed to classify in certain ways rather than others.

Now for common sense the most basic thought about physical reality is the thought that some specified body has some specified property. The first ingredient of this thought (the specification of a body) is linked to our criteria of bodily unity, and the second ingredient (the specification of a property) is linked to our principles for classifying bodies. We have just seen that, according to Quine and others, the classificatory ingredient is rooted in the innate disposition to classify in distinctive ways. One can scarcely resist the speculation that perhaps the other ingredient, that related to our criteria of unity, is likewise rooted in the innate disposition to adopt certain criteria of unity rather than others. The general scheme we then wind up with is this: As our innate sense of similarity stands to our principles for classifying bodies, so does our innate sense of unity stand to our criteria of unity for bodies.

It will be instructive to try to make out what Quine's reaction might be to this proposal. Some of his remarks may certainly seem to suggest that he too believes in an innate sense of unity. He says that "body-unifying considerations, though complex, are rooted in instinct,"[7] and he refers to our "instinctive body-mindedness."[8] But this is puzzling, since the view standardly attributed to Quine is that, besides such obvious general faculties as perception, intelligence, and motor behavior, quality space is essentially the only innate endowment that can confidently be related to the process of learning language. Not that Quine is at all adamant about this; he seems quite open to other possibilities, even perhaps to some of Chomsky's suggestions.[9] But it would certainly be extremely odd to attribute to Quine the unheralded

7. Quine, *The Roots of Reference*, p. 55.
8. Ibid., p. 56.
9. See Quine's "Philosophical Progress in Language Theory," in H. E. Kiefer and M. K. Munitz, ed., *Language, Belief, and Metaphysics*, p. 6.

position that working side by side with the language-learner's innate quality space is the quite distinct disposition to adopt certain identity criteria. That is in fact the position that I want to maintain, but I have to doubt that this is Quine's position.

Actually if we look more closely at that section in *The Roots of Reference* from which I previously quoted, we find that when Quine refers to our "instinctive body-mindedness" he probably does not mean to introduce an innate disposition distinct from our sense of similarity. Rather he seems to be suggesting that our body-mindedness is itself the result of our innate sense of similarity.

Thanks to [the child's] instinctive body-mindedness, he is an apt pupil when the general terms are terms for bodies. He is able to appreciate not only that the second-order similarity of a dog to a dog exceeds that of a dog to a rabbit, but also that the latter in turn exceeds that of a dog to an apple or buckle. . . . And then there is the yet slighter degree of second-order similarity, residing in just those very general body-unifying considerations that preserve the identity of each dog, each rabbit, each apple, each buckle, in short each body. This would be a second-order similarity basis for the child's ostensive learning of the general term "body" itself, or "thing," to take the likelier word.[10]

What Quine seems to be saying here is that our "instinctive body-mindedness" is actually nothing more than our disposition to appreciate the complicated similarity relations that obtain between those space-time portions of reality which we count as bodies.

But there is something wrong here. To operate with the ordinary concept of bodily unity is not just a matter of appreciating various similarities between those portions of reality which qualify as bodies. Imagine someone who did *not* operate with the ordinary concept, but who operated instead with that technical notion of an object which, as I mentioned earlier, Quine ultimately favors over the ordinary notion. Someone who operated with this revised concept would be treating all portions of reality, whether disconnected or whatever, as units on a logically equal footing. But certainly he might very well appreciate the relevant similarities between those select portions of reality which common sense dignifies as bodies. To be body-minded, in the way

10. Quine, *The Roots of Reference*, p. 56.

that common sense is body-minded, is to adopt an ontology that *excludes* all of those portions of reality which do not qualify as bodies. Common sense simply does not credit such portions of reality. Our commonsense adoption of this exclusionary ontology cannot be regarded as merely a corollary of our disposition to appreciate certain similarities.

Perhaps someone will be tempted to suggest that we exclude portions of reality other than bodies because our sense of similarity provides no basis for comparing or contrasting such portions of reality, and hence we cannot classify them in any way. But this is wrong. If we did credit such portions of reality as units we certainly could classify them in various ways. If, say, there is a brown table and a brown tree in my backyard and there is a brown table and a brown tree in your backyard, then we could say that my table-*cum*-tree is similar to your table-*cum*-tree at least with respect to the property of being brown, or, even more obviously, with respect to the property of being a table-*cum*-tree (i.e., the property of being exhaustively composed of a table and a tree). In these respects both items could be said to contrast with any table-*cum*-tree that is not brown, or with any chair-*cum*-tree. Of course we do not ordinarily draw any such comparisons and contrasts. This is because we do not ordinarily credit any such unit as a table-*cum*-tree. But that fact is in no way explained by our sense of similarity.

It is unclear, then, what connection Quine intends to educe between our body-mindedness and our sense of similarity. I think that part of the trouble here is that Quine does not distinguish between two questions. One is a question about why our language is the way it is; the other is a question about how our language is learned. The first question is: "Why does ordinary language contain just these particular criteria of unity?" The second question is: "How do children learn these criteria of unity?"

It is the first question that I raised at the outset of this chapter. It was this question that I also expressed by asking why it is that common sense is body-minded. Now what we have just seen is that Quine certainly offers no answer to this question. There is no way that a sense of similarity can be seen as delivering common sense into body-mindedness.

On the other hand Quine may have provided a viable answer

to the second question, about how a child acquires the criteria of unity implicit in our language. The child must learn to distinguish between those portions of reality which do, and those which do not, satisfy the criteria. This he may be able to do, so long as his classificatory impulses are attuned to the complex considerations that enter into these criteria. That is, if the child's sense of similarity reveals a general contrast between what qualifies in our language as a unitary body and what does not, he may be in the position to imbibe the rule that only the bodies are referred to as units, the rest being excluded. Thus he may be able to pick up the body-minded way of talking. There are many complications here, of course, as Quine readily admits. But the general idea may seem workable. What cannot be explained along these lines, however, is why the language, which is being passed on to the child, contains just those criteria of unity.

III. Conventionalism

The answer to this question that I am advocating is that our language contains those criteria of unity because of our innate disposition to see the world in a certain way, where this disposition must be distinguished from our sense of similarity. Now one possible alternative to this answer would be to maintain that there is in fact no reason why our language had to contain just those criteria of unity, but that this is nothing more than an arbitrary convention of language. Our ordinary body-mindedness, according to this "conventionalist" position, is merely one scheme for conceptually dividing the world into units, and any number of other schemes might have done just as well. The scheme that we have gets passed on from generation to generation, in the manner suggested by Quine.

At the very outset of Köhler's discussion of the topic of unity in his book *Gestalt Psychology,* he peremptorily dismisses this conventionalist alternative in the following words:

On the desk before me I find quite a number of circumscribed units or things: a piece of paper, a pencil, an eraser, a cigarette, and so forth. The existence of these visual things involves two factors. What is included in a thing becomes a unit, and this unit is segregated from its surroundings. *In order to satisfy myself that this is more than a verbal affair,* I may try to form other units in which parts of a visual thing and parts of its environment are put together. In some cases such an attempt will end in complete failure.[11]

I think we may assume that a case of "complete failure" in Köhler's terms would occur if we tried to see a tree, or some part of it, as forming a unit together with a nearby table, or some part of it. Köhler's line of reasoning seems to be as follows. I cannot get myself to see the tree and the table as forming a unit, though I can of course easily utter the words "The tree and the table form a unit." This shows that a judgment of unity is "more than a verbal affair," more than an arbitrary linguistic convention. Unity is something that we experience; it is, as Köhler says a few sentences later, a "visual fact."

The conventionalist is not likely to be convinced by this argument. The issue is not whether we experience unity; obviously we do. As I look around me I can see that some portions of the scene add up to a unitary object and some do not. This the conventionalist would not deny. His suggestion, however, is that the way that I experience unity is determined by the arbitrary conventions of my *primary language*, i.e., the language I habitually speak and in terms of which I think. Of course I cannot alter my experience merely by mouthing some *strange* sentence (e.g., "The tree and the table make up one thing"), because it is my primary language that matters. Hence Köhler's stark dichotomy between "visual facts" and "verbal affairs" does not speak to the issue.

Köhler's failure to address the possible influence of language on our experience is a flaw in his whole treatment of sensory organization. Some of his most impressive observations pertain to the way that we see things as forming groups or clusters, a phenomenon which he sometimes refers to as the formation of "group-units." Though this phenomenon of "group unity" is not directly relevant to the topic of bodily unity under discussion, it may serve to highlight the problematical relationship between our language and the structure of our experience. Köhler points out that, when we look at Figure 1, we see two groups of dots, each group containing three dots. We do not see three groups of two dots each, or two groups divided in some other way. What we see very clearly are two groups of three dots each. Here

11. Köhler, *Gestalt Psychology*, pp. 137–38; my italics.

Fig. 1

the phenomenological datum is so striking that one is immediately inclined to share Köhler's assumption that our language can have nothing to do with the matter.[12]

But is this really so clear? Consider that in order for us to describe our experience of Figure 1 we must make use of the English word "group" (or some equivalent word like "cluster," "collection," "arrangement"). Two *groups* are what (we say) we experience. We must, then, have learned at some point what the criteria are for applying the English word "group," where these criteria presumably coincide with just those "principles of grouping" which gestalt psychologists try to elicit. Is it not possible that, in learning how to use the word "group," we learned these principles of grouping, and that, had we spoken a different kind of language, we might have experienced Figure 1 quite differently? I am not saying that this is plausible; I doubt that it is. But the question needs to be focused on properly.

I would like to apply some of these points to the topic of unity through time, a topic which Köhler essentially ignores. There is a comment that Sydney Shoemaker makes about unity through time which seems to parallel Köhler's dismissal of conventionalism:

It is a striking fact that motion, though it involves the persistence through time of the moving object, is often directly observed rather than inferred. . . . And I think it is partly because there is an experience of motion that spatiotemporal continuity occupies the central role it does as a criterion of identity. . . . It does not seem to be just a matter of convention that we use spatiotemporal continuity as a criterion of identity. On the contrary, when I see motion (as opposed to

12. See Köhler, ibid., p. 142.

inferring it) there seems to be no way in which I could describe what I see except by saying "It (or: something) is moving," and in saying this I imply the persistence of something through time.[13]

What does Shoemaker mean when he says that *what I see* could only be described in terms of the ordinary proposition "It (or: something) is moving?" Here the expression "what I see" has the characteristic kind of ambiguity that Wittgenstein discussed under the heading of "seeing as." [14] Of course if I am asked to describe the *way* I ordinarily experience a moving object I must employ just those ordinary notions which are constitutive of my ordinary experience. But the conventionalist would hold that, had we learned a different kind of language, with different identity criteria, we might have experienced a moving object in a radically different way (under a radically different "aspect"). Shoemaker's comments merely dismiss this possibility.

To flesh out the conventionalist's point we would have to sketch an alternative language, one which did not make use of our ordinary identity criteria, and explain how the world might have been experienced in terms of that language. Strange languages, of the general sort required, are of course not unknown to philosophical literature. An alternative language that is especially relevant to the present purpose is one that employs Quine's technical notion of an object, a notion I have mentioned several times before. From the vantage point of that "space-time language," any space-time portion of reality, however disconnected or noncohesive, qualifies as a unitary object. The space-time language is, in an important sense, a *language without criteria of unity*. In the sense that a club that allows anyone to join has no criteria of membership, a conceptual scheme that allows any space-time portion to qualify as a unit can be said to have no criteria of unity. What would the world look like from the space-time standpoint?

Well, in a sense everything remains the same. If there is a mouse moving across the floor, then, from the space-time vantage point, there is that particular spatially and temporally extended chunk of reality which corresponds to common sense's moving

13. Shoemaker, *Self-Knowledge and Self-Identity*, pp. 203–4.
14. Ludwig Wittgenstein, *Philosophical Investigations* (The Macmillan Co., N. Y., 1953), pp. 193–214.

mouse. But that chunk of reality would be seen as crisscrossing and overlapping a myriad of other "objects," such as an object that consists of an early stage of the mouse together with a later stage of a nearby table, or an object that consists of an early stage of the mouse together with a later stage of the mouse's head. Hence that space-time chunk of reality which corresponds to common sense's moving mouse would not *stand out* as it does for common sense, because it would be seen as embedded in a reality swarming and whirling with an endless number and variety of objects corresponding to every shift in one's attention. There would scarcely be, from this standpoint, a "moving object" in anything like the ordinary sense.

This description of the space-time standpoint pretty quickly fades into impressionism. But that is to be expected on any account since we are trying to construct a language that goes against the deepest habits of our thought. What the conventionalist would insist is that, if we had learned that language in childhood as our primary language, we could have seen the world that way.

Now my aim is not to defend conventionalism, but only to try to get somewhat clearer as to what the issues are. Actually, as I stated earlier, I favor the position that our criteria of unity are rooted in an innate disposition, what I called our "sense of unity." This seems to be Köhler's position, and it is also, I believe, implicit in Shoemaker's remarks. I think that what is really behind Köhler's and Shoemaker's abrupt dismissal of the conventionalist idea is the intuition that this idea is too incredible to be taken seriously. And it does indeed seem to me intuitively incredible that, had I only been trained to speak differently, my experience of unity might have been completely different. Still, it would be better not to have to rely entirely on this intuition, but to have some argument to lean on.

One possible argument against conventionalism would be of an anthropological sort. If it could be established that every language known to us contains criteria of unity essentially like ours, then this would evidently be a problem for the conventionalist. Of course, if a philosopher holds, as Quine apparently does, that how we translate a foreign language (how we choose a "translation manual") is itself (something like) a convention, then it seems that we could never hope to establish, as a factual matter, that our criteria of unity are universal. But I am assuming, as I think most philosophers would, that it is a factual question, and in principle an answerable one, whether other people operate with a concept of bodily unity like ours. If, then, an affirmative answer to this question were forthcoming, this would seem to be a strong objection to the view that our criteria of unity are merely arbitrary conventions.[15]

Another line of attack against the conventionalist, which I will take up presently, might draw on speculations about how children see the world before they learn a language. Before pursuing that point, however, I want to consider another possibility that is found in Köhler's discussion.

IV. An "Empiricist" Explanation

Interestingly enough, although Köhler immediately dismisses the conventionalist approach, he addresses himself at length to the "empiricist" (or, as Köhler calls it, the "empirist") explanation that our judgments of unity are based on previous learning.[16] What "previous learning" must mean here, if this position is to be distinguished from conventionalism, is learning about the world rather than learning about language. The empiricist position, in the sense relevant to Köhler's discussion, is that the criteria of unity in our language are neither innately determined nor arbitrarily conventional, but are rather the result of our having derived these criteria from something that we learned about the world. As against this, Köhler wants to argue that our criteria of unity are innate rather than learned and that,

15. But perhaps not a decisive objection: see Hilary Putnam's suggestion that perhaps all languages have a common origin, in "The 'Innateness Hypothesis' and Explanatory Models in Linguistics," *Synthese*, 7, 1 (March 1967), p. 18.
16. For his (somewhat unclear) distinction between the two terms "empiricist" and "empirist," see Köhler, *Gestalt Psychology*, p. 113. I will use the more familiar word "empiricist" to signify the third alternative to the conventionalist and innateness positions that have been discussed, though obviously an "empiricist," in some more general sense, could easily hold either of these latter two positions. (Cf. Quine's remarks about "empiricism" in the passage cited in ftn. 9, above.)

therefore, our ordinary experience of unity is elementary rather than derivative.

The reference to previous learning can still be interpreted in two ways. It might mean that each human being must derive the criteria of unity from something that he learns about the world; or it may mean that prehistoric people over the millenia derived the criteria from what they learned about the world, and then passed these criteria down to us through our language. On either interpretation the essential difficulty is to explain how our criteria of unity could have been derived from anything learned about the world.

A crude but not unfamiliar explanation is depicted by Köhler in the following words: "Since early childhood we have often observed that sets of sensations which have approximately the same color, and differ in this respect from their environment, tend to behave as units, i.e., to move and be moved, to appear and disappear, at the same time. Such is the case with stones, with papers, with plates, with shoes, with many animals, with the leaves of plants. . . . It is only an example of the well known generalizing power of memory if, as a result of such experiences, we treat all homogeneously colored areas as units."[17]

Köhler's own critique of this position is quite complicated and relies on a variety of somewhat specialized phenomenological data. But it seems that his discussion overlooks the obvious and decisive objection to the proffered explanation.

The explanation is premised on our having often observed that certain "sets of sensations . . . tend to behave as units." Of course one would immediately like to know how the word "sensation" is being used here. But, even more to the point, we need to ask how the idea of something "behaving as a unit" can possibly operate within this explanation. Something behaves as a unit if its parts move together, appear and disappear together, and, in general, are causally interdependent. This is essentially the condition that I earlier called "dynamic cohesiveness." So the idea is that we treat certain conditions (such as color homogeneity) as criteria of unity because we have learned to associate those conditions with dynamic cohesivenes. But why, then, do we treat dynamic cohesiveness as a criterion of unity? How did we ever

17. Köhler, *Gestalt Psychology*, p. 141.

learn *that*? Evidently not the slightest gesture is being made to answer this question.

Furthermore, to make matters much worse, the criterion of dynamic cohesiveness itself presupposes various other criteria of unity. To judge that the parts of a thing move together we must be able to trace those parts through time. For this we require various criteria of unity through time (e.g., qualitative and spatiotemporal continuity). Hence the proffered explanation of how we derive our criteria of unity really presupposes many of these criteria from the start.

When one reflects on these difficulties it becomes clear that there cannot be any remotely straightforward way of explaining how our criteria of unity might have resulted from previous learning. The sort of "empiricist" who believes in such an explanation must describe an elementary level of experience which does not already presuppose our ordinary criteria of unity. He must then go on to explain how at that level we learn something about the world which somehow gets us to adopt these ordinary criteria. It is far from clear how one could even begin to formulate such an account.

Traditionally, sense-data languages and the like were often taken to provide a level of experiential judgment more elementary (more "immediate") than that of common sense. It is not clear, however, that sense-data descriptions can have any bearing on the present topic. For one thing, these descriptions require criteria of unity for sense data, and these criteria seem generally to be simply borrowed haphazardly from our ordinary criteria of bodily unity. Futhermore, the sense-data maneuver relates to the "problem of the external world," which is not the problem we are discussing. When I originally introduced the case of the table and the tree, my question was not "How can I be sure that this is not a hallucination?" or "How do I know that this sort of scene ever exists unperceived?" but rather "How do I know what criteria to employ in dividing the scene into units?" This latter question pertains to the external world, and traditional sense-data dialectics about how we get to external reality seem quite irrelevant to answering the question.

We might try to think of the space-time language as providing a level that is elementary in a sense relevant to the present discussion. For, as I explained earlier, the space-time language might be said to contain no criteria of unity, since at that level we would not exclude any portion of reality from qualifying as a unit. Perhaps we might then focus on the following question. Suppose that we (as infants or as prehistoric people) started out by experiencing the world from the space-time vantage point. Could we at that level have discovered something about the world which would have taught us to adopt our ordinary criteria of bodily unity? That is, could we have discovered something that would have induced us to convert to commonsense body-mindedness?

It seems fairly clear that purely theoretical motives could not provide this inducement. Neither science nor metaphysics, the two repositories of good theory, have ever been much enthralled by our commonsense criteria of unity. This relates to the point that I made earlier vis-à-vis Kant: that the commonsense concept of a body cannot be equated with the scientist's or metaphysician's concept of underlying matter. A creature with purely theoretical needs, who started out without any criteria of unity, might possibly develop some concept of matter conservation, or he might plunge directly into the physics of fields and space-time manifolds. At any rate, he could scarcely have any reason to take a detour through the specific conceptual concoction that constitutes commonsense body-mindedness.

A more likely suggestion would be that practical rather than purely theoretical needs might motivate the adoption of our ordinary criteria of bodily unity. Such a suggestion seems rather common in pragmatist literature. For example, William James says: "But what are things? Nothing . . . but special groups of sensible qualities, which happen practically or esthetically to interest us, to which we therefore give substantive names, and which we exalt to this exclusive status of independence and dignity."[18] The hint of phenomenalism in James's remark is not relevant to the present issue. What is relevant is James's suggestion that our practical (and aesthetic) interests are what induce us to "dignify" certain portions of reality as unitary things. Translated into the model I am considering, James's idea is that,

18. William James, *The Principles of Psychology* (Henry Holt and Co., N. Y., 1890), I, p. 285.

if we had originally started out with the space-time standpoint (i.e., without any criteria of unity), our practical concerns would eventually convert us to body-mindedness.

I do not think that James's suggestion can withstand careful reflection. Our concerns and interests are almost never directed toward objects taken one at a time, but are directed rather toward a multiplicity of objects related in various complicated ways. A typical concern, as ordinarily conceived, would be to alter the relations between objects, say, to bring them closer together or farther apart, to attach or detach them, to replace one with the other, and so on. But any such concern might be said to embrace that whole portion of reality which includes those objects or their relevant stages. If, for example, I want to bring a chair nearer to a table, the target of my concern might be described as that space-time chunk of reality which includes the table and the chair (or perhaps their stages during the period when their increased proximity is of concern to me). One might say roughly that my concern here is to replace a wider or less compact table-*cum*-chair with a narrower or more compact table-*cum*-chair. Of course that is not how I would ordinarily describe my concern. When I ordinarily describe my concern I do so by conceptually dividing reality in the ordinary way; I talk about a unitary chair and a unitary table, and not about any such thing as a table-*cum*-chair. This is because the ordinary concept of unity is already given, and I describe the target of my concern in terms of that concept. But there is apparently nothing in the concern as such which could explain why I operate with that concept of unity, why I divide reality up in just that way. And this same point could be made for virtually any example one cares to consider. Contrary to James's suggestion, there appears to be no clearcut connection between our interests or purposes and our concept of unity.

It is perhaps true that we tend to classify objects, especially artifacts, in terms of their aptness to fulfill human purposes. But this is a comment about our classifying tendencies, not about our unifying tendencies. The units are already given, and we classify them from a practical standpoint. There are all kinds of space-time portions which, if we only treated them as units, we could easily classify in practical terms as well. James's idea is that an object is a portion of reality which is especially spotlighted by our needs and interests. But the fact is that our human concerns striate space-time in a manner that crisscrosses and overlaps the space-time paths of objects in every imaginable way. There seems to be nothing in our practical standpoint which can account for the specific concept of unity we have.

It seems to me that there is no way that the "empiricist" position under discussion can overcome these difficulties. If we imagine ourselves as having started out without our ordinary criteria of unity, there is nothing that we might have learned about the world, or about our practical relationship to the world, which could have yielded those particular criteria. In criticizing the empiricist position, I have been using the word "learning" in a rather loose and intuitive way. Certainly the prospects for the position would be immediately diminished if one limited learning to the sort of stimulus-response model that Quine sometimes seems to favor. But my criticism of the position does not rely on any particular analysis of what learning consists in. Taking the concept of learning in what seems to be the broadest sense relevant to this discussion, as roughly equivalent to "inference" or "rational derivation," the crucial point remains just this: If we had started out by describing the world without our ordinary criteria of unity, then there seems to be no inference of any sort whatever that could have led to our adopting those criteria.

My argument against the empiricist view has taken the rather extreme form of denying not only that we do in fact arrive at our criteria of unity by some kind of inference; I deny that we could even in principle have arrived at these criteria in any such manner. According to my version of the innateness hypothesis, we are innately disposed to adopt the criteria of unity that we have; but, apart from this specific and complicated disposition, there is nothing about the world which could have taught us to adopt our criteria of unity, since there are no considerations, theoretical or practical, which mark off just those criteria as being especially right or reasonable. It might seem initially tempting to maintain an innateness view somewhat different from mine. It might be maintained, contrary to my view, that our criteria of unity are rationally derivable in principle, that they are the peculiarly right criteria for us to have, and that precisely for that reason we have evolved the innate propensity to operate with those criteria.[19] But, if my arguments in this section against the empiricist position have been successful, then they show that our criteria of unity are not even derivable in principle.

V. Focusing on Objects

I have discussed three general approaches to our concept of bodily unity. According to one approach, our criteria of unity are essentially arbitrary conventions which could easily have been otherwise. This idea seemed intuitively implausible, though I have yet to present a definite argument against it. A second possibility was that these criteria are somehow derived from some facts about the world, facts that one could describe without presupposing the criteria. I tried to argue in the last section that this view in untenable. So we are left with the third possibility, which is that our criteria of unity are neither arbitrary conventions nor learned, but are determined by our innate disposition to experience the world in terms of just those criteria.

It should be understood that the issue posed by these alternatives relates most directly to the bare foundations of our concept of bodily unity. To believe in an innate sense of unity is to suppose that our most basic and general criteria of unity result from an innate disposition. This does not preclude the possibility that these criteria may be enriched and elaborated in various ways, indeed in ways that are likely to include an element of convention as well as an element of practical and theoretical reasoning. The conventionalist and the "empiricist" are not saying merely that various nuances of our fully developed concept of unity may result from convention or inference. They are denying an innate status to *any* of our criteria of unity, even such seemingly fundamental criteria as cohesiveness and continuity. The position I have been arguing for is that these most fundamental criteria must be innate.

19. This seems in fact to be Köhler's position; see Köhler, *Gestalt Psychology*, pp. 162–64. My own position might be compared to Chomsky's view that "there is no a priori 'naturalness' to such a system [of innate grammatical principles], any more than there is to the detailed structure of the visual cortex." See Noam Chomsky, *Language and Mind* (Harcourt Brace Jovanovich, Inc., N. Y., 1968), p. 88. For further discussion of the rationality of our identity criteria see above, Chapter 5, Section V.

Earlier, when discussing the conventionalist position, I suggested that one might try to clarify some of these issues by reflecting on how children are likely to experience unity before the learning of language. In this connection one naturally thinks of Jean Piaget's discussions of the child's development of the object concept.[20] According to Piaget's scheme, the child's concept of an object invariably passes through a succession of stages. The principle of transition from one stage to the next is characterized by Piaget in a somewhat elusive manner. In some cases the transition seems to be essentially nothing more than maturational development, but the more fundamental idea seems to be that each successive stage resolves with increasing success various conceptual conflicts and tensions that arise at earlier stages. We are invited to compare this process to the development in theoretical science of increasingly more adequate ways of thinking about the world. All of this would obviously repay close examination. My concern at present, however, is less with Piaget's account of these transitions, than with his depiction of the very earliest stages. Would Piaget agree with my contention that our experience is from the very start governed by our most basic commonsense criteria of unity?

In the initial stages, according to Piaget, the child's orientation is essentially solipsistic; the infant does not initially appreciate that objects can persist when they are not perceived. Piaget bases this interpretation of the infant's experience on his (somewhat controversial) findings that infants at an early stage do not engage in any "search behavior." If an infant at this stage "is reaching for an object that is interesting to him and we suddenly put a screen between the object and him, he will act as if the object not only has disappeared but also is no longer accessible."[21] The infant, as here depicted, seems to treat the object in rather the way in which we would treat an after-image, as something whose *esse* is *percipi*.

Now the most striking feature of this account, from my present standpoint, is the way that Piaget unabashedly describes the

---

20. Jean Piaget, *The Construction of Reality in the Child* (Balantine Books, N. Y., 1954), ch. 1; *Genetic Epistemology* (Columbia University Press, N. Y., 1970), pp. 43–44, 52–57; *On the Development of Memory and Identity* (Clark University Press, Worcester, Mass., 1968), pp. 17–37.
21. Piaget, *Genetic Epistemology*, p. 43.

infant as reaching for an object, as being interested in the object, and as, apparently, noticing the object's disappearance from his field of view. In fact, Piaget consistently describes infants in very early pre-linguistic stages as focusing on objects and following them as they move. These descriptions seem perfectly natural, even inevitable. But it is important to see that these descriptions imply that the infant's experience is directed toward units approximating to our ordinary things, units that he can focus upon, reach for, follow with his eyes, lose sight of, and so on. In the initial stages, at least according to Piaget, these units are treated as having a status akin to after-images (or akin to the philosopher's sense data), and, like after-images, their unity seems to be defined in terms of such familiar criteria as cohesiveness and continuity. Hence Piaget apparently would agree that our experience is at the very earliest stages—certainly before the acquisition of language—governed by our most basic commonsense criteria of unity. Indeed it may not even be completely clear that the child's drift away from solipsism, as characterized by Piaget, deserves to be counted as a development in the child's concept (*definition*) of unity, rather than merely an alteration in the child's beliefs about the unperceived persistence of the units he has picked out.

It may be somewhat incautious of me to try to relate Piaget's highly complex thesis to the present discussion. I can, however, more confidently cite the recent work of T. G. R. Bower, in which a modified version of Piaget's developmental scheme is expounded and impressively argued. The point that presently concerns me is Bower's depiction of the infant's experience in early pre-linguistic stages.

The evidence that infants do segregate their environments into units is clear. A large number of studies on the eye-fixation behavior of infants has shown that infants will fix on the external contours of objects in their visual field. If the objects are moved, the infants will track them. If after moving together, the contours of an object break and begin to move independently, very young infants will display massive surprise. This indicates that the common motion (common fate) has specified for them a single unit.[22]

22. T. G. R. Bower, *Development in Infancy* (W. H. Freeman and Co., San Francisco, Cal., 1974), p. 102.

The condition that Bower calls "common motion" (or "common fate") is essentially what I earlier called "dynamic cohesiveness." As I pointed out, this condition presupposes various criteria of unity through time, such as qualitative and spatio-temporal continuity. So Bower is in effect saying that the infant's experience is pre-linguistically organized around units that are defined in terms of such fundamental commonsense criteria as cohesiveness and continuity.[23]

To speculate about the experience of infants may seem a rather dubious undertaking for a philosopher. But I would submit that the facts I am here rehearsing are, for the most part, so commonplace, and seem so central to our intuitive grasp of what human nature consists in, as almost to invite the designation "transcendental." Try to imagine a person whose eyes and hands do not fixate upon objects in an essentially ordinary way, but whose attention meanders about without ever settling on (what we ordinarily regard as) a single object. Can we imagine what it would be like to initiate such a creature into our ordinary thought-world? Where could we begin?

I am now taking back my earlier tentative concession to Quine that perhaps the child's quality space is essentially all that is required to explain how the child can learn the body-minded way of talking. Something else that is required is the child's instinct to focus on objects in the ordinary way. This instinct is just another form of what I have been calling our "innate sense of unity." In order for the child to learn the ordinary way of talking, he must already be focusing on objects in a manner that exhibits his disposition to adopt our basic criteria of unity.

The easiest case to reflect upon is one in which the infant is tracking a moving object. Here the characteristic alterations in the infant's eyes, face, and body vividly display the effort to keep an object in focus. For the infant, as indeed for us, a moving object evidently stands out as something to be focused upon.

23. For the purposes of the present discussion I am deliberately leaving it quite vague just what our "fundamental criteria" are, except to suggest that they would undoubtedly involve some appeal to continuity and cohesiveness. I attempted a more thorough presentation of these fundamental (or basic) criteria in Chapter 3 above, and especially Section VI. (For some weird complications, however, see Bower, *Development in Infancy*, pp. 189–92.)

When a moving object passes through our field of view, we, even as adults, experience the unmistakable impulse to fix our gaze on it and follow it as it moves. Our various purposes, expectations, concerns—our whole "mental set"—will eventually determine where we look, and for how long. But the primitive power of an object, especially a moving object, to fix our attention is unmistakable.

A point that I especially want to stress, in the light of Quine's approach to this topic, is that our quality space (our sense of similarity) cannot account for our disposition to focus on objects in the way we do. The infant who is tracking a moving object is not merely registering passively some complex similarities between the presented scene and various other space-time portions of the world which, as he later learns, are called "moving bodies." He is exhibiting the quite irreducible instinct to direct his attention in a distinctive way, by correlating the position of his eyes (or hands) with the position of the object he is tracking. It is, I am inclined to say, strictly a logically contingent fact that the focus of the infant's (and our) attention tends (however briefly) to follow the path of an object, rather than to meander through space-time in any number of other imaginable ways. However, as I remarked a moment ago, this fact seems completely central to our way of experiencing the world.

What it means for us to focus (our attention) on an object can be explained partially by reference to the manifest correlations between the movements of our eyes and hands and the movements of the objects in our surroundings. At a deeper, and somewhat more nebulous, level our focusing propensities can be seen as providing us with a general epistemic orientation toward the world, with a general schema for learning. Consider, for example, how readily we learn about the shape of an object, though an object's shape is equivalent to a complicated fact about the interrelations between the object's parts. Compare this with the relatively slower and more arduous process of learning about the interrelations between things that do not add up to an object, as ordinarily conceived. Or consider how readily we discern the various changes (e.g., the patterns of movement) of a single object, though these changes are equivalent to complicated interrelations between the object's temporal stages. It is generally far more difficult for us to size up the interrelations between object-

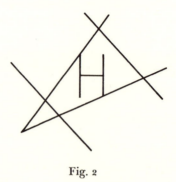

Fig. 2

stages that do not add up to what we ordinarily regard as a single persisting object. We can say, in general, that the qualities and internal constitution of a unitary object, as ordinarily conceived, are far more readily discerned than the qualities and internal constitution of any other kind of space-time portion. (In behavioral terms we can say that we are far more likely to "respond" to the former properties as "stimulus," than to the latter.) Our heightened readiness to focus upon, and hence to learn about, an object, rather than any other kind of space-time portion, is evidently central to what it means for us to regard a portion of the world as a unitary object.

Some of the points that I have just been discussing can be illustrated by reference to Figures 2 and 3 (which are adapted from Köhler). The reader will readily discern that there is a central portion of Figure 2 shaped like the letter H. Let me call that portion "α." On the other hand, one is not apt to notice that, embedded within the center of Figure 3, there is also an H-

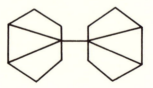

Fig. 3

shaped portion. I will call that portion of Figure 3 "β." The evident fact, then, is that we readily tend to focus on α, but not on β.

This fact about our focusing propensity, to recast an earlier point, cannot be accounted for by reference to our sense of similarity. What is peculiar about β is not that we fail to see it as similar to this or that, but rather that, in a sense, we fail to see it, *period*. Once β is pointed out to us, however, we readily see it as being similar to various things (if nothing else, at least to corresponding portions of replicas of Figure 3).

This distinction between α and β can be expressed in terms of our disposition to learn. If presented with Figure 2, we would be apt to learn various things about α, for example, that it is shaped like an H, or that it contains three line segments, or that it is not round. By contrast, we are not likely to learn anything at all about β when we are presented with Figure 3. (In behavioral terms, the idea would be that α's properties are far more likely than β's to elicit a response from us.)

Now a space-time portion of the world which does not correspond to what we ordinarily count as a unitary object can be compared to β: we do not readily focus on (or learn about) such a portion of the world. One might almost say that, primitively, a unit is just this: a portion of reality that we naturally focus on. Or, to put this from another angle, one might almost say that the root impulse behind our body-minded ontology is to exclude those portions of reality which "we do not see," in the peculiar sense in which we do not see β.

I have been suggesting that there is a close connection between the following two ideas: (1) "experiencing (and thinking about) bodily unity in an essentially ordinary way" and (2) "exhibiting essentially ordinary focusing and tracking behavior in the presence of bodies." I am uncertain just how close we ought to say this connection is.[24] (This seems of a piece with the un-

---

24. If the connection is sufficiently close then, it may be suggested, at least an indirect or derivative pragmatic justification of our criteria of unity may after all be possible, for our focusing and tracking behavior (it will be said) surely serves our practical concerns. I do not rule out the possibility of developing such an argument, but I would stress two requirements for the argument to be convincing: first, some *alternative* patterns of focusing and track-

certainty one feels about the closeness of the connection between, for example, anger and anger-behavior.) Even most modestly construed, the connection seems amply to warrant the conclusion that before the acquisition of language very young infants experience bodily unity in a manner akin to adults. Most modestly construed, the connection is explanatory: We explain people's focusing and tracking behavior by reference to their experience of unity. Put in these terms, my point about infants is this: A seemingly plausible (indeed a seemingly compelling) explanation of the infant's focusing and tracking behavior, and the similarity of that behavior to our own, is that the infant experiences the world as broken up into units in essentially the way that we do. Someone who wants to reject this explanation certainly has the burden of suggesting an alternative.

VI. Conclusion

My argument against the empiricist position consisted in maintaining that there is nothing about the world which could have taught us to adopt our ordinary criteria of unity, had we started out without those criteria. My argument against the conventionalist view was basically to suggest that children experience unity in an essentially ordinary way before they acquire language. Perhaps this latter argument also works to some extent against the empiricist view, for it may seem immediately implausible to suppose that very young infants have already arrived at their experience of unity by way of learning.

Our concept of bodily unity, or at least the basic core of that concept, is rooted in our primitive, pre-conventional experience of unity. And it seems that only our innate constitution can plausibly account for the specific and complicated conditions that a portion of the world has to satisfy if it is to be experienced primitively as a unit. As far as defining what enters into this element of innateness, one point I have repeatedly stressed is that

---

ing behavior must be described, and second, it must be *carefully explained* why our ordinary focusing and tracking behavior is more expedient than any of the alternatives.

our quality space, our sense of similarity, cannot explain why we experience unity in the way we do; nor can it account for our correlative focusing and tracking behavior. The conclusion suggested by this whole train of argument is that an innate sense of unity is a quite irreducible feature of our experience of the world.

9
Natural Kinds
and Natural Units

I. Kinds and Units

A NATURAL kind, as this notion has been employed in some recent literature, is a class of things that it seems in some sense natural to bring together under a general concept. As Quinton puts this: "[T]he members of some of the collections of things which it is formally possible to construct must have a natural affinity for each other, there must be some collections of things which it is natural to class together in contrast to other collections whose association is arbitrary."[1] Otherwise it seems that we could never even learn how to use a general term, for we would have no basis to extrapolate from old cases to new cases.

Just what to make of this "natural affinity" between the members of a natural kind is one aspect of the traditional problem of universals. If we permit ourselves to talk about properties, then we can say that a natural kind is a class of (all and only) things sharing some property or, perhaps better, some "genuine" property. I assume that both the class of tigers and the class of lions would be regarded as natural kinds, but that none of the following are natural kinds: the class of things which are either tigers or lions; the class of things which are not tigers; and the class of things which are not lions. We do not regard the latter classes as natural kinds because they do not intuitively strike us as being defined by "genuine" properties. Evidently our judg-

1. Quinton, *The Nature of Things*, p. 262. Quinton talks here about natural *classes* rather than natural *kinds*, but I doubt that this has any significance.

ments about which classes are natural kinds are closely correlated to our judgments about which terms signify genuine properties. Indeed the only immediate advantage of talking about "natural kinds" rather than "genuine properties" is that the former notion might be acceptable to a nominalist who eschews properties while admitting classes. Such a nominalist might be content to characterize a natural kind as a class of things that are in some sense "sufficiently similar" to each other. I shall return to that characterization shortly.

My use of the notion "natural kind" may depart somewhat from the use associated with Kripke and Putnam. In the writings of these philosophers the notion of a natural kind is often associated with a distinctive form of semantic analysis of such terms as "lion" and "tiger," which are said to refer rigidly to underlying structures as opposed to superficially observable qualities.[2] But I want to stipulate that this association is not to be taken as definitive of what a natural kind is. One can hold that such terms as "spherical object," "red object," and "painful sensation" denote natural kinds, in the sense that concerns me, even if it is assumed that the application of these terms depends wholly on superficially observable qualities. In this sense, natural kinds, and the properties which define them, may be either manifest or hidden, and they may be referred to in any number of ways. A similar point is brought out by Quine, who distinguishes between natural kinds of two varieties, which he calls "intuitive kinds" and "theoretical kinds."[3] As an illustration of this difference he mentions color classifications: the class of red things constitutes a natural kind from an intuitive common sense standpoint but perhaps not from a more theoretical standpoint. In what follows I will be talking about "natural kinds" in Quine's broad sense, and indeed my emphasis will be on kinds at a rudimentary intuitive level.

The notion of a natural kind is surely problematical. I want, however, to take this notion pretty much for granted in the present discussion, and to explore certain possible points of connection between it and a seemingly kindred notion. Our basic

2. Kripke, *Naming and Necessity*; Putnam, "Is Semantics Possible?," reprinted in *Mind, Language and Reality*.
3. Quine, "Natural Kinds," in *Ontological Relativity and Other Essays*, p. 131ff.

form of proposition, according to an enduring tradition, is one in which the subject-part picks out some concrete thing, and the predicate-part classifies that thing as being of one kind or another. If there is with respect to the predicate function a distinction between natural and artificial classifications, one might hope to find a parallel distinction with respect to the subject function. And looking in that direction one readily sees the possibility for drawing such a distinction. A concrete thing, such as a tree or a cat, is comprised of the contents of a particular portion of space and time. Evidently, however, not just any arbitrary space-time portion of reality constitutes what we would naturally regard as a thing. Suppose that a cat is lying a few feet away from a tree. We would not naturally regard the cat together with the tree as making up some unitary thing, a thing composed of the cat and the tree. Nor less would we naturally regard some early stage of the cat's history together with some later stage of the tree's history as comprising the history of some unitary thing, a thing which was first a cat and then a tree. A cat, it appears, is a natural unit, as is a tree; but the result of combining in thought a cat, or some stage of a cat, with a tree, or some stage of a tree, is not a natural unit.

A natural unit, then, is a concrete portion of reality which, at some level of common sense or science, we treat as a unitary thing. Paralleling the distinction between natural kinds and artificial classes we have the distinction between natural units and artificial portions of reality. As before we can distinguish further between units at a relatively nonspecialized commonsense level and more theoretical units; and, again, my concern will be primarily with the former.

The notion of a natural unit, as I intend to employ it, encompasses only such items as philosophers call "concrete" or "substantial." Concrete things have, I assume, a special and central connection to the subject-role of our basic subject-predicate proposition. And the point is that apparently not every portion of reality which could in principle be treated as a concrete thing is naturally so treated. It is indeed true that some philosophers, notably Quine, have recommended metaphysical systems in which any space-time portion of reality, however discontinuous or noncohesive, is to be treated as a concrete thing on a par with an ordinary body.[4] In these metaphysical systems the sum of a cat and a tree is a concrete thing, as is the sum of a cat-stage and a tree-stage. Even these philosophers would agree, however, that at the level of common sense, as well as at various scientific-theoretic levels, not just any arbitrary portion of reality is treated as a concrete unit. Relative to these levels, at any rate, we have a distinction between natural units and artificial portions of reality.

II. Kinds and Similarity Classes

This discussion, as I have already said, presupposes the notion of a natural kind and aims primarily to connect this notion to that of a natural unit. There are, however, several essential assumptions about natural kinds which I must make explicit before proceeding.

a. The *naturalness* of a "natural kind" seems to convey two somewhat different ideas. On the one hand there is the idea that *we find it natural* to regard certain things as forming kinds. On the other hand there is the idea that certain things form kinds *in the natural order*, apart from how these things relate to our human purposes or attitudes or interests. I think that both of these ideas are generally implied by philosophers who employ the notion of a natural kind. A natural kind is thus a class of things that strike us as forming a kind independently of our human activities.

The antithesis of a natural kind is an artificial class, the members of which strike us as not just "going together" in the natural order of things, but rather as being "*put* together" by us. One sort of example, mentioned earlier, is classes defined on the basis of essentially disjunctive or negative descriptions. A rather different sort of example of an artificial class is one defined on the basis of a description that implicitly or explicitly refers to our human activities. Thus the term "article of clothing" would not, I assume, be said to define a natural kind, on the grounds that articles of clothing have nothing distinctively in common but their relationship to some human activity. Many other examples are much more difficult to assess. Should we say that the class of

4. Quine, *Word and Object*, p. 171; "Worlds Away," *Journal of Philosophy*, 73, 22 (1976).

tables is a natural kind, on the grounds that even apart from our human activities tables are similar to each other (e.g., in shape and size)? This does seem somewhat plausible, at least in the "weak" sense of natural kind which I will explain in a moment.

So membership in a natural kind must not depend on how a thing relates to our human activities. But should we in fact make the much stronger remark that membership in a natural kind must not depend on *any* of a thing's external relationships? Something like this may often be tacitly assumed (at least in the choice of examples), though the motivation for such an assumption is far from clear. In any case this question need not be resolved for the limited purposes of the present discussion.

What is essential to note, however, is that a natural kind certainly *can* be defined on the basis of *internal* relationships, that is, on the basis of a description of the sorts of parts a thing has and how these parts are interrelated. Thus "molecule of H_2O" denotes a natural kind, membership in which depends on whether a given molecule is made up of certain kinds of atoms related in certain ways. Membership in a natural kind will very typically depend upon a thing's internal structure. Indeed it seems to me reasonable to suppose that *any* description of an internal structure will define a natural kind, so long as the description does not depend on essentially disjunctive or negative properties. Thus the class of things which are partly red and partly green ought to count as a natural kind (at least at a rudimentary level).

b. This leads directly to another point. Certainly we must not assume that in order for a term to define a natural kind the term must be in any sense *logically simple*. The most typical natural kinds are based on terms of some relatively high degree of logical complexity; terms such as "molecule of H_2O," "tiger," and "spherical object" are evidently in no sense simple or indefinable.

A consideration of such examples suggests indeed that any *conjunctive* term, built up out of terms which define natural kinds, itself defines a natural kind. Thus if "(bit of) H_2O" and "solid" define natural kinds, so does "solid bit of H_2O" (i.e., "ice"). And if "cubical" also defines a natural kind, then so does "solid cubical bit of H_2O" (i.e., "cube of ice"). There seems to be no intuitive reason to place any general limitation on such constructions.

That a natural kind may have even a high degree of logical complexity follows directly from one of our earlier characterizations of what a natural kind is, viz. a class of things which are sufficiently similar to each other. Obviously if cubical things constitute a similarity class, and bits of H_2O constitute a similarity class, then without question cubical bits of H_2O also constitute a similarity class.

So complex descriptions of internal structure as well as complex conjunctive descriptions can typically define natural kinds. On the other hand, two forms of logical complexity which typically cannot define natural kinds are, as mentioned several times earlier, disjunction and negation. This too follows immediately from the characterization of a natural kind as a similarity class. For we cannot say that things which are either tigers or lions form a class in virtue of being sufficiently similar to each other, nor that things which are not lions form such a class.

c. There is, however, a difficulty in defining what we mean by a similarity class, or a class formed on the basis of the similarity of its members. A tempting definition is this: S is a similarity class if anything outside of S is less similar to something inside S than any pair of things inside S are similar to each other. (That is, if x is not a member of S, then there is a y such that y is a member of S and such that for any z and w which are members of S, x is less similar to y than z is to w.) Can we now simply equate the notion of a natural kind with this notion of a similarity class?

Quine argues against this on the grounds that we would then have to say that disjunctions of overlapping conjunctions define natural kinds.[5] Consider, for example, the class of things which are either red and spherical, or red and solid, or spherical and solid. This will qualify as a similarity class on the previous definition, because any pair of members of the class must at least be similar with respect to one of the three properties, whereas anything outside the class will lack even this degree of similarity to some members. But such a class, Quine insists, should not count as a natural kind.

I shall not, however, follow Quine in this point of terminology, but shall stipulate instead that any similarity class does qualify as a natural kind. This stipulation accords, I think, with one

5. Quine, "Natural Kinds," pp. 119–23.

tendency in current philosophical usage, though the termino-logical point as such has of course no great importance. (In fact the reader who wishes may substitute "similarity class" for "nat-ural kind" in all that follows.) I do not question Quine's intui-tion that there is an important difference between the similarity class last mentioned, which was defined on the basis of a dis-junction of conjunctions, and a full-blown natural kind such as, perhaps, the class of spherical objects. We might mark this difference by distinguishing *weak* natural kinds from *strong* natural kinds.[6] It has often been noted that Wittgenstein's notion of a "family resemblance" is closely related to a disjunction of overlapping conjunctions.[7] My usage will allow us to say that a natural kind (of the "weak" variety) can be based on a family resemblance. This seems correct at least insofar as it is obviously in some sense natural to bring under a general concept objects which are related by a family resemblance.

III. Is the Class of Units a Kind?

Let us now consider some possible connections between natural kinds and natural units. One question that might be asked is whether the class of natural units is itself a natural kind. This question is surely obscure and difficult, but I think it may be worthwhile trying to address it.

The question might be compared with asking whether the class of beautiful objects constitutes a natural kind. This would amount to asking whether there is, apart from our human atti-tudes and purposes, some point of similarity between all and only those objects which we regard as beautiful. In the same vein we are now asking whether there is, apart from our attitudes and purposes, some point of similarity between all and only those portions of reality which we naturally treat as concrete units. What we are seeking, it might be said, is an elucidation of

6. For *degrees* of natural kinds see Anthony Quinton, "Properties and Classes," *Proceedings of the Aristotelian Society*, 58 (1957–58), pp. 47–48.
7. See, e.g., Renford Bambrough, "Universals and Family Resemblances," re-printed in George Pitcher, ed., *Wittgenstein* (Anchor Books, New York, 1966), p. 189. In order for us to have a similarity class, or a family resemblance, we must have a disjunction of *extensively* overlapping conjunctions, roughly a term which applies to a thing only if it satisfies *most* of some list of conditions.

the relationship between our similarity intuitions and our unity intuitions.

As stipulated earlier, a natural unit must be concrete. Does this amount to saying that, at least for common sense, the class of natural units coincides with the category of a body, so that all and only bodies are natural units? The answer to this question would hinge on several nebulous points. First of all, one would have to decide whether persons are bodies, since persons are surely to be regarded as natural units. Furthermore, one would have to clarify the notion of concreteness or substantiality before one could assess the substantive status of various items, for example, particular sounds and flashes, marks on bodies (such as a figure drawn on paper), and segregated clusters of bodies (such as a flock of birds). Even if we conceived of the class of natural units as encompassing, besides bodies (and persons), these other sundry items, it might still be possible to maintain that all of these things have something in common which marks them off from other portions of reality that are not natural units. However, the issue in these terms seems fairly intractable.

Let me in fact simplify our question significantly by focusing exclusively on bodies as natural units. Bodies (together perhaps with persons, if these are to be kept distinct) seem to be, in any case, our most basic paradigms of concrete units; and it may even be arguable that the class of natural units can properly be regarded as forming a natural kind if and only if the class of bodies can be so regarded. The simplified question, then, is whether the class of bodies is a natural kind. Should we say that there is some point of similarity that marks bodies off from all other portions of reality?

An affirmative answer to this question is indicated by some of Quine's remarks about the child's acquisition of the concept of a body. Quine suggests that there are some "very general body-unifying considerations that preserve the identity of each dog, each rabbit, each apple, each bundle, in short each body." These general body-unifying considerations, he says, constitute a "similarity-basis for the child's ostensive learning of the general term 'body' itself, or 'thing,' to take the likelier word."[8]

8. Quine, *The Roots of Reference*, p. 56.

To know how to apply the term "body" requires that one should know how to judge of the unity of a body; one must know when to count a space-time portion of reality as constituting a single self-same body. Quine's remarks imply that if a child learns how to apply the term "body" (or "thing") to a fair assortment of bodies then he can go on to apply the term correctly to new cases, basing himself on the similarity between bodily unity in the new cases and bodily unity in the old cases. A body, according to Quine, is a distinctive kind of space-time portion, one whose spatial and temporal parts are structured in some distinctive way. This is tantamount to saying, at least in the rough terms of the present discussion, that the class of bodies is a natural kind.

Wiggins's sortal theory of identity, on the other hand, would seem to imply the opposite, that the class of bodies is *not* a natural kind. Wiggins holds that a judgment about bodily unity must always be mediated by some "substance-sortal" concept, where a substance-sortal is some relatively specific noun such as "cat," "tree," or "car." Wiggins's view implies that there are no "general body-unifying considerations" of the sort that Quine refers to, that there is no "similarity basis" which could permit one to extrapolate from the unity conditions of one body to that of another, where these bodies fall under different substance-sortals. This is why Wiggins repeatedly insists that a term like "body" (or "thing" or "object") is only a "dummy sortal" which cannot operate independently of the specific nouns subordinate to it.[9] One might indeed say that for Wiggins the term "body" is in effect equivalent to some long disjunction of the form "either a tree, or a cat, or an apple, or . . . ," where each different substance-sortal enters as a disjunct. The term "body," so regarded, could not be said to denote a natural kind.

As regards this apparent controversy between Quine and Wiggins my view would be that Quine is right at one level and Wiggins at another. Quine is surely correct in supposing that there are some body-unifying considerations which can operate independently of our various sortal differentiations. An example I have discussed previously is that of an Eskimo who has never before seen (or heard of) a tree, and who is now presented with

9. Wiggins, *Identity and Spatio-Temporal Continuity*, pp. 29, 33, 35.

a tree for the first time.[10] Though he lacks the general concept of a tree there can be no doubt, I think, that the Eskimo is immediately in the position to make such judgments as the following: "There is a tall, queerly shaped, mostly brown body (thing) over there, with a cylindrically shaped central portion, out of which there is jutting at various angles a number of twisted parts of various shapes and sizes, at the very ends of which are some green things." This judgment reveals the Eskimo's basic grasp of the tree's spatial extent, of the tree's unity through space. And other judgments would no doubt reveal the Eskimo's basic grasp of the tree's temporal extent, the tree's identity through time.

What we can appreciate when we reflect upon this sort of example is the extent to which our judgments of unity need not depend upon any sortals: we can often base a judgment of unity on body-unifying conditions that are not linked to any sortals. Perhaps this sort of example does not conclusively show that the sortal-neutral body-unifying conditions are *similar* from one case to another. For it might be possible to suppose that when the Eskimo confronts the tree, he just finds it natural or reasonable to apply some wholly new criteria of unity, criteria essentially different from any that he has previously employed in other cases. Certainly, however, the far more plausible explanation of the Eskimo's judgments is that he bases himself on some analogy, on some point of similarity, between the unity of the tree and other cases of bodily unity which he has encountered. So it seems that Quine is right in saying that there are some general body-unifying considerations that are the same for bodies of all sorts. And presumably we could, with some care, even formulate more or less what those considerations are. Quine indeed makes the rough suggestion that a body's unity is determined by its "synchronic continuity" and its "diachronic continuity of displacement and deformation."[11] This suggestion needs a great deal of elaboration, but surely it points in the right direction.[12]

10. See above, pp. 75–78.
11. Quine, *The Roots of Reference*, p. 54.
12. A more elaborate sortal-neutral formulation might be in terms of the "basic rule" and the "principle of articulation"; see above, Chapter 3, Sections II and VI.

So there are, as Quine suggests, some general body-unifying considerations which can operate independently of sortals. It seems, however, that Quine may overrate the scope of such considerations. For the fact is (and this is Wiggins's point) that cases can arise where one's ignorance of the applicable sortal (one's ignorance of "what the thing is") will give rise to mistaken judgments. Our Eskimo, for example, who has no idea what a tree is, could not be expected fully to share our sortal-relativized view of just what kinds of changes the object he picked out can suffer without ceasing to exist.[13] Quine's account, one might say, answers to our most basic, our most unsophisticated, concept of bodily unity. This is the concept we would apply when exploring some wholly new terrain and, like the Eskimo in the previous example, have no sortals to apply. But this most basic concept of bodily unity is eventually refined by our sortals, and the sortals, when they are available, can make a difference to our identity judgments. Wiggins is right therefore in denying that our most sophisticated judgments of bodily unity can always be based on some general similarities between bodies coming under different sortals.

So we can conclude, perhaps, that whereas our most rudimentary concept of bodily unity does denote a natural kind (of at least the "weak" variety), to the extent that the concept is complicated by sortal differentiations it no longer does denote a natural kind.

IV. Kinds and Individuation

Whether or not we judge the class of natural units (which, for simplicity, I continue to identify with the class of bodies) as a natural kind, it seems clear that many natural units belong to some natural kind or other. If x is a lion then x belongs to the natural kind of lions, and if x is a tree then x belongs to the natural kind of trees, and so on. This point might suggest the possibility of explaining the notion of a natural unit in terms of the notion of a natural kind. Could we not say, perhaps, that a natural unit is just a portion of reality wich belongs to some natural kind? This suggestion may seem plausible, for if a por-

13. Cf. above, Chapter 3, Section III, on the "limitations of the basic rule."

tion of reality does not belong to any natural kind, and hence cannot be classified in any natural way, this might explain why we do not regard that portion of reality as a unit.

There are two questions that we can raise about this suggestion. First, is it true that every natural unit belongs to a natural kind? And, second, is it true that every artificial portion of reality fails to belong to a natural kind? The answer to the first question would be trivially affirmative if we could assume that the class of natural units is itself a natural kind. But given the more nebulous position arrived at in the last section, it may not be immediately obvious what the answer to the first question is. I shall not pursue this, however, for I think that the more important and revealing issues arise in connection with the second question.

Consider, as an example, a discontinuous portion of reality which is comprised of two trees that are standing next to each other (surrounded, let us say, by other trees). This portion of reality, which I will call a "tree-*cum*-tree," is evidently not a natural unit. According to the above suggestion the reason why the tree-*cum*-tree is not a natural unit is that it fails to belong to any natural kind. But what of the classes denoted by the terms "(mostly) brown" and "(mostly) wooden"? Presumably these classes are natural kinds, and it seems that the tree-*cum*-tree belongs to both of them.

It might be answered that the terms "brown" and "wooden" must be understood as equivalent to "brown *body*" and "wooden *body*," so that the tree-*cum*-tree, which is not a body, fails to qualify under these terms. But what about the terms "brown portion of reality" and "wooden portion of reality"? Obviously the tree-*cum*-tree qualifies under these terms, and it seems that these terms denote natural kinds. For it seems that we ought to say that all brown portions of reality have some property in common, as do all wooden portions of reality.

It would do no good to suggest that the class of brown portions of reality, and the class of wooden portions of reality, are not natural kinds precisely because some of their members (e.g., the tree-*cum*-tree) are not natural units. If one simply stipulates, as part of the definition of "natural kind," that the members of natural kinds must all be natural units, then one has obviously given up the hope of explaining what a natural unit is in terms of the independently understood notion of a natural kind. The only legitimate procedure here is to retain our earlier intuitive characterization of a natural kind, as a class whose members are in some sense sufficiently similar to each other, and see whether on that basis one can explain what a natural unit is. It seems, at this point, that one cannot.

It might still seem possible to attempt a slightly different approach. A natural unit is a portion of reality which we find it natural to pick out as a distinct and unitary thing. Now it seems that the most fundamental way to pick something out is by an expression of the form "that F," e.g., "that tree." In order for a term F to function properly in the expression "that F," the term must be *individuative*, where we might say, for present purposes, that a term is individuative if and only if it typically happens that exactly one instance of the term is present in a given region of space. Hence "tree" is individuative, since there might typically be exactly one tree in the observable region, or one tree in the direction that someone is pointing. This is why the expression "that tree" can often serve to pick out a tree. Clearly such terms as "brown portion of reality" and "wooden portion of reality" are not individuative. You could never pick something out by way of the expression "that brown portion of reality," or "that wooden portion of reality," because wherever there is a brown or wooden portion of reality there must be an indefinite number of such portions of reality.

Let it be granted, it might now be said, that the terms "brown portion of reality" and "wooden portion of reality" do denote natural kinds. It follows from this that a tree-*cum*-tree does belong to some natural kinds. It does not follow, however, that the tree-*cum*-tree belongs to any *individuative* natural kind (where a natural kind is individuative if it is denoted by some individuative term). Perhaps the reason why the tree-*cum*-tree does not qualify as a natural unit is that it does not belong to any individuative natural kind, and therefore cannot be picked out in any natural way.

The present suggestion, then, is that a natural unit is a portion of reality that belongs to some individuative natural kind. But this suggestion fails too, I think. For consider the term "tree-*cum*-tree" (or, equivalently, "portion of reality that is comprised of two trees.") This term is quite definitely individuative; you can just as easily point out a particular tree-*cum*-tree by way of the expression "that tree-*cum*-tree," as you can point out a tree by way of the expression "that tree." Consequently the class of tree-*cum*-trees is an individuative natural kind, if, that is, it is a natural kind at all. But why would it not be a natural kind? If trees are (sufficiently) similar to each other, then it seems that tree-*cum*-trees ought to be (sufficiently) similar to each other. (To make this even clearer, we might stipulate that the trees in a tree-*cum*-tree must be similarly situated with respect to each other, say a few feet away from each other.) So it seems that a tree-*cum*-tree, which is decidedly not a natural unit, does after all belong to an individuative natural kind. And, in general, it seems that, contrary to the above suggestion, various artificial portions of reality will belong to individuative natural kinds.

Let me try to bring this point out in a slightly different way. We can classify not only unitary things but *pairs* of things, and it seems plain that some of these classifications will constitute natural kinds (i.e., similarity classes) and some will not. Suppose that S is the class of all pairs of trees (or, if one wants, pairs of trees a few feet away from each other), and S' is the class containing pairs of trees and pairs of tigers. It seems plain that S is a natural kind (of pairs), whereas S' is an artificial class. Suppose it is now asked why we do not treat the pairs in S as constituting unitary things. The answer cannot be that we are prevented from doing so because these would-be units could not then be classified as belonging to any individuative natural kind. On the contrary, if we *did* treat the members of S as constituting units then S would itself provide us with the required classification.

Though I have been carrying on this discussion from an elementary commonsense standpoint, I think that these points would remain essentially intact even if we shifted to a somewhat more theoretical level. From a biologist's standpoint there is, I take it, no such thing as a tree-*cum*-tree. We might be tempted to explain this fact by saying that, for biology, there are no kinds, or no individuative kinds, to which a tree-*cum*-tree might belong. But this explanation is doubtful since it is not clear why the class of tree-*cum*-trees could not itself qualify as a biological kind. If any tree has the same underlying structure as any other tree, would it not follow that any tree-*cum*-tree has the same underlying structure as any other tree-*cum*-tree? (This would surely seem to follow if a thing's underlying structure is a function of its atomic structure.) And, as before, it would not help to answer that the class of tree-*cum*-trees is not a biological kind precisely because the members of this class are not biological units. For we would then be explaining kinds in terms of units, rather than the other way around, which was what we wanted. Taking kinds simply as similarity classes, the point is that there is apparently no way to explain the biologist's sense of unity by reference to his sense of biological similarity.

It might be said that the biologist eschews tree-*cum*-trees because biological theory is simplified by not acknowledging (not quantifying over) any such units. Actually I think it is quite unclear that the biologist is here motivated by intuitions about theoretical simplicity, rather than straight-out intuitions about unity. Perhaps, though, this is not a critical question, since one might say in general that our "unity intuitions" form one important aspect of our overall "simplicity intuitions." Be this as it may, the important point for my present purposes is that there seems to be no reason to regard the biologist's units as dependent upon his kinds, rather than vice versa.

What I want to conclude from this discussion is that the notion of a natural unit cannot be explained or reduced in terms of the notion of a natural kind. And I take it as obvious that a reduction in the opposite direction is impossible. That we find it natural to regard only certain portions of reality as units, is one fact about us. That we find it natural to regard these units as classifiable, as similar to each other, in only certain ways, is another fact about us. These are two fundamental features of our thought, neither of which can be explained in terms of the other.

V. The Basis of Kinds and Units

We might now ask how these features of our thought originate. How do we arrive at our intuitions about kinds and units? With respect to kinds Quine has in several places sketched an account which seems plausible.[14] The sketch, with some minor modifica-

14. Quine, "Natural Kinds," p. 123ff.; *The Roots of Reference*, p. 19ff.; *Word and Object*, pp. 83–84.

tions of my own, goes something like this. We start out with an innate quality space, an innate sense of similarity, relative to which certain classifications seem natural and others not (or, more likely, certain classifications seem more natural than others). It is easy to conceive that, of those classes which could be deemed natural kinds relative to the innate starting point, some emerge as more important than others. These would be the kinds that figure most prominently in our commonsense practical principles and low-level laws of nature. One might speculate that there is some rough correlation between the importance of a kind and the likelihood of our having a single word in our language that denotes it. The commonsense kinds are eventually reshaped by scientific posits of deeper structures and properties, yielding theoretic kinds which may diverge rather sharply from the commonsense kinds.

I would suggest that a roughly comparable account ought to be given of the genesis of our natural units. Studies by developmental psychologists, such as Piaget and Bower, suggest that the neonate is innately disposed to single out only certain portions of reality as units.[15] The conditions defining these most primitive units probably include some of those same basic body-unifying conditions that, as maintained earlier, one would appeal to in the absence of any relevant sortals. If Piaget is right the child's most primitive notion of unity undergoes a succession of transitions to increasingly more sophisticated notions. These transitions can be seen as motivated in part by the aim of achieving a simpler and more precise system of units, and this same aim yields at scientific levels theoretic units such as atoms and electrons.

Both our units and our kinds emerge, according to these speculations, from instinctive roots, and evolve through various levels of common sense and science. There seems, however, to be a crucial difference between the two cases. It seems to be a matter of a priori necessity that any language-learner should start out with a sense of similarity, that is, with a propensity to classify in certain ways rather than others. Otherwise there could apparently be no way to learn the use of a word, for there would

15. Cf. above, Chapter 8; Piaget, *The Construction of Reality in the Child*, ch. 1; *On the Development of Memory and Identity*, pp. 17–37; and Bower, *Development in Infancy*, p. 102ff. and ch. 7.

be no basis for extrapolating from observed cases of the word's application to new cases. It does not seem equally clear that, as a matter of a priori necessity, a language-learner, or even a learner of *our* language, must start out with a propensity to pick out only certain portions of reality as units. We can apparently imagine someone who starts out by regarding any portion of reality as equally a unit, and who then classifies these units in various ways. One such classification might indeed distinguish between units that are bodies and units that are not bodies. The final step to ordinary language would be to repudiate the non-bodies as units, thus arriving at our commonsense ontology of bodies. This would seem to be one conceivable route to common sense, though it is quite certainly not the route actually taken by ordinary human children.

It appears, then, that natural kinds are necessarily implicit in language-learning in a way that natural units are not. There is a closely related point. As mentioned before, many philosophers, including Quine, have espoused metaphysical systems in which all portions of reality count equally as units. As Quine puts it, a physical object is simply "the material content of any portion of space-time, however scattered and discontinuous." Hence: "There is a physical object part of which is a momentary stage of a silver dollar now in my pocket and the rest of which is a temporal segment of the Eiffel Tower through its third decade."[16] This seems as much as to say that, according to Quine, at the highest level of philosophical theorizing the distinction between natural units and artificial portions of reality simply falls away.

Could there be a philosophical system in which, in a comparable way, the distinction between natural kinds and artificial classes falls away? In at least one sense this seems evidently impossible. Any philosophical system must begin with some stock of primitive terms (i.e., terms which are not defined within the system), relative to which things are classified in certain ways

16. Quine, "Worlds Away," p. 859. Has my talk throughout this whole discussion of "space-time portions of reality" committed me all along to Quine's position? Not really; for such talk can be taken innocuously, as merely an expository device amenable to various interpretations in terms of set-theoretical constructions out of bodies, places, times, etc. But Quine's view is that any space-time portion has the same metaphysical status, the same status of concrete unity, as a body.

rather than others. If a class of things is denoted by a primitive term, or conjunction of such terms, then it might be said to constitute a kind within the system; whereas artificial classes are denoted only by disjunctive or negative constructions. This characterization is very rough, but does it not at least suffice to show that the core distinction between natural kinds and artificial classes must remain intact?

These considerations may seem to suggest that the notion of a natural kind is more fundamental than that of a natural unit. For it seems that natural kinds are necessarily indispensable both to language-learning and to metaphysics, in a way that natural units are not.

But let us reflect more closely on these points. The fact that any philosophical system must contain some primitive vocabulary does not entail that this vocabulary must include any such term as "kind" or "similarity class" or even "similarity." That is, the fact that we classify things in certain ways does not entail that we must go on to classify our *ways of classifying* in terms of the distinction between kinds and artificial classes. No such distinction need be acknowledged.

Of course we can simply define a natural kind as a class which corresponds to some primitive term or conjunction of such terms. But this would not establish that there is any *objective basis* for distinguishing between natural kinds and artificial classes. A philosopher might maintain that this distinction is wholly dependent on our classificatory apparatus, and that there is nothing in the objective world corresponding to the distinction. Let me call such a philosopher an Extreme Nominalist. This philosopher will accept the existence of classes (and perhaps even the existence of properties), but he does not accept any objective distinction between natural kinds and artificial classes (or between "genuine properties" and "mere constructions"). Since a natural kind is (or is at least closely related to) a similarity class, the position of Extreme Nominalism can also be expressed by saying that there is no objective similarity relation. I think it is fairly clear that Nelson Goodman is an Extreme Nominalist, and perhaps Quine is too.[17]

17. See Nelson Goodman, "Seven Strictures on Similarity" in *Problems and Projects* (The Bobbs-Merrill Company, Inc., Indianapolis and New York, 1972), especially pp. 444–46. In "Natural Kinds," Quine maintains that it is

It is important not to jump to the conclusion that the Extreme Nominalist must adopt an idealistic or subjectivistic attitude about facts in general. His position might rather be this: "There is an objective fact of the matter as to whether something is a lion, just as there is an objective fact of the matter as to whether something is either-a-lion-or-a-tree. But there is no objective fact of the matter as to whether the class of lions, or the class of lions-or-trees, constitutes a kind. That just depends upon our classificatory practices."

The essential argument for Extreme Nominalism derives from the fact that our judgments about kinds, or about similarity, are often highly nebulous, uncertain, and contingent upon our interests.[18] I personally doubt that these considerations can ever really convince us that there is no objective sense in which, say, the class of grue things is artificial.[19] However, my main concern now is not to assess Extreme Nominalism, but rather to see how this position bears on the comparisons I was making earlier between kinds and units.

Let me return to the question I raised earlier: Could there be a philosophical position with respect to kinds that parallels Quine's position with respect to units? It may now seem that there could be such a position, and that Extreme Nominalism is it. But the parallel is not really exact, as I now want to explain.

It is necessary to be clear in what sense Quine's position involves a rejection of the ordinary distinction between units and artificial portions of reality. Certainly Quine does not deny that there is an *objective basis* to the ordinary distinction. On the contrary, he even tries to explain what that objective basis is: From the ordinary standpoint we regard as a unit only a portion of reality which satisfies certain continuity (etc.) conditions, whereas a portion of reality which does not satisfy these conditions is not regarded as a unit. Quine maintains, however, that a metaphysically more perspicuous standpoint would treat all

---

a "mark of the maturity of a branch of science that it no longer needs an irreducible notion of similarity and kind" (p. 138).

18. See Goodman, "Seven Strictures on Similarity."

19. See Nelson Goodman, *Fact, Fiction, and Forecast,* 3rd ed. (The Bobbs-Merrill Co. Inc., Indianapolis and New York, 1973), p. 74, where the predicate "grue" is defined as applying to all things examined before a given time just in case they are green but to other things just in case they are blue.

portions of reality equally as units; for why should we meta-physically despise those portions of reality which do not satisfy the continuity (etc.) conditions? We can treat all portions of reality as units, as referents of concrete nouns and as bearers of qualities and spatiotemporal relations, and still distinguish be-tween those portions of reality which satisfy the continuity (etc.) conditions and those which do not. We can reject the ordinary distinction between units and artificial portions of reality while still holding on to the objective facts that underlie that distinc-tion.

This position is almost the exact reverse of what the Extreme Nominalist is saying about kinds. Whereas Quine does not ques-tion the objective basis of the ordinary notion of a unit, the Extreme Nominalist does question the objective basis of the ordi-nary notion of a kind. Furthermore, whereas Quine wishes to dispense with the distinction between units and artificial por-tions of reality it is not clear that the Extreme Nominalist wishes to dispense with the distinction between kinds and artificial classes. To regard the distinction as subjective (or relative to our interests or language) is not necessarily to dispense with it.[20]

Indeed it seems that the distinction between kinds and arti-ficial classes is indispensable for language-learning, as I noted earlier. And this of course is only one aspect of the more general point that the distinction is indispensable for inductive general-ization. In fact both Quine and Goodman stress the indispen-sability of the distinction in these respects, even while in the same breath disparaging the distinction's objectivity.

The notion of a kind, or similarity is . . . disreputable. Yet some such notion, some similarity sense, was seen to be crucial to all learning, and central in particular to the processes of inductive generalization and prediction which is the very life of science.[21]

[W]e must recognize that similarity is relative and variable, as unde-pendable as indispensable.[22]

20. The Extreme Nominalist might even be able to say "Lions constitute a kind apart from their relationship to our human activities" in the sense "Lions *strike us as* constituting a kind apart from their relationship to our human activities." Compare with an ethical subjectivist who says "The pain of animals is bad apart from its relationship to us."
21. Quine, "Natural Kinds," p. 133.
22. Goodman, "Seven Strictures on Similarity," p. 444.

The Extreme Nominalist is saying that, though our ordinary similarity intuitions do not correspond to any objective facts, they are nevertheless indispensable to our thought. On the other hand Quine's view with respect to units is that our ordinary unity intuitions do correspond to some objective facts, but we can more perspicuously describe these facts without our ordinary concept of unity.

If there could be a position with respect to units that more accurately parallels the Extreme Nominalist's position with respect to kinds, it would have at least to entail that there is no objective basis for the ordinary notion of a unit. The only semblance of an argument that I can think of for such a position might run along the following lines. To the extent that the unity of a thing can be said to depend upon the sortals that apply to the thing, the unity of a table depends on the fact that the thing is a table, depends, that is, on how the thing relates to our human interests and purposes. This may seem to imply a sense in which the unity of the table is not fully an objective matter. Whatever the merits of this argument, however, it obviously casts no aspersion on the objective unity of such non-artifacts as lions, tigers, and trees. So at least if we reserved the notion "natural unit" for nonartifacts the objectivity of the notion could apparently not be called into question.[23]

And let us ask, finally, what could be the accurate counterpart with respect to kinds of Quine's view with respect to units. This position would have to hold that our ordinary judgments about kinds, or similarity, *are* objectively based, but that they can be more perspicuously rendered in some different terms. I cannot readily imagine what this position could amount to.

Let me conclude this chapter by considering again the question: Which is more fundamental, the contrast between kinds and artificial classes or the contrast between units and artificial portions of reality? A case might be made out in either direction. It might be held that the former contrast is more fundamental

---

23. Notice that even if the class of natural units is not a natural kind, this in itself casts no aspersion on the *objectivity* of unity. The class which contains tigers and trees is not a natural kind but it is a wholly objective matter which things belong to the class. In the same way it might be an objective matter which portions of reality are natural units even though the class of natural units is not a kind.

because it is more obviously indispensable to thought; or it might be held that the latter contrast is more fundamental because its objective status is less disputable. My own opinion is that the contrast between kinds and artificial classes is more fundamental. For I think, contrary to the Extreme Nominalist, that this contrast is objectively based, as is indeed the contrast between units and artificial portions of reality; but the former contrast seems indispensable to thought in a way that the latter contrast does not.[24]

---

24. The contention that thought must necessarily contain *some* contrast between kinds and artificial classes (*some* standard of similarity) does not entail that thought must necessarily contain *our* contrast between kinds and artificial classes (*our* standard of similarity). Only the stronger claim could support the judgment that our natural kinds are (in terms of the distinctions of Chapter 6) metaphysically more basic than our artificial classes. The position I am here advancing would obviously not support the judgment that our natural units are metaphysically more basic than our artificial portions of reality. (Cf. ftn. 9 of Chapter 6.)

10

Constraints on Self-Identity

THE ORDINARY distinction between "me" and "not-me," between that which does and that which does not lie within the boundaries of a single self, seems at least on first reflection completely inevitable. It is difficult even to understand the suggestion that this distinction might be arbitrary, or that it might legitimately be redrawn in some other way. Here, if anywhere, a "conventionalist" attitude is likely to strike us as intuitively incredible.

Even here, however, our intuitions can be seriously challenged; it is possible to argue that there is in fact nothing which constrains us to think of the identity of the self in the way we do. One rather direct way to broach this issue is actually to try to imagine what it would be like for people to operate with a conception of the self radically different from ours, and then to ask what, if anything, would be wrong with such a conception. In the first section of this chapter I will construct one such alien conception as an illustration.[1] Of course many other illustrations

1. The illustration is somewhat akin to that discussed by Sydney Shoemaker, in "The Loose and Popular and the Strict and Philosophical Senses of Identity," in Care and Grimm, eds., *Perception and Personal Identity*, p. 117ff.

The illustration could be generalized to apply to the case of bodily identity, and as such it might serve to elucidate the issue of conventionalism with respect to bodily identity which was discussed in Chapter 8. There are indeed close parallels between the discussion of Chapter 8 and that of the present chapter, and a connection between the two discussions will be drawn later in Section V of this chapter. But it seems advisable to address the case of personal identity separately, because of the quite special—and especially strong —intuitions that we have about this case.

are possible; mine perhaps has the virtue of being logically simple and easily generalizable. This alien conception is designed to strike us intuitively as utterly bizarre and crazy; and the philosophical problem will then be to explain what these intuitions amount to. In subsequent sections of the chapter I will discuss various ways of responding to this problem.

I. A Strange Identity Concept

It will be useful to develop the fantasy of this alien conception as involving two stages. Suppose that there is a community of people who, to begin with, speak ordinary English. At the first stage we imagine that these people introduce a set of linguistic conventions, which I will tentatively characterize, subject to further discussion, as altering their descriptions of the identity of the self. We might say that as a result of these linguistic conventions they wind up with a new language. At the first stage we imagine that English remains their primary language; perhaps they speak the new language only on special occasions. At the second and more critical stage of the fantasy we will try to imagine that English is forgotten and only the new language is used. Let me indicate how this new language works.

Suppose that A and B are two people who come into physical contact with each other (say, they shake hands). Then in the new language the term "person" will denote neither A nor B, as ordinarily conceived, but will denote instead two individuals A′ and B′ who stand to A and B in the following sort of way. The history of A′ will contain all the stages of A's history during periods when A is not touching another person, together with the stage of B's history during the period when A and B touch; correlatively, the history of B′ will contain all the stages of B's history during periods when B is not touching another person, together with the stage of A's history during the period when A and B touch.

More generally, suppose that A is a person who throughout his entire life-history (as ordinarily conceived) makes physical contact with only the people B, C, D, . . . etc. Then in the new language the term "person" will denote an individual whose whole life-history consists of all the stages of A during periods when A is not touching another person, together with all the stages of B during periods when A is touching B, together with all the stages of C during periods when A is touching C, together with all the stages of D during periods when A is touching D, . . . etc. Crudely put, the idea is that in the new language it is a rule of "personal" identity that when two "people" come into physical contact, each takes over the physical and mental characteristics of the other, and then when they cease to be in contact they again exchange their physical and mental characteristics. (What happens if someone is simultaneously in contact with two or more people? Let us stipulate that this will not qualify as contact in the sense relevant to the rule of identity.) We imagine correlative changes in the use of personal pronouns, and in nouns subordinate to "person." For example, in the new language it would be correct to say: "A person must use the word 'I' to refer to that person."

Let us consider a few examples of this language in operation. We might call the language "Contacti." Suppose that a man, who is not touching anybody, approaches a woman, who is not touching anybody, and they embrace. Let us imagine that the man is standing to the left of the woman. We can picture the situation as in Figure 1. In the diagram the full arrows represent our ordinary identity relations, whereas the broken arrows represent the Contacti identity relations. We imagine that at 1 P.M. neither the man nor the woman is touching anybody; at 2 P.M. they are touching each other; and at 3 P.M. they are again separate.

This situation could be described in Contacti as follows: "At 2 P.M. a man embraces a woman. At the moment of embrace the first person, who was previously a man standing to the left, becomes a woman standing to the right; whereas the second person, who was previously a woman standing to the right, becomes a man standing to the left." When they cease to embrace the description in Contacti would continue: "The first person now reverts to being a man, whereas the second person reverts to being a woman."

Since it is a rule of Contacti that "a person must use the word 'I' to refer to that person," during the embrace the man could say in Contacti, "A few moments ago I (who am now a man) was a woman." The woman, in turn, could say, "A few moments ago I was a man." After the embrace (e.g., at 3 P.M.) the man

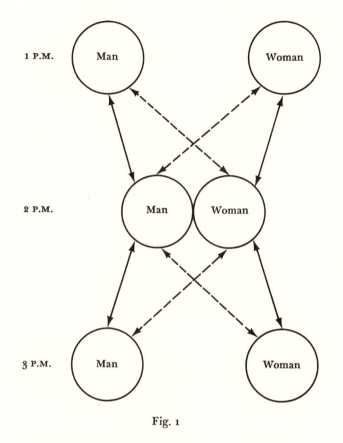

Fig. 1

could say, "A while ago I was a woman embracing a man, and before that I was a man standing alone." And the woman could say after the embrace, "A while ago I was a man embracing a woman, and before that I was a woman standing alone."

Let us suppose, further, that prior to the embrace the man, but not the woman, was feeling disconsolate. Then during the embrace the man could say in Contacti, "This woman whom I am embracing was feeling disconsolate a few moments ago (when she was a man), and I can well remember what that feeling was like." She, on the other hand, would say, "I was feeling disconsolate a few moments ago, or so I'm told." But if she were asked, "Can you remember your feeling of disconsolation?" she

would reply, "Of course not! How could one conceivably remember while touching somebody what one felt when not
touching anybody?" We imagine, in short, that their use of
"remember" (as well as various other psychological verbs) is made
to accommodate their criteria of "personal" identity.[2] To remember an event is, roughly, to be able to make a judgment that
stands in a distinctive kind of causal relationship to the event.
Now we are certainly not to imagine that speaking Contacti
alters any such causal relationships. The point is rather that the
peculiar concept of "personal" identity in Contacti requires that
the causal chains constitutive of memory be regarded as typically
traversing the boundaries between one "person" and another.

There are many details and niceties here that I skip over. I
think, however, that for present purposes the general idea of
Contacti ought to be clear enough.

We are imagining that in the first stage the speakers of Contacti
still regard English as their primary language. We can even
imagine that they speak English silently under their breaths,
and then translate into the appropriate Contacti sentences. In
the second stage, however, English is completely forgotten. Let
us imagine indeed that a whole new generation of speakers is
raised on Contacti. These people have never even heard of
English, and we will assume that they do not at any level (conscious or unconscious) derive their Contacti sentences from
English; they "think in Contacti," as we might put it.

Now here is the difficulty. The speakers of Contacti apparently
describe the identity of the self in an abnormal way. We would
like to say (if we are not conventionalists) that they are wrong
and we are right. But how can they be wrong when their statements are logically equivalent to ours? Suppose that E is a true
English statement, and that C is the crazy-seeming counterpart
of E. For example, E might be the statement "I am now touching somebody (while neither of us touches anybody else), and I
felt disconsolate a few moment ago (when not touching anybody)," while C is the statement "I am now touching somebody
(while neither of us touches anybody else), and that person felt
disconsolate a few moments ago (when not touching anybody)."

2. For the sort of revision in the concept of memory that would be required
in Contacti, see Shoemaker's notion of "quasi memory," in "Persons and
Their Pasts."

Since E is true and C is logically equivalent to E, then C must also be true. This is completely obvious at the first stage, since at that stage someone who utters C will be silently translating from E. But if the point holds at the first stage it must apparently also hold at the second stage. For the advent of the second stage does not alter the truth conditions of any statements in Contacti. These statements remain logically equivalent to their English counterparts.[3]

The first stage need not puzzle us. At this stage they still think in English; that is, they still think about the identity of the self in the normal way. At the first stage Contacti can be dismissed as merely a strange "code" of some sort. (We might even imagine that Contacti was introduced during a prolonged war in order to confound the enemy.) Our puzzle arises, however, at the second stage. At this stage they are not thinking about the identity of the self in the normal (English) way. Yet their statements remain logically equivalent to ours. How, then, can they be wrong when we are right? How can a change in language convert truth into falsehood (or sanity into craziness)?

Someone might object to my characterizing the Contacti speakers, at the second stage, as conceiving of the identity of the self differently from the way we do. Why, it might be asked, should we say that they conceive of *the self* at all? Since their use of "person," and correlative terms, is so very different from ours, perhaps we should not associate these uses with one another; perhaps we should not say that they have any concept (like our concept) of a person.

But this point is not crucial. It does not matter whether we say that they have a different concept of a person or no concept

---

3. Note that I *take it for granted* as part of the fantasized example that the Contacti statements are indeed logically equivalent to (have the same truth conditions as) the English statements that would typically be uttered in the same contexts. I make no pretense of offering some general (e.g., behavioral) test which would enable us to verify such an assumption in practice, or to exclude other possibilities (such as that the Contacti speakers are deluded about the causal relations between people who touch each other). Of course my characterization of Contacti will invite various questions about "radical translation." Some of these questions will be implicitly dealt with in what follows. But my general assumption is that it makes sense to characterize a language as containing sentences with certain specified truth conditions, and terms with certain specified denotations.

of a person. In either case they evidently do not have our concept of a person; they evidently do not conceive of the self as we do, whether they can be said to conceive of the self at all. And this threatens us with the conventionalist conclusion that it is arbitrary for us to have our concept of a person, that it is arbitrary for us to describe the identity of the self as we do.

There is one feature of the Contacti example that I have so far left open. I have said nothing about their behavior and attitudes. This feature of the example might be filled out in several ways, but, in order to prepare for a later point, I want at present to fill it out as follows. I want to imagine that their behavior and attitudes will seem completely normal from our (English speaking) point of view. Suppose, for example, that a certain Contacti speaker is about to shake hands with someone who is obviously limping with intense pain. Then the first person will say, "When I shake hands with him I will have great pain," but that judgment would not trouble him in the least. If we ask him why the judgment does not trouble him he would reply, "Because (obviously!), though I will have great pain, the person whom I will be touching will have no pain." In this sense, their behavior and attitudes, apart from their speech, remain just like ours.

If we complete the fantasy in this fashion then we increase the dissimilarity between their talk of "persons" and ours, since their "person"-talk and ours would not be linked up to behavior and attitudes in a comparable way. This would reinforce the suggestion that perhaps we should not regard them as having any concept of a person at all, that perhaps we should not associate their use of "person" with ours. But, as I said a moment ago, that point is not crucial, since, in any case, they certainly do not conceive of persons as we do.

Contacti is evidently just one of an indefinite number of languages that can be constructed along similar lines. It seems that we can imagine any number and variety of conceptual schemes that dispense with our ordinary concept of the self, conceptual schemes that combine in a single individual the successive stages (or even the simultaneous states) of what we normally regard as different persons. Any such conceptual scheme might contain statements that are logically equivalent to our ordinary statements about the self. The decisive problem is to explain how it would be wrong to adopt such a conceptual scheme.

II. Metaphysical Constraints

Certainly our first, and perhaps inexorable, impulse is to insist that Contacti must be ruled out on *metaphysical* grounds. To speak Contacti, it will be said, is simply to misdescribe the ultimate nature of the self.

This response as it stands, however, appears to miss the point. For let the ultimate nature of the self be whatever you like. Our problem still remains to explain how it could be wrong to shift from one statement about the self to another logically equivalent statement. Whatever might be the nature of the self it remains clear that insofar as our ordinary statements of self-identity are true, so must be the Contacti statements. So it is not immediately obvious how our problem can even be addressed by appealing to some facts about the nature of the self.

Nor should it be suggested that Contacti runs afoul of some *explanatory* requirements. For we can explain in Contacti precisely what we can explain in English. If E_1 explains E_2, these being English statements, then C_1 explains C_2, where these are the Contacti equivalents of E_1 and E_2. We do not lose our explanations just by putting them into different words.

A suggestion that seems more seriously tempting is that the second stage of the Contacti fantasy ought to be dismissed as logically or metaphysically impossible. Though we can indeed describe (and explain) the facts in terms of Contacti it is, according to the present suggestion, impossible that Contacti should be our primary language. This is because our use of the Contacti concept of personal identity necessarily depends upon our prior use of the ordinary concept.

But should we concede this alleged necessity? Let us reflect that according to many philosophers our ordinary concept of personal identity can be explained somewhat as follows: A succession of person-stages constitutes a persisting person if the succession is R-interrelated, where the relationship R consists of some combination of physical, psychological, and causal continuity. R, it should be noted, is not itself the relationship of identity, since R relates *different* person-stages. But we can say, perhaps, that the ordinary concept of the identity of a person is *based* upon R (that personal identity is, perhaps, a "logical construction" out of R).

Along these same lines it might be suggested that in Contacti a succession of person-stages constitutes (what they call) a persisting person if the succession is R′-interrelated, where R′ involves both the continuity relation R and various facts about human contact.[4] So the Contacti concept of personal identity is based upon R′.

How could it now follow that our employment of the Contacti concept of personal identity must necessarily depend upon our prior employment of the ordinary concept? It could be maintained, with at least a fair degree of plausibility, that anyone who has the concept of R′ must necessarily already have the concept of R. (Even this may not be completely clear; but I will assume it for the sake of the argument.) It would be a non sequitur, however, to conclude from this that anyone who has the Contacti concept of personal identity (which is based on R′) must necessarily already have the ordinary concept (which is based on R). Why should it be impossible for someone to proceed directly from R and R′ to the Contacti concept of personal identity, without taking any detour through the ordinary concept? Why, that is, should it be impossible for someone to proceed directly from the thought of certain kinds of continuity and contact relations to the Contacti conception of personal identity?

The issue I am here raising is related to a certain traditional question about the nature of the self. Derek Parfit has expressed this question as follows: "Does personal identity just consist in bodily and psychological continuity, or is it a further fact, in-

---

4. Roughly: The person-stage x-at-t_1 is R′ to the person-stage y-at-t_2 if either (a) x-at-t_1 is not exclusively in contact with anyone, and y-at-t_2 is not exclusively in contact with anyone, and x-at-t_1 is R to y-at-t_2, or (b) x-at-t_1 is exclusively in contact with z-at-t_1, and y-at-t_2 is exclusively in contact with w-at-t_2, and z-at-t_1 is R to w-at-t_2, or (c) x-at-t_1 is exclusively in contact with z-at-t_1, and y-at-t_2 is not exclusively in contact with anyone, and z-at-t_1 is R to y-at-t_2, or (d) x-at-t_1 is not exclusively in contact with anyone, and y-at-t_2 is exclusively in contact with w-at-t_2, and x-at-t_1 is R to w-at-t_2.

dependent of the facts about these continuities?"[5] In Parfit's terminology the "Complex View" holds that personal identity consists in just continuity, whereas the "Simple View" holds that there is some further fact, independent of continuity.[6] Now I think it is tempting to suppose that there is a close connection between this issue of the Complex View versus the Simple View and the problem of explaining why our ordinary concept of the self is peculiarly right. One might be inclined to reason as follows:

"If the Complex View is correct, then a person reduces to a succession or bundle of momentary stages related by continuity. Then it does seem that we might have used the word 'person' to denote some *other* kind of succession, which is what they do in Contacti. But if the Simple View is correct, then the identity of a person is ultimate and unanalyzable, so that the only way to talk about persons is the way we do."

This line of reasoning may seem convincing, but I question whether it is really cogent. Consider the following point. If we accept the Simple View then we regard personal identity as consisting in something other than continuity. There is, however, nothing in this idea which prevents us from regarding a person as a succession of stages that are related to each other in *some* way. We can even give a name to this relationship, say "person kinship."[7] We can then say, on the Simple View, that a person is a succession of stages related by person kinship, where person kinship is independent of continuity. Hence it seems that even the Simple View would allow us to think of a person as a "mere bundle" (and would therefore allow us to think of collecting together other kinds of bundles).

It seems, in other words, that both the Simple View and the Complex View can accommodate the general formula: A succession of person-stages constitutes a single person if the succession

5. Derek Parfit, "Personal Identity," in Jonathan Glover, ed., *The Philosophy of Mind* (Oxford University Press, 1976), p. 162, ftn. 37; reprinted, with added footnote, from *Philosophical Review*, 80, 1 (1971).

6. For this terminology, see Parfit's "On 'The Importance of Self-Identity,'" *Journal of Philosophy*, 68, 20 (1971).

7. Cf. Quine's use of "river kinship" and "water kinship" in *From a Logical Point of View*, p. 66.

is R-interrelated. The disagreement only concerns the nature of R. But this disagreement has no obvious bearing on our question about the viability of Contacti as a primary language. The Contacti conception of personal identity is based on the relationship R', where R' is defined in terms of R and contact. It seems that even on the Simple View we are still left with the question why it would be impossible for someone to proceed directly from the thought of R and R' to the Contacti conception of personal identity.

I am quite certain that many proponents of the Simple View will want to insist that our ordinary concept of a persisting person must necessarily precede any concept we form of person-stages and their interrelations, or any such deviant concept of personal identity as that of Contacti. But we need to understand whether this is just *another* claim, in addition to the claim that personal identity is not a matter of continuity. It is unclear how these claims are related to each other.

I am therefore not confident about how to connect the Simple View to the issue of the present chapter. In any case my own inclination is to favor the Complex View. And the Complex View certainly does not seem to provide any explanation as to why a language like Contacti must be ruled out as a primary language. So the upshot of this argument seems to be that the preeminence of our ordinary concept of self-identity lacks any clear logical or metaphysical ground.

(Some philosophers might want to appeal to the traditional distinction between "superficial grammatical form" and "true logical form" to defend the claim that Contacti is necessarily dependent on ordinary thought. The superficial grammatical form of a Contacti identity statement, it will be suggested, distorts the true logical or metaphysical form of the facts; whereas the superficial form of an ordinary identity statement adequately reflects the true logical form. This is why Contacti is necessarily only a code, which must depend upon a language like English, but could not possibly itself serve as a primary language.

One may question the principle, evidently assumed in this suggestion, that our grasp of a statement whose superficial form deviates from logical form must necessarily depend on our grasp of another statement whose superficial form reflects logical form.

Actually, however, I suspect that this principle is only a tautology, which in effect defines the technical distinction between "superficial form" and "true logical form" in terms of the idea that our grasp of one kind of statement necessarily depends on our grasp of another. Be this as it may, my main response to the above suggestion is already implicit in my earlier argument. First of all, if we hold the Complex View, which is my inclination, then there seems obviously to be no basis for regarding the superficial form of our ordinary English identity statements as especially suggestive of the "true logical form"; we might then even be led to say—in the spirit of Hume and others—that *both* our English statements *and* Contacti statements distort logical form. And second, even if we hold the Simple View—defined in terms of the independence of identity and continuity—it is still not clear what we should be led to say about the "true logical form" of self-identity.)[8]

III. Pragmatic Constraints

It might now be suggested that we ought to look for a more "pragmatic" approach to this issue. Even if I have raised doubts as to whether there are any purely logical or metaphysical reasons which constrain us to employ our ordinary concept of personal identity, there are, it may be said, compelling *practical* reasons to consider. According to this pragmatic approach our ordinary concept of the self performs various essential roles in structuring an individual's relationship to himself and to others. And to dispense with, or radically to alter, these roles would be, as a practical matter, unthinkable.[9]

Take Contacti, for example (our "pragmatist" might continue); such a language must lead to total havoc. For one of the essential functions of our concept of the self is to enable us to

8. The flimsiness of our intuitions about "the logical or metaphysical form of the facts," especially as regards such crucial examples as personal identity, may generate scepticism about the general usefulness of this traditional notion. Cf. Chapter 6, Sections IV and VI, and ftn. 9.

9. Two papers which suggest this pragmatic approach are: Terence Penelhum, "The Importance of Self-Identity," *Journal of Philosophy*, 68, 20 (1971); J. M. Shorter, "Personal Identity, Relationships, and Criteria," *Proceedings of the Aristotelian Society*, 71 (1970–71).

retain our separate identities in the course of complex social interactions, including of course physical contact. In Contacti this would be impossible. People who spoke that language would feel impelled to touch each other, or not to touch each other, in ways that are completely irrational or even socially harmful. For example, if someone were in pain, no one would want to touch him, including the doctors. On the other hand, everyone would be anxious to touch the rich and successful (which is *already* something of a problem). The whole idea is evidently insanely unworkable.

It is all too easy to acquiesce to this kind of argument. Consider, however, that I stipulated earlier that the Contacti speakers would feel and act, apart from their speech, just as we do. I mentioned, in particular, that a Contacti speaker would not be at all troubled by the thought he would express as "When I touch him, I will be in pain." The previous argument seems to overlook this stipulation.

To clarify some of the issues here, it might be useful to introduce a certain distinction. When we fantasize about some language such as Contacti there are two directions in which we might try to develop the fantasy, which I will call the *emotive* and *nonemotive* directions. If we develop the fantasy in the emotive direction then we imagine that a given sentence (e.g., the sentence "When I touch him, I will be in pain") tends to be linked up to the emotions and behavior of Contacti speakers in much the same way that it is linked up to our emotions and behavior. Hence, on the emotive interpretation, a Contacti speaker *would* be troubled by the thought he would express as "When I touch him, I will be in pain." Taking the fantasy in the nonemotive direction, as I did earlier, we imagine that a given sentence does not have the same emotional significance for a Contacti speaker as it does for an English speaker. Rather, on the nonemotive construal, a given sentence tends to have the same emotional significance for a Contacti speaker as its *English equivalent* has for an English speaker. On this construal a Contacti speaker might be troubled by the thought he would express as "When I touch him, he will be in pain," which is equivalent to the English statement "When I touch him, I will be in pain." (More strictly, the Contacti statement "I am not touching anybody now and when he and I are touching only each other, he will be in pain" is logically equivalent to the English statement "I am not touching anybody now and when he and I are touching only each other, I will be in pain.")

To take another example, suppose that when I shake hands with a certain person he squeezes my hand till it hurts. Escaping from his grip I might say "You hurt me when we were shaking hands"; and that fact would make me angry. If I spoke Contacti, what I would say in that circumstance is "I hurt you when we were shaking hands." So who would be angry at whom? On the emotive construal, *he* would be angry at *me*. For it would be he who could say "You hurt me when we were shaking hands." On the nonemotive construal I am angry at him, just as if I spoke English.

Taking the fantasy in the nonemotive direction, life goes on in the normal way; only the words change. The pragmatist must explain why this would be an impossibility. So far his remarks seem only to apply to the emotive construal. My main concern, on the other hand, is with the *non*emotive construal.

If we tried to develop the Contacti fantasy in the emotive direction, then we imagine people whose lives are in countless ways bizarre and grotesque, from our ordinary point of view. I am not in fact even confident that we can make the fantasy fully intelligible in this direction. In any case, my primary question is not "Why do we have to live the sorts of lives that we do?" but rather "Given the sorts of lives that we live, why do we have to talk (and think) about personal identity as we do?" The pragmatist must explain why we could not speak a language like Contacti and go on living as we do. Why should it make a practical difference whether we utter certain sentences in English or utter their logical equivalents in Contacti?

The inevitable suggestion will be that a language like Contacti would have to be too cumbersome and complicated. Consider one of our moral principles, such as "You ought to be punished for a bad deed only if you yourself did the deed." This principle obviously involves our ordinary concept of personal identity. The fantasized people who speak Contacti, construed now nonemotively, would also be committed to the content of this principle, but would have to express the principle in terms of *their* concept of personal identity. This might lead to a very complicated formulation of the principle. And in general, it will be said, all of their talk about persons would have to be too complicated.

I think that this point needs to be approached with a good deal of scepticism. What does it mean to say that the Contacti statements are "too complicated"? Of course Contacti strikes us as *mind-boggling*; that is, we have the greatest difficulty in even grasping how the language operates. This fact is indeed the point of departure of this whole discussion: we are trying to understand why the language strikes us as mind-boggling. It is not enough just to repeat this fact.

But perhaps it will be suggested that the Contacti statements are too complicated in the obvious sense of being *too wordy*. It does in fact seem that many of the things that we normally say would require more words to be said in Contacti. But can this point by itself bear any serious weight? It must not be supposed that English is somehow ideally suited to minimize the number of words that we utter. Obviously we could introduce various abbreviations into English which would further condense our statements. And, by the same token, we could undoubtedly introduce abbreviations into a language like Contacti which would make the typical statements of that language relatively condensed.

Let me reinforce this last point by mentioning one abbreviatory device that might be available in Contacti. Suppose that the language contains a symmetrical relationship, say "C-partnership," defined as follows: "x and y are C-partners" means: Either x and y are exclusively in contact with each other (i.e., each is touching the other and no one else), or $x = y$ and x is not exclusively in contact with anyone. In other words, I am the C-partner of anyone with whom I am exclusively in contact, and, as a degenerate case, I am my own C-partner if I am not exclusively in contact with anyone.

The reader can now verify that any English statement of the form "There is a person x such that x is A at t_1 and x is B at t_2" is equivalent to the Contacti statement "There are people x, y, and z such that x and y are C-partners at t_1, y and z are C-partners at t_2, x is A at t_1, and z is B at t_2."

On the basis of this equivalence virtually any typical statement of English can be rendered in fairly manageable Contacti. For example, the English principle "You ought to be punished for a bad deed only if you yourself did the deed" comes out in Contacti "You ought to be punished for a bad deed only if (the person who is) your C-partner at the time of punishment once had a C-partner who did the deed." Of course this latter formulation remains utterly mind-boggling. And our philosophical problem is to understand why this is so. My point is that it would surely be incorrect to answer that it is mind-boggling because it contains too many words.

Perhaps it will next be suggested (still in a somewhat pragmatic vein) that even if Contacti is not absurdly *impractical* it is absurdly *arbitrary*. For we are imagining that Contacti is just like English except for the different rule of personal identity. Only in this one case do contact relations play their distinctive role. Is it not absurd for a language to contain a rule of identity which diverges arbitrarily from the general pattern?

Of course this argument may merely encourage us to alter the Contacti fantasy so that contact relations figure in *other* identity rules as well. But even if we stick with the original fantasy the argument has, I think, little force. Suppose that we confronted a Contacti-speaker with this argument, in the hope of persuading him that his way of talking is absurd. Surely we can imagine him responding that, on the contrary, people are special and therefore deserve an exceptional identity rule, indeed a rule which highlights the special importance of human contact. For the Contacti-speaker it might seem completely natural and inevitable that personal identity revolves around contact relations.

Consider, furthermore, that many languages contain various "irregularities," e.g., of conjugation or pronunciation. These languages thrive nonetheless. Indeed any student of a foreign language must be struck by how the nuances of a language, even (or perhaps *especially*) its "irregularities," can come to have a distinctive sense of fittingness and elegance. Surely the same might be said for Contacti.

IV. Psychological Constraints

So where does this leave us? The preceding discussion suggests that there may be neither metaphysical nor pragmatic constraints which determine us to draw the boundaries of the self as we do.

If this is so, are we then forced to embrace the conventionalist position? This position would imply that our ordinary concept of the self is an arbitrary convention, which could be replaced by various other radically alien conceptions. According to the conventionalist, a language like Contacti strikes us as impossible, as mind-boggling, only because of the deeply entrenched habits of our ordinary thought.

The most vividly implausible consequence of this position is that we could *in actual fact* raise our children to speak a language like Contacti, and they would be none the worse for it. Presumably we (or at least some of us) could train ourselves to translate very quickly from English into Contacti, and to do this silently (i.e., under our breaths); so that, if we wished, we could speak only Contacti in the presence of our children. What would happen to these children? According to the conventionalist they would grow up speaking Contacti as their primary language, and their lives would be quite unaffected by this fact.

I know that many readers will share my own incredulity about this outcome. Of course the intuitive incredibility of conventionalism may not by itself constitute a decisive reason to reject the position; but it will certainly prepare us to look favorably on another alternative.

The alternative to conventionalism which I want to consider consists in the following hypothesis: We conceive of the self as we do because this is a basic kind of *psychological necessity*. Another way to express this hypothesis is that it is a basic *part of human nature* to conceive of the self as we do. According to this position our concept of the self is indeed not constrained by some metaphysical or pragmatic considerations; nor, however, is the concept merely an arbitrary convention. Rather it is a (more or less) specialized and irreducible fact about our nature that we must think about the self as we do. Precisely what this means is of course far from clear; and I do not pretend that I will be able to clarify it fully. But in the remainder of this chapter I will try to draw out some of the implications of this idea.

We can, to begin with, associate the idea with some of Chomsky's views about "universal grammar." Chomsky holds that, as a matter of empirical fact, there are certain features which must be present in any human (primary) language. These universal features are said to be determined by some "innate properties of the mind."[10] What this means is that any human being is innately disposed to speak a language containing the universal features, though, as Chomsky stresses, both maturational processes and environmental stimulations might have some role in the natural development of this disposition.[11] Applying these views to the present topic, we might speculate that, as a matter of empirical fact, any human being is innately disposed to speak a language in which the boundaries of the self are drawn in the normal way. Chomsky holds that there is no a priori justification for why certain linguistic features, rather than others, must be universal; this is just a certain kind of contingent fact (perhaps a very deep kind of contingent fact).[12] In the same vein we would hold on the present proposal that it is essentially a contingent fact about our human nature that we must speak about the self in the ordinary way.

This idea might be developed along the following lines. If two statements are logically equivalent then we can say that they have the same *factual content*. Statements having the same factual content may nevertheless fail, in some sense, to be synonymous (to have the same meaning). One important way in which this can happen (and the only way that need presently concern us) is that statements having the same factual content need not even refer, via their singular and general terms, to the same things. For example, a statement that refers to triangles may have the same factual content as a statement that refers only to the sides of triangles. Let us say that such statements have different *referential contents*, though the same factual content. This was the relationship that we found to obtain between English and Contacti statements. For any English statement about the self there is a Contacti statement with the same factual content. But no Contacti statement has the same referential content as any English statement about the self, for no Contacti statement refers to a person as ordinarily conceived.

Suppose we ask what it is that fixes, that places a constraint

10. Chomsky, *Language and Mind*, p. 95.
11. Ibid., pp. 81ff., 72–73.
12. Ibid., pp. 61–62, 88.

on, the factual contents of our statements. One wants to answer: the facts, reality, the world. That is to say, if we are going to have any knowledge at all then we must make true statements about the world, and this imposes a constraint on the factual contents of our statements. But what can constrain the referential contents of our statements? Since for any true statement there are an indefinite number of statements with the same factual content, but differing only in referential content, it seems that the demands of knowledge as such could not fix referential content. According to the present proposal it is an innate property of the mind which fixes referential content. Or this is so at least with respect to reference to the self.

This proposal should be contrasted with the view criticized earlier in Section II of this chapter, according to which it is logically or metaphysically impossible for people to speak a language like Contacti as their primary language. The present proposal implies instead that the relevant kind of impossibility is natural or causal rather than logical or metaphysical. It is logically conceivable that people should speak Contacti as their primary language, and their view of reality would not therefore be metaphysically less adequate than ours. But this is, for human beings, psychologically impossible; Contacti is not the humanly natural way to think. On the present position we see no metaphysical significance in the difference between English and Contacti, but we do see psychological significance in this difference.

The psychological significance of our ordinary way of referring to the self lies most obviously, on the present proposal, in the fact that we are innately disposed to refer to the self in just this way. But we might speculate that this does not exhaust the sense in which our ordinary mode of referring to the self is psychologically significant. It seems plausible to suppose that there are various psychological laws that relate our emotions and behavior to our thought about the self. For example, there seems to be a law roughly to the effect that a person will tend to feel angry if he thinks that someone has injured him. Perhaps there is another law roughly to the effect that a person will tend to feel guilty if he thinks that he has injured someone. In terms of the view being advanced, we might formulate these laws as follows: A person will tend to feel angry, if he accepts as true a statement (or judgment) having the factual and referential content of the English statement "That person has injured me"; and a person will tend to feel guilty, if he accepts as true a statement (or judgment) having the factual and referential content of the English statement "I have injured that person."

Imagine, somewhat fancifully, that it is possible, by way of drugs or brain surgery or whatever, to alter the "deep structure" of someone's language, so that he actually winds up speaking (and thinking in) Contacti. Suppose that such a Contacti-speaker is injured by someone during physical contact, say, while shaking hands. After the contact is over, he could say in Contacti, "I hurt that person when we were shaking hands (and now I am not touching anybody)," which has the same factual content as the English statement "That person hurt me when we were shaking hands (and now I am not touching anybody)." But what would his emotional response to this situation be? Given the previous speculation, we would not assume that, just because his Contacti statement has the same factual content as the anger-inducing English statement, he would therefore feel anger. For we would regard it as significant that his statement does not have the same referential content as the anger-inducing English statement. Nor could we expect him to feel guilty, for his Contacti statement does not even have the same factual content as the guilt-inducing English statement "I hurt that person." Since his thought about the self is abnormal, we could not expect to find any obvious correspondence between his responses and ours. Perhaps all we could expect, given his extreme "identity confusion," is that his responses will seem unintelligible to us.

The position I am advancing is evidently in line with some of Chomsky's views. It is also more vaguely in line with a whole strand of psychological literature which takes the development of a sense of self-identity to be subject to psychological law. To mention one example, which seems fairly close to our philosophical concerns, Margaret Mahler and her associates announce in one study the aim "to learn how healthy children attain their sense of 'individual entity' and identity."[13] That question seems pretty unmistakably related to the present discussion. So does Mahler's

13. Margaret S. Mahler, Fred Pine, and Anni Bergman, *The Psychological Birth of the Human Infant* (Basic Books, Inc., N. Y., 1975), p. x.

assumption that "the innate given is the drive toward individuation."[14] I take this philosophical-sounding remark to imply that the "given" is our innate tendency to conceive of the self in the normal way. ("Here is where justification comes to an end.")

In Mahler's account, we find that the innate drive toward individuation requires, for its normal development, various maturational processes, and also various prototypical interactions with the environment. Where, for one reason or another, the drive toward individuation is stymied, the result is a "disturbed sense of identity."[15] In cases of "extreme disturbance" the outcome is psychosis, in less extreme cases, various forms of neurosis. I shall not here attempt to address the difficult question as to what extent such terms as "psychosis" and "neurosis" are normative. I assume, however, that at least the notion of psychosis contains an important descriptive element, which includes such things as: being confused and incoherent, being unable to provide for one's physical well-being, and, typically, suffering in a peculiarly terrible sort of way. This, on Mahler's account, appears to be the inevitable outcome for any human being whose concept of the self is not at least essentially normal. (If we try to imagine a human being who thinks in Contacti, then we are certainly imagining someone with an "extremely disturbed" sense of identity, and therefore someone who, on Mahler's assumptions, would have to feel and behave like a psychotic.)

Mahler's kind of account supports the earlier conjecture that there are essential linkups between our ordinary concept of self-identity and our most rudimentary patterns of feeling and behavior. It is not just that we are innately determined to think about the self in a certain way, but that this way of thinking is essentially tied to our sanity.

To summarize, according to the position I am now proposing, human beings are, as a contingent fact of psychology, innately disposed to develop an essentially normal concept of the self. I have also suggested, in keeping with psychologists like Mahler, that developing a normal self-concept is constitutive of human sanity. So there is, after all, a deep constraint on our concept of the self.

14. Ibid., p. 9.
15. Ibid., p. 11ff.

V. The Sense of Self

The position outlined above is obviously highly tentative, and would need to be significantly elaborated. Let me, in this final section, indicate a few directions for further consideration.

a. I maintained previously in Chapter 8 that our most basic criteria of bodily identity (e.g., continuity, cohesiveness, boundary contrast) are innately determined. It is tempting to try to draw a connection between that idea and the position I am now advocating. One obvious difficulty in the way of drawing such a connection is that our concept of bodily identity does not appear to coincide exactly with our concept of personal identity. This seems to be suggested by "brain-transfer" cases, and the like. Still, it might be possible, for the purposes of drawing the connection, to downplay such problematical cases and to emphasize that at least normally our concept of personal identity does indeed coincide with our concept of bodily identity. It might seem, therefore, that the innateness of our concept of bodily identity (argued in the earlier chapter) could provide essentially all the psychological resources required to explain the innate basis of our concept of personal identity.

There are a number of difficulties here, but I want especially to emphasize one of them. It seems that we can imagine an "impersonal" language, in the sense of a language which contains no personal pronouns. I want to imagine that, apart from containing no personal pronouns, the general concept of a person which operates in that language is exactly like ours. Someone who speaks that language would refer to himself by way of definite or demonstrative descriptions, such as "the (this) person who is such-and-such," or by way of a proper name. But he would never refer to himself by way of a first-person pronoun.

This "impersonal" way of thinking about oneself certainly strikes us as significantly different from our normal way. Part of the difference can be brought out by reference to the following sort of example.[16] Imagine that someone judges, "That person whose trousers are on fire is in danger," but, because he does not realize that he is looking in a mirror and seeing himself,

16. See Hector-Neri Castaneda, "He: A Study in the Logic of Self-Consciousness," *Ratio*, 7 (1966), p. 141ff.

he does not judge, "I am in danger." Then, we could not say, "He believes that he himself is in danger"; nor would we expect him to act accordingly. It seems that in order for someone to ascribe a property to himself, in the fundamental sense of believing that he himself has that property, it is not in general enough that he should conjoin a definite or demonstrative description of himself to that property. Nor, by much the same argument, would it suffice for him to conjoin a proper name of himself to the property. What is required, apparently, is that he should conjoin the first-person pronoun to the property, that he should judge, "I am such-and-such." It seems, therefore, that the "impersonal" language would not even permit a person to "think about himself" in the most fundamental sense.

Evidently much more would need to be said to show convincingly that personal pronouns, in particular the first-person pronoun, are indispensable to our ordinary thought.[17] But if this point is granted, then it follows that in order to conceive of oneself in the normal way, it will not suffice that one should have the ordinary general concept of the identity of a person. Something else required is that one should employ a term or concept having the special role of "I" (that is, roughly, the special role of demonstratively picking out the person who employs the term or concept). This seems to establish an essential gap between the innateness theory being proposed in the present chapter and the innateness theory of bodily identity I proposed in Chapter 8. It seems the most we could possibly say, to bring the two theories together, is that the innate disposition to conceive of oneself in the normal way consists in the general disposition to adopt our ordinary criteria of bodily identity, together with the special disposition to employ a term or concept with the role of "I." Even this might overstate the connection between the two theories; so, for now, I shall have to leave this connection open.

b. I hope it is clear that when I suggest that the normal way of thinking about the self is "natural" or "innately determined" I am talking only about our most primary and spontaneous level

---

17. For further discussion of related points, see Shoemaker's critique of the "disguised description theory" in *Self-Knowledge and Self-Identity*, pp. 99–106; see also John Perry's account of "self locating knowledge" in "Frege on Demonstratives," *Philosophical Review*, 86 (1977), p. 492ff.

of thought. What happens after that, at more inferential and theoretical levels, is of course another story. Psychologists like Mahler frequently employ such expressions as "a sense of identity," or "a feeling of self," or even "an experience of I" to convey the immediacy and spontaneity of our judgments about the self. This point can be brought out by considering the familiar joke that many people have been certified for saying some of the things that Descartes said. Descartes's position, on at least one classic formulation, was that the word "I" designates the soul. This position would have led Descartes to say such things as "I am not here in this room. I am invisible and intangible. No one can see me or touch me." The literature of psychopathology is replete with just such statements.[18] The difference between the pathological cases and Descartes's case is that presumably Descartes's "feeling of self" was (more or less) normal. That is, Descartes did not just find himself spontaneously thinking that no one could really see him or touch him, which would be the pathological case, but rather he arrived at his philosophical judgments by way of a complicated piece of ratiocination. I imagine that often Descartes spontaneously thought such things as "The queen has seen me. Let's hope she doesn't want to touch me." While philosophizing, however, he would censor these spontaneous judgments (these "feelings") for the sake of what he regarded as a better theory.

There may be cases which are in a way the opposite of Descartes's, i.e., cases in which someone's considered judgments about the self are normal even though his sense of self is distorted. Someone who suffers from such symptoms as "depersonalization" or "dissociation" may report the inclination to make bizarre judgments about his identity, but, if he is not psychotic, he will "know the truth," which in this context may mean little more than that he knows the ordinary way to talk. Perhaps it would be more accurate to say that in these cases the patient's sense of self is in conflict, in that the patient experiences a conflict between two spontaneous judgments, one normal and one abnormal.

Obviously a great deal of further clarification is required here,

18. See, e.g., the discussion of the "unembodied self," in R. D. Laing, *The Divided Self* (Penguin Books Ltd., Middlesex, England, 1965), p. 65ff.

from both a philosophical and a psychological standpoint. Certainly we need a more secure grasp of what is meant by a "spontaneous judgment about the self," and the correlative notion of a "sense (or feeling) of self." It may turn out, upon deeper analysis, that there is no such thing as *the* normal sense of self," but rather a range of significantly different cases that fluctuate around a central paradigm. Nevertheless I think it is plausible to suppose that there are severe psychological constraints on such fluctuations, that there are severe limits on the extent to which a person can, within the bounds of sanity, alter his sense of self. And this leads directly to one final point.

c. Derek Parfit has argued that what matters is not personal identity as such, but rather those continuity relations which (on the Complex View) underlie identity. The importance of personal identity is only derivative, stemming from the links between identity and the inherently important continuity relations. Hence if a situation should arise (e.g., the case of the person who divides) in which our concept of identity has no definite application, we can still express our reasonable concerns by reference to the continuity relations.[19]

Let me say that someone has a "Parfitian attitude" insofar as his judgments of concern are couched in terms of the continuity relations, rather than in terms of personal identity. Someone with this attitude might say "How terrible, tomorrow a person who is continuous with my present state will be in pain!" rather than "How terrible, tomorrow I will be in pain!"

One of Parfit's points is that we might be confronted with an exceptional situation (e.g., the case of division) in which it would be reasonable for us to adopt a Parfitian attitude. Perhaps I can agree with this. What I want to question, however, is the pervasive suggestion in Parfit's work that it would be possible, perhaps even beneficial, for us to adopt the Parfitian attitude as

---

19. Parfit, "Personal Identity," and "On 'The Importance of Self-Identity' "; see also "Lewis, Perry, and What Matters" in Amelie Rorty, ed., *The Identities of Persons* (University of California Press, Berkeley and Los Angeles, Cal., 1976).

Parfit maintains that if a person divides into two people in such a manner as to preserve all of the relevant continuities with each of the resultant people, then this would not be in any sense that matters a case of ceasing to exist, even though the original person could not be unambiguously identified with either of the resultant people.

our *primary orientation.* Here I am no longer picturing some-one who on some rare occasion translates his ordinary identity-related concerns in terms of the continuity relations, but rather someone whose most spontaneous and unreflective judgments of concern are typically couched in terms of the continuity relations. The sort of hypothesis I have been considering implies that it is psychologically impossible for a sane human being to have a Parfitian attitude as his primary orientation. If one has a normal sense of self then one's spontaneous judgments of concern must at least typically be couched in terms of the ordinary concept of self-identity. The Parfitian attitude can be at most an occasional and sophisticated modulation of the more basic identity-related orientation.

Let me emphasize that the issue here is not a priori. I am not saying that it *ought* to be impossible for us to adopt a Parfitian attitude as our primary orientation, or that this is a priori inevitable. I am only saying that, given the sort of psychological hypothesis I have been advancing, it is, as a matter of fact, im-possible for human beings to adopt a Parfitian attitude at the primary level.

My impression is that Parfit, and others who have taken up his question about "what matters in identity," are not sufficiently alive to the possibility that the way we are able to think and feel about identity, at least at the most primary and spontaneous level, may be severely restricted by psychological constraints quite unrelated to the terms of philosophical justification. The machinery of human sanity is complex and delicate. That may not be an a priori fact, nor even a desirable fact; but it appears to be a fact. And if my speculations here have been correct, an essential element, or prerequisite, of sanity is that one should spontaneously think of the self in a certain way, in essentially the ordinary way.

Index